# Documentary as Exorcism

I HOPE THIS BOOK WILL INSPIRE
YOU TO KEEP THE FAITH AND
FIGHT THE POWER!

BEST WISHES

ROBERT

30/1/2014

# Documentary as Exorcism

## Resisting the Bewitchment of Colonial Christianity

ROBERT BECKFORD

B L O O M S B U R Y
LONDON • NEW DELHI • NEW YORK • SYDNEY

**Bloomsbury Academic**

An imprint of Bloomsbury Publishing Plc

| | |
|---|---|
| 50 Bedford Square | 1385 Broadway |
| London | New York |
| WC1B 3DP | NY 10018 |
| UK | USA |

**www.bloomsbury.com**

**Bloomsbury is a registered trade mark of Bloomsbury Publishing Plc**

First published 2014

© Robert Beckford, 2014

Robert Beckford has asserted his right under the Copyright, Designs and
Patents Act, 1988, to be identified as Author of this work.

**British Library Cataloguing-in-Publication Data**
A catalogue record for this book is available from the British Library.

ISBN: HB: 978-1-84706-391-5
PB: 978-1-84706-392-2
ePub: 978-1-44112-719-8
ePDF: 978-1-44112-070-0

**Library of Congress Cataloging-in-Publication Data**
A catalog record for this book is available from the Library of Congress.

Typeset by Newgen Knowledge Works (P) Ltd., Chennai, India
Printed and bound in Great Britain

*Thanks to Charlie English, Yvette Hutchinson, Sekai Makoni, John Wilkinson, Sarah Chukwudebe, and Chris Shanahan. This book is dedicated to my friend, the preacher and scholar, Rev. Dr Tammy Williams.*

# CONTENTS

# Introduction: Black steel in the hour of documentary

*Each generation out of relative obscurity must discover their mission, fulfil it or betray it.*

FRANTZ FANON[1]

Outside New Church, Sunday morning, May 2007:

'I like the work that you do, you got steel man!'

'What do you mean?' I asked.

'You stood up to the BNP (British National Party) and you gave them no flex man. . . .

Then you went inside that BNP pub and tried to reason with those racists . . . You got steel.'

It took me a few seconds to realize that he was referring to a film of mine on the subject of the 'diversity industry' in Britain, called *Ghetto Britain*.

'I hear you. . . . That's a real compliment coming from you.'

I said this, fully aware from a previous but less personal encounter (listening to his particular testimony at a men's meeting) that the tall, muscular, dark-skinned Christian 'brother' with the welcoming smile was a former football hooligan who chose a career in the British Army to escape the lure of criminal life. Battle-hardened, he had a military view of inner strength (steel) in the midst of adversity. He took a step closer towards me and whispered . . .

'You want us to do that, don't you?'

'What are you saying?' I replied, looking up to catch his eye but still sounding reserved, to tease out his undisclosed thoughts.

'You're speaking to Christians like me. You want us to rise up.'

By that he meant . . . generally become more active against injustice and specifically against racism in Britain.

Respectful of his analysis, I came back with,

'You got it, blood . . . It's all there in code.'

He smiled, I smiled, and we gave each other the black male telepathic head nod, a prosaic physical gesture that conveys an emotional intelligence – a mutual respect.

As a black theologian and documentary filmmaker (developing and presenting programmes), I was pleased to hear the church brother's acute observation. Normally people would comment on how good it was to see a black academic on television or criticize an aspect of one of my films, but on this occasion someone understood that while using the medium and language of the mainstream, I was also addressing black Pentecostals.

From the outset, I made a conscious effort to encode[2] as many documentary films as possible with themes that would speak to black Pentecostals. The process began in the very first film I made in 1999 (*Britain's Slave Trade*) and continued to my last one in 2010 (*Revelation*). While it is impossible to guarantee that the intended audience would receive the message in the way that is hoped for by the sender, the church brother's ability to juxtapose Pentecostalism with 'resistance' suggests that at least one member of the audience was able to decode the way that my documentary filmmaking intersects the fields of theology and politics.

Despite its connection with reality and the factual events in the historical and social world, encoding *is* possible in documentary film. Put simply, a documentary is a non-fiction film – a representational mode of filmmaking that seeks to 'document' or capture reality.[3]

It has the lofty ambition of accurately reflecting the historical and social world. But this is a misplaced expectation: reflecting the real is shot through with difficulties including the inevitable distortion of real-life events. As we shall see later, documentaries experience interference at every level of production and as a result it is best to think of this genre as a lived tension between the 'real' and the 'reel'. It is this tension that creates a space for the encoding of messages.

## What is this book about?

The book reveals how, through developing and presenting television documentaries, I also encoded the documentary narrative in order to challenge and empower black Pentecostals. So who are the black Pentecostals and what is the predicament that concerns me? Well, black Pentecostalism in Britain consists of numerous denominations and tens of thousands of adherents. These denominations are now headed by a second generation of leaders who rose to prominence in the late 1990s, with a numerical shift away from a West Indian migrant clergy, and towards indigenous black British leadership. The second generation has inherited an expansive denominational network, hundreds of buildings and spheres of influence in every major urban conurbation in Britain. Furthermore, while there are numerous ongoing political struggles within black Pentecostalism (class, gender, sexuality), this book reveals how my documentaries make their point of departure in the deep-seated issues related to the colonial history and legacy of these churches. Indeed, the Pentecostal history travelled in this book begins with the colonial experience of African Caribbean men and women rather than African Americans and the Azusa Street Revival of 1906, the traditional start date for the birth of the Western Pentecostal tradition. Beginning with the slave and colonial experience is necessary in order to identify the soil in which black British Pentecostalism was birthed and how it continues to be hampered by inadequate theological nutrients from its Caribbean Christian origins. This wider Pentecostal history also enables us to address the root causes of problematic theological ideas in the deep tissue of black Pentecostalism. So what are the deep-seated issues?

This book critically theorizes how black British Pentecostalism, due to its colonial Christian heritage, fell prey to an insular anti-intellectualism and apolitical stance that enervated its ability to productively engage the wider culture, and advocate for its poorest and most marginalized members.

In light of this plight, in this book I employ liberating modes of thinking and acting that can free Pentecostals from particular theologies and practices that constrain them from promoting social change in their communities. I underscore these dimensions of Pentecostalism through language. I intentionally 'use' widely recognized religious terms in provocative and evocative ways so that they 'perform' cultural and political work. Admittedly, I redefine terms that are highly revered in Pentecostal lexicons – such as 'bewitchment' (here used to describe the oppression or social ineffectiveness of many Pentecostal churches) and 'exorcism' (used in this book to describe the often visceral process of liberation or renewal) – in a manner that would be unrecognizable to many Pentecostals. My purpose in using bewitchment and exorcism as visual, primary metaphors throughout this text is that Pentecostals and a broader readership might recognize powerful, concealed meanings that come to light when we name social realities in radically new ways. The resolution of the deep-seated issues takes place in documentary film.

This book is also about visual theology: my documentaries are vessels for a theological critique of black Pentecostalism. It represents a culmination of researching theology and popular culture that I began as a graduate student, and elaborated as a university teacher in works such as *Jesus Is Dread: Black Theology and Black Culture in Britain* (1998) and *Jesus Dub: Music, Theology and Social Change* (2006). *Documentary as Exorcism* continues this research enterprise by revealing how documentary films are inscribed with theological meanings that not only engage or exorcize black Pentecostalism but also indirectly create a new way of doing documentary film as a 'conjure' or a religious documentary etched with a theological-political narrative aesthetic.[4] The book is therefore more 'academic' in form and content than the films it surveys, but just as revelatory. In light of my task, I give important weight to theory – the selective intellectual frameworks and concepts that undergird and structure my content and methodology – in the deliberate and consequential way in which I carry out my work.

Finally, by doing theology in documentary with the express aim of decolonizing black Pentecostalism, this book is also theology in action. It communicates a distinctive intersection between thought and action through the matrices of theology and popular culture. The intersection between theology and popular culture has numerous modalities and scholars have rightly invested a significant amount of time cataloguing the relationships and outcomes.[5] However, as a black liberation theologian and documentary filmmaker, my approach is best described as *praxis*. The praxis approach stands within the political school of black theology[6] and also the 'committed-art school' of artistic endeavour in African diaspora cultures, where art is never a neutral aesthetic, but always situated and a vehicle for social change.[7] As a result, in the praxis approach, aesthetic consideration and abstract formulation are subordinate to instrumentality and theological-political struggle.

In sum, as an interdisciplinary study, *this book reveals how I set about doing theology in documentary film in order to make primary the 'emancipation' of black Pentecostalism, that is, enable it to shake off the colonial theological shackles that enslave it, so that, in the words of anti-colonialist, Frantz Fanon, it is no longer 'overdetermined from without'.*[8] However, while the primary focus of this book is black Pentecostalism, the arguments, perspectives and recommendations are not exclusive to it. Instead, my hope is that black Christians of every denomination and also progressive white Christians (those seriously committed to racial justice and articulating white liberation theology[9]) will also embrace aspects of this book that speak to their experience and ministry.

My motivation is not to disparage the Pentecostal tradition nor its current leadership, but to engage in constructive criticism, which challenges the status quo for the sake of seeking improvement. As such, my critical analysis does not make me an opponent of the Pentecostal faith; indeed, nothing could be further from the truth. Instead, constructive criticism is a way of being a teacher determined to inspire this church tradition to live up to the dictates of the 'good news' of the Gospel. I base my Pentecostal credentials and disposition on a particular reading of Pentecostal origins. My Pentecostalism does not rest on a foundation that slavishly peddles Bible passages as the only source for Pentecostal theology (and as a way of justifying one's credentials as a black Pentecostal).[10] Instead, my faith rests on the political praxis of the Western Pentecostal origins. As mentioned elsewhere, while there are a number of perspectives by which we can evaluate

Pentecostal origins (the Azusa Street Revival of 1906), I have chosen a theological-political interpretation.[11] A theological-political interpretation identifies how the structures of 'race', class and 'gender' are mediated through the emergence of glossolalia (speaking in an unknown tongue). In short, a new egalitarian praxis accompanied the movement's defining leitmotif. It was a new Christian ecclesiastical arrangement made even more remarkable by its opposition to the inherent discrimination of the prevailing 'American apartheid' of the early twentieth century. While the fledgling movement's radical commitment to 'race', class and gender inclusion was short lived, the nexus of glossolalia, social justice and Pentecostalism were not completely abandoned as the movement spread across the United States and the rest of the world.[12] Thus, my reading of the origins inextricably connects faith and practice, Bible and social transformation and provides an alternative way of being a *black Pentecostal* in Britain. That is to say, the version of Black Pentecostalism expressed in this book is one that is not only committed to upholding the redemptive power of Scripture, a belief in the sanctified life, but also living the intersection of the Spirit and social transformation. It is fair to say that while black Pentecostals have excelled in the first two areas (affirmation of scripture, and Christian holiness) they lag behind their African American and Latin American counterparts in the third.[13]

## Research methods

This book makes use of a variety of research tools. I make use of diachronic (over time) and synchronic (one point in time) analysis of textual sources and also post-colonial theological interpretations of biblical texts. However, two additional methods are foregrounded. These are 'autoethnography' and narrative analysis. The first method investigates the significance of personal experience in space and time and the second probes the way that we make use of stories to interpret the world. Combined, these approaches validate both my personal experience(s) and my voice as author – important episteme (ways of knowing) that are all too often neglected in knowledge validation systems in the university.[14] In fact, in my case, these additional research methods give more weight to the author than the text and audience as the criterion of meaning. In other words, this book is also an affirmation of 'auteur theory', that is, the view that the author is a key factor in understanding the meaning(s) of a cultural product. The author as the decisive voice or locus is given little attention in cultural studies and there are several reasons for the neglect. Generally, in the prevailing intellectual climate, theorists argue that other locations (the text or site of the image and the audience) account for the meaning(s) and effects of a cultural product.[15] Therefore, textual analysis and reception theories are given more weight in determining the significance of a product. However, in this book the emphasis on the author, that is, authorial intention[16] does not negate the importance of textual analysis or audience reception but instead seeks to add to the body of research in the theology of culture, *a body of work that is currently under-represented in studies by auteurs reflecting on their practice.*[17]

# Outline

*Documentary as Exorcism: Resisting the Bewitchment of Colonial Christianity* explores how I went about encoding documentary film, showing how black Pentecostalism is bewitched by colonial Christianity and how it must exorcize its 'demons'. The book consists of two parts, 'set on' and 'cast out'. The first part, set on, explores context and the predicament facing black Pentecostals – the continued impact of colonial bewitchment. The second part reveals how I encoded this impasse and its overcoming or exorcism in a collection of films.

## *Part I*

In Chapter One, I explore issues often ignored in documentary film studies, that is, how one gets into the industry and how one positions oneself in the field. This is also another way of thinking about documentary theory, by exploring positioning. I begin by describing my chance entry into documentary filmmaking as a black liberation theologian. Appearing on *Right to Reply*, a British television programme in 1996, inspired me to enter the world of television documentary, but distinguish myself from other black presenters and also the dominant representations of the black church on British television – choirs and conflicted individuals. In order to do so, I based my filmmaking craft on an emancipatory framework. Chapter Two introduces the emancipatory framework as the central paradigm that informs my filmmaking and consequently the structure of this book. The chapter explains the evolution of the framework and its central components. The evolution is necessary because these themes arise from the experience of hearing duppy (ghost) stories as a child and also from going to church every Sunday. The components are a belief in *bewitchment* or malevolent forces in the social world – and remedy through *exorcism* or the tradition of Jesus the healer. These core ideas are then embellished in the chapters following it to provide a framework for considering bewitchment and exorcism.

In Chapter Three, I develop an understanding of bewitchment. Bewitchment or witchcraft is a complex and varied concept and practice with a plethora of interpretations from a multitude of contexts around the globe. As a result, it is difficult to find one singular definition that everyone can sign up to. Due to its variety, it is best to define the subject contextually – how we come to experience it. Taking this view, I construct a unique understanding of bewitchment by combining perspectives from Christian theology and also anthropological studies of African witchcraft. I construct a distinctive contextual understanding that gives new meaning to the witchcraft idioms of the 'cannibal and zombie' that is to say, how these figures, when wrestled away from their unreliable and fantastical representation in popular culture, are a serious reminder of colonial subjugation. The purpose of the chapter is a particular interpretation of witchcraft that reverses the 'witch hunt', so that it is Western expansion, slavery and colonialism that are analysed as witchery. Chapter Four explores the antidote for witchcraft, that is, exorcism. Exorcism has a history in the Bible and is not outside of power relations, especially questions of conquest and occupation. The chapter begins by tracing the evolution of the practice from an underdeveloped idea in the Old Testament to a worked out theology in the New Testament. The centrepiece of the chapter is Jesus as a practitioner of exorcism, in which the expulsion of evil can be read both as an individual and yet, more importantly, a social practice or a social action.[18]

The next step is to show how (1) bewitchment is a feature of colonial Christianity and (2) how it further continues to inform black Pentecostalism *today*. The reason for doing so is to show that the soil in which Christianity was developed in the Caribbean was polluted and the impact of the degradation has powerful resonance in the present. Regarding the first step, how bewitchment became a negative feature of European Christianity, Chapter Five describes how Christianity became complicit with empire in the age of European expansion. It analyses textual sources in order to implicate both Catholicism and Protestantism in the rapacious and avaricious activities of Western European empires. Viewed through the bewitchment framework of Chapter Three, the church becomes party to the occult or hidden power of empire – its cannibalism and zombism. Cannibalism and zombism describe the rapacious and avaricious nature of colonialism, how it literally devoured African substance in the transatlantic slave trade and industrial plantation system of the Caribbean. The next two chapters are contemporary studies of the continued impact of colonial Christianity in black British Pentecostalism. Chapter Six explores the continued influence of the colonial *devouring* of black life, particularly its influence on a political passivity in black Pentecostalism that I name as non-prophetic ministry. It does so by outlining an archaeology of Western *cannibalism* from slavery to contemporary Britain. In other words, how the memory of the consumption of African substance is retained and re-imagined over time. The influence of the church is highlighted throughout, including a contemporary case study of the service at Westminster Abbey in 2007 to commemorate the bicentennial of the abolition of the transatlantic slave trade in Britain. In this final manifestation, flesh eating is expressed as a memory cannibalism – a struggle to maintain a particular interpretation of the slave past by marginalizing/consuming other perspectives. Memory cannibalism permits non-prophetic ministry to flourish. Chapter Seven turns the spotlight on the bewitching idiom of the zombie and the continued influence of colonial Christianity in a practice I name as academic-theology phobia. The zombie denotes a form of consumption but in this case it is a mindless body experience of African slaves. Through a comparative analysis of the Haitian zombie and a case study of black Pentecostal worship, I show how the idea of the zombie as a mindless body enlightens and reframes how we talk about black

Pentecostal attitudes towards academic theological education. That is to say, that 'zombie worship' signals worshipping traditions in black British Pentecostalism that marginalize and criticize critical theological thinking – or academic-theology phobia.

## *Part II*

In the second part of the book, I return to the role of the emancipatory framework as a central feature of documentary filmmaking. I begin by translating the emancipatory framework into a visual practice. To accomplish this task, Chapter Eight constructs a method of conversion based on techniques imbedded in the church cultures of black Pentecostalism. Using the example of the doctrine of sanctification, I reveal a signifying practice. That is, how the doctrine of sanctification is encoded in perception of music/broadcast equipment, dress codes and the décor of these churches. I use this method to legitimate my practice of encoding my theological focus, the emancipatory framework into documentary film. However, having crafted a new approach to the religious documentary – as a form of encoding, I reframe this practice as conjure. Conjure, while a varied and complex practice of thought and action, has a particular history in African diaspora cultures, as a form of spiritual encoding of cultural products. Thought of this way, cultural products, including documentary film, are perceived to have a certain transforming dynamic or power – and this is the way that I rethink the religious documentary encoded with the emancipatory framework. However, having articulated a view of documentary from the perspective of authorial motivations and positioning in Chapter One, I return to the subject to identify the location of conjure within the documentary genre. Chapter Nine continues the exploration of documentary that began in Chapter One, by focusing on documentary theory and practice. The chapter defines the genre, identifies the tension at its core and outlines its central modes. I locate conjure in the documentary's narrative and make use of the poetic mode of documentary, with its emphasis on textures or layers of meaning, as the best way of categorizing this approach to documentary.

The final chapters disclose the presence of the emancipatory framework in documentary film. Chapter Ten begins by showing how I encode the *bewitchment* of colonial Christianity in my early documentaries made for Channel 4 and the BBC. The first three documentaries, *Britain's Slave Trade, Black Messiah* and *Ebony Towers*, identify the encoding of bewitchment, that is, the complicity of colonial Christianity and also its continued influence as *cannibalism* and *zombism* in contemporary, black British Pentecostalism. *Britain's Slave Trade*, is a three-part series identifying the history, economic gain and continued influence of slavery in Britain. In this film, using the language of economics, I describe the church's complicity with the rationality of slavery. *Black Messiah* is a one-hour film comparing the rise of Black churches in America and Britain. Through the contrast, I identify how one tradition has rid itself of slavery's enforced political passivity and how one tradition remains captive. Finally, *Ebony Towers* is another Black Atlantic comparison, but this time the subject is education. The film reveals how African Americans made academic learning central to struggle to overcome the proclivities of the post-slave world and how, in comparison, black Britain lags behind. Central to this comparison is the role of the church.

In radical contrast, Chapters Eleven and Twelve explore how I went about encoding *exorcism* in documentary. Chapter Eleven explores two political films, with the expressed aim of challenging the continued political passivity of black Pentecostalism. The films are, *Empire Pays Back* and *The Great African Scandal*. In both of these films, exorcism is explored as a form of prophetic ministry that seeks to unmask injustice and proffer justice and as a result combat the non-prophetic ministry of black Pentecostalism. Thus, while not directly mentioning black Pentecostalism, these films modelled an alternative theological-political practice that is a repudiation of the continued influence of the political oppression of colonial Christianity. Likewise, Chapter Twelve explores the Bible documentaries *Who Wrote the Bible* and *Revelation: The Final Judgment*. *Who Wrote the Bible* explores the construction of sections of the Old and New Testament in order to demonstrate the historical and cultural forces at work in the development of Scripture. Likewise *Revelation: The Final Judgment* also engages in historical criticism to critique literal readings of the book. On another level, these films are exorcisms of academic-theology phobia by highlighting a hermeneutic of suspicion and a social justice optic. Having identified how exorcism works in film, in the conclusion to the book, I turn my attention to the context of the church. I want to also show that there are concrete recommendations for black Pentecostals, as also for progressive white Christians in Britain, that arise out of this study. I do so by first arguing that the study affirms the importance of serious reflection on political engagement. This is not a new call but it is expressed on the basis of this study – an emancipatory framework. Also, I call on black Pentecostal churches to reconsider how they go about the business of training ministers and also conducting Christian education in churches. However, the final recommendation is one that concerns aesthetics. To signal the commitment and engagement with the overcoming of colonial Christianity, I call for the introduction of an explicit visual culture of exorcism in places of worship.

This book is by no means written as the definitive or exhaustive study of the subjects at hand. Instead, it is offered as a distinctive methodology and practice for those seeking to find new ways of combining theology and the arts, revising the meaning of works by authors and, moreover, rethinking the meaning and practice of black Pentecostalism. Finally, although I have written this book with black Pentecostals in mind, they are the primary but not exclusive audience. That is to say, my intention is that the frameworks, models and practices explored in this book will find resonance with not only black Christians of other denominations but also with progressive white Christians and activists searching for new ways in articulating political theology and theology and culture.

# CHAPTER ONE

# Beyond the ubiquitous black choir

*A person's knowledge can only exist by virtue of a vast range of past experiences, which have been lived through, often with the most intense feelings. These experiences, including textual experiences (books, lectures, lessons, conversation, etc.), we have been taught to disguise so that our utterances are made to seem as though they emerge from no particular place or time or person but from the fount of knowledge itself.*

H. ROSEN[1]

'How did you break into television?' people have asked on numerous occasions. Implied in the question is inkling that I am either well-connected or simply lucky. My standard reply is: 'It's not a case of "how" but "why" . . . Because I wanted to challenge the way things are.' Imbedded in my reply is a bottom-up notion of power: that even in the face of an allegedly omnipotent media, the masses have agency.[2] However, it would be disingenuous to deny that social shifts have played their part in the opportunities afforded me. For instance, my entry into the field coincided with an increased promotion of diversity in broadcasting. As a result, it was easier for people like Aaqil Ahmed, a commissioning editor at Channel 4, to 'sell' the idea of a black presenter for religious broadcasting than it may have been just a few years before.

This chapter describes my entry into television broadcasting. It is a view of documentary filmmaking from the perspective of the author and concerns positioning. Here I want to think of positioning in relation to broadcasting, that is, presenting television documentaries. Specifically, it indicates where I position myself in relation to other presenters and black Christian representation on terrestrial television. Explaining one's position is more than 'navel-gazing'. It is to locate one's place in relation to matrices of power relations and to develop an approach.[3]

My position emerges from the initial forays into television and this chapter discusses how two issues, black presenters and the representation of black Christians, shaped my approach as a broadcaster. The first issue, black presenters, emerged immediately after filming *Right to Reply*, and is intimately related to the 'politics of containment' and 'misrecognition' – how black presenters negotiate their presence in the face of a white hegemonic media. The second issue, black Christian representation, surfaced several months later when I was asked to comment on black music on a special edition of the BBC's *Songs of Praise*. After providing an interview on the history of the black church in Britain, I reflected on the meanings of the dominant images of black Christians on British television. Determined to move beyond the politics of containment and recognition, and also the dominant images of black Christians, I decided to carve out an alternative representation that foregrounded black liberation theology.

# Entry into television broadcasting: *Right to reply,* 1996

It all began in the mid-1990s when I appeared on a viewers' complaint programme, *Right to Reply*, on Channel 4. I went on because of a growing frustration over a perceived change of emphasis in black programming at the channel. By the mid-1990s there was a shift towards representation tainted with 'racialized'[4] motifs. This new perspective, possibly informed by a more commercial environment for black programming,[5] was not always the case with Channel 4.[6] For instance, like many black people of my generation, I grew up admiring the channel because, after its launch in the early 1980s, it became a leading space to explore complex issues confronting black people including the dynamics of racism(s) and cultural politics. Committed to constructive black representation, the channel commissioned programmes such as the magazine *Black on Black* and the political show *The Bandung File*. In addition, the channel broadcast a raft of documentaries exploring a range of popular and esoteric themes in black history from the domestic and international arenas. Thus, for a decade, the channel was the only broadcaster devoting a significant amount of time and resources to black people's perspectives in the mainstream.

However, by the mid-1990s there was a distinct change in attitude – the gloves came off and the previously supportive perspectives with their explicit anti-racism were beaten aside.[7] In their place emerged a new gaze on black social and cultural life. While not completely denying the efficacy and existence of racism, the new emphasis de-emphasized its importance. While the motivations for this cultural shift at the channel remain opaque, the change bears an uncanny resemblance to a political philosophy called 'post-racial liberalism'.[8]

Post-racial liberalism arises in late modernity from liberal political thinkers in Western societies with long histories of racial discord.[9] While proffering a complex articulation of 'race'-relations, it is accused of reducing the importance of 'race' as a factor in black disadvantage. It does so by promoting diversity rather than equality, colour-blindness rather than affirmative action and 'culture of poverty' theories (the idea that disadvantage is fundamentally an individual matter based on lack of education or bad life choices[10]) rather than structural and historical analyses. An indication of this new outlook was evident in a number of documentary films broadcast on subjects as diverse as single parenting, mixed identity and criminality. On the cusp of this change was the emergence of *Badass TV*.

*Badass TV* was a magazine show that combined satire, parody and late-night titillation that I read as a glamorization of the blaxploitation genre – past and present. The programme embodied post-race liberalism by failing to provide context to the genre and also identifying the role of racism in the development of the complex use of hyper-real and black power motifs.[11] Initially, a critical view looked inevitable when the programme-makers cast West Coast gangster rapper Ice T and black British presenter Andrea Oliver to assume the roles of the protagonist and antagonist respectively. Unfortunately, the balancing act never materialized. With Ice T's sharp pithy statements, machismo and educated taste in all things, blaxploitation dominated the studio links and set the tone for the series. Consequently, viewers expecting some element of critical investigation of the genre were disappointed. Instead, the producers served up a weekly diet of ahistorical, salacious voyeurism of hyper-real sexualities and a bizarre ghetto-centric cultural production. Even artists rooted in serious black artistic endeavours could not escape these production values. Take for instance the programme's discussion of the work of the award-winning artist, Chris Ofili. His artwork was presented to the audience as a modern-day example of blaxploitation because of his use of elephant dung. The programme, however, failed to fully acknowledge why he used the waste product – a pragmatic African philosophy undergirding his aesthetic.[12]

I decided to complain about the programme and left a voice message on the channel's viewer complaint line. To my surprise, I was invited to present my case to *Right to Reply*. This weekly programme aimed to achieve broadcaster accountability by allowing viewers to challenge programme-makers, thereby making visible, to a degree, behind-the-scenes decision-making. I went on the show to register general displeasure at the move towards a more antagonist approach to black programming and a specific objection to *Badass TV*. Alongside Bola Fayola, another concerned viewer, I tackled the Commissioning Editor for Youth Programmes, David Stevenson, and co-presenter Andrea Oliver. Our segment on the show was a mere 10 minutes, recorded live and broadcast the next day.

The discussion began with Fayola claiming that the program was negative, especially in relation to the portrayal of black women. Andrea Oliver, consistent with her viewpoint in the series, countered by arguing that the programme was satire. She gave an example of how an interview with African American rapper 'Sir mix-a-lot' lying on a bed, carousing with semi-naked women, was a sophisticated attempt to unmask and ridicule his misogyny. Then David Stevenson, supporting Andrea, chipped in to argue that such images do not stereotype black men as hyper-masculine but attempt to portray them through the programmer's 'multi-textured approach'. I was not convinced. Ice T's transparent love of and identification with the genre, and Oliver's inability in each programme to seriously deconstruct the cultural products, seriously reduced the capacity for satire or irony. As a result, from my perspective, the programme had simply fallen in line with the new mood at the channel and reproduced some of post-racial liberalism's motifs in and through the blaxploitation genre. Supporting Fayola's gender critique, when asked by the show's presenter, Roger Bolton, about my concerns, I said:

> In the first programme, five out of the seven items . . . looked at black women and sex. Now to me that was an overwhelming attempt to represent black women as sexual objects, as commodities to be exploited. And I think that's very dangerous on television.

I went on to say that there was the potential alignment of these racialized images with other forms of racist discourse on black people. I continued:

> I think this [kind of programme] is dangerous in a climate where negative, racialized images are used to justify the mistreatment of black people. If you present black people as being no more than people who are somehow pathological, who have something internally wrong with them, then you run the risk of enforcing views which are held by parts of the [national] community we would not want to be associated with.

Both David Stevenson and Andrea Oliver denied this was the case and that the programme was in no way 'racialized'.

At the end of recording, I left with Fayola and we continued the discussion on the tube journey back to central London. Both of us were struck by the representational politics at work in the meeting. Representational politics refer to the intersection between representation and power or 'the ability to influence and dominate others'.[13] In this case, it refers to how presenters represent themselves on television and how the representation connects with matrices of power. We reflected on our own performances on the show and, generally speaking, the perils and pitfalls that encounter black presenters working in mainstream media, namely, how to negotiate their presence in a hegemonic white, middle-class workplace. I reflected on the discussion and arrived at two explanations of what we had witnessed and how my positioning is developed as a challenge to them.

# Representational politics

One on level, I was aware that black people have to negotiate their presence in mainstream media because, as a working-class African Caribbean man raised by Jamaican immigrants in the inner city, I was experienced in the complex cultural rituals that minorities enact in order to negotiate resistance, especially in spaces where they are monitored.[14] One way of describing the predicament is the 'politics of containment'.[15]

> . . . a new politics of containment honed this intersection of fixity and change. While continuing to be organized around the exclusionary practices attached to racial segregation, the new politics simultaneously uses increasingly sophisticated strategies of surveillance.[16]

The politics of containment describes how black middle-class people, especially women, have to comply with prevailing norms in the workplace, no matter how incongruous. At the nub of compliance is a contradiction: their relative visibility masks exclusionary practices. Faced with these confines, black women have to navigate situations that claim to be empowering, which in reality are sites of disadvantage. Applying the politics of containment to black people on television we may say that while some are fully aware of the racialized representations at play they decided to negotiate resistance by participating, albeit under duress. Sometimes, some black presenters let you know that they are uncomfortable with the narrative or subject direction by conveying an *African diaspora kinesis* – the non-verbal communication such as physical posture or facial gestures to convey solidarity with us despite being on the other side of the argument.[17] These 'black looks' convey the 'burden' of the politics of containment to the intended audience. But there is also another predicament that lacks the reflexivity exhibited in those negotiating the politics of containment, that is, misrecognition.[18]

Misrecognition is a form of forgetting within a cultural field, wherein individuals in question collude with the hierarchical order of things and unwittingly legitimate their own oppression:

> The agent engaged in practice knows the world . . . too well, without objectifying distance, takes it for granted, precisely because he [sic] is caught up in it, bound up with it; he inhabits it like a garment. . . . he feels at home in the world because the world is also in him. . . .[19]

Misrecognition describes a state of false consciousness where the individual succumbs to the dominant order of things. Moreover, it is acceptance and approbation of the way things are. Misrecognition is dangerous because it may lead to 'symbolic violence', or 'the violence which is exercised upon a social agent with his or her complicity'.[20] What this means in everyday life is that, unwittingly, by failing to recognize oppressive forces, some individuals leave themselves open to abuse. Accepting 'misrecognition' in black media professionals including the roles of television presenters suggests at best, naiveté and, at worst, complicity.

As a result of appearing on *Right to Reply*, I was determined that if I were given the chance to make programmes, I would oppose the politics of containment and misrecognition. I would do so by choosing to adopt a perspective that facilitated counter-politics – and I will sum up this position in my discussion of Black Liberation Theology later in this chapter.

Another opportunity to appear on television arose soon after my appearance on Channel 4, as my appearance alerted other broadcasters of my existence as a fledgling black theological voice in Britain. I appeared as a contributor on *Songs of Praise*, the BBC's flagship religious programme, during a special on black Christianity, to speak on black theology in Britain. This programme alerted me to a second form of representational politics: the controlling stereotypes of black Christians.

# The dominant representations of black Christianity on British television

During my appearance on *Songs of Praise*, I was interviewed along with other contributors to explain aspects of the black Christian tradition. Interestingly, there were no historical or theological questions; instead, questions were directed towards me about the style of worship. At one point, the interviewer asked me if black worship was 'happy clappy'? The question was asked in order to clarify the dynamics of black worship and was not intended to cause offence. Ironically, while no one took offence, the accusation did signal another related fact: *the representation of the black church on British television is stereotyped.* Black Christianity, despite being on the periphery of the public square, is more visible in popular culture and in visual media. It is over-represented in at least two ways: these are the choir and the 'conflicted'.

## The choir

Arguably the most popular image of black church life in the 1990s and beyond in television culture is the choir. Whether in a semi-comedic television commercial (Cornflakes cereal or mobile phone adverts), backing a musician or band on a popular music television show or singing 'spirituals' on a 'special edition' of the BBC's *Songs of Praise*, the choir has come to personify the black church. While it is true that the choir is an important feature of the black church (especially Pentecostal and evangelical traditions), it is misleading to reduce the choir to its aesthetic. Choirs have a social and theological role. Choirs were established for more than artistic endeavour,[21] inasmuch as the first wave of choirs was a means of securing church and denominational solidarity, particularly among young people.[22] Later, interdenominational choirs provided an occasion for informal ecumenical links that were forged between second- and third-generation black British people. For instance, the London Community Gospel Choir (LCGC) was founded on a desire to unite in musical harmony young people from across the black churches in London.[23] In recent years, this inclusive impulse has led Christians from white and other church communities to join what were once exclusively black choirs. Furthermore, we should not forget that in both North America and the United Kingdom, the gospel choir and its re-articulation of the 'spirituals' is fundamentally didactic in practice: it is a musical mediation of deep spiritual truths.[24] Despite its varieties of purpose, the aesthetic has become the main feature of the choir, and the choir a face of black Christianity in Britain.

So what are we to make of this media fascination? On the one hand, the over-representation of the choir can be read as a success story – it exemplifies the way that black popular culture has infiltrated the British mainstream. On the other hand, this over-representation is potentially problematic. That is, it could also be viewed as a type of 'blackface ideology'.[25] 'Blackface ideology' is a complex history of black representation based on the caricature or stereotype of a black person. Blackface can apply equally to whites imitating blacks as well as blacks imitating blacks. Either way, blackface comedy seeks to project a 'laugh at us' rather than a 'laugh with us' humour. While I am *not* suggesting that black choirs perform with the express aim of demeaning or denigrating black people, *I am* proposing that *the British media 'blacks up' the black choir* so that it functions as a stereotype of the black church. Stereotypes have power; 'they establish differences and these differences allow power to be exercised by one group over another'.[26] In this case, the stereotyping of the black church as smiling, clapping, singing black Christians reduces a complex religious tradition and its intersections with slavery, community, resistance and pedagogy to nothing more than dark-skinned people who 'sing so well'.

## Conflicted Christian body

The choir is not the only dominant image of black Christianity. Another leading image is the conflicted individual. The conflicted individual motif emerges from a misinterpretation of black Christian ethics through an unsophisticated surface reading of black religious cultural forms that leads to yet another representation. The misunderstanding is this: the traditional preaching and teaching of the black Pentecostal church, particularly its traditional affirmation of non-market values of conservative morality and personal integrity, are portrayed in the media as reactionary or socially oppressive, especially through the prism of a post-Christian, secular society. As we shall see, in such cases faith and 'race' collide to produce a view of black faith as problematic or unreliable. It is only the black Christian body that is marked in this way. In contrast, the white Christian body on screen, while also the subject of stereotype and even ridicule, is not 'raced' and is therefore marked in a very different way.[27] Thus, the appearance of the black Christian body on screen signals conflict and uncertainty.

The conflicted individual, in its problematic and unreliable modalities, is particularly prevalent in drama series and comedy productions. For example, blackness and sexual misdemeanour (themes that have a long and controversial history in biblical interpretation[28]) were reproduced in the 1990s' *Brothers and Sisters*, to date the only television drama set in a black church. The show had as its central narrative the inner conflicts surrounding the sexual preferences of a closet gay black minster. More recently, however, in 2007, in the BBC drama series *Casualty*, a black Jehovah's Witness family was faced with the dilemma of blood transfusion. After a significant amount of criticism of their beliefs, the hospital had to discover a way of allowing the family to retain their principles but save their daughter. Similarly, in 2010, the BBC's soap opera *East Enders* met with severe criticism from the black press over a character who was a mad, black, murdering Christian.[29]

Black performers are not averse to capitalizing on the conflicted for sardonic effect. One of the most successful black British comedy series of the 1990s, *The Real McCoy*, ran a weekly sketch of a black preacher played by the actor Felix Dexter. The character was torn between preaching moral virtues and containing his lust for the unholy. Likewise, in 2009 a black church sister, 'Miss Kingston', with a propensity for unpredictable verbal profanity, was a staple of the comedy series *The Little Miss Jocelyn Show*. The character was always the focus of a loss of trust or betrayal of trust, and subsequently played on the stereotype of the unreliable, unstable, black Christian body.

However, all is not what it seems; the ethics of the black church are more sophisticated than what is represented on screen. The ethical frameworks of these churches are forged between missionary morality and African retentions,[30] and reveal a tension between a strict morality and a pragmatic faith. The former is often dogmatic while the latter is transformative and flexible.[31] Sadly, the media tends only to capture the former and the result is the conflicted individual.

A useful way of thinking about the predominance of the conflicted image is through the modality of the 'wounded black'.[32] The 'wounded black' is a way of explaining how black bodies in pain or conflict are positioned in mainstream culture. The 'wounded black' is, however, an ambivalent image. On one level, it can be a figure of resistance. Take, for example, the way that images of less-than-perfect black bodies oppose the media fascination of hyper-black bodies in sports and popular music. However, on another level, that of oppression, the 'wounded black' registers a pathologization of the black body, wherein the over-representation of black bodies as weak, conflicted or contradictory, in some regards, is a way of signalling inferiority:

> The figure of the black wounded man builds on cultural ideas that equate bodily difference with inferiority. The wound serves as the mark of difference. Lurking beyond the wound is the notion of the not wounded, the intact, normal body by which the wounded body is measured insufficient.[33]

Using the wounded black to evaluate the conflicted black body on British television leads to two possibilities. On the one hand, the conflicted can be read as an alternative to black hyper-masculine braggadocio and self-assured images in sporting arenas and hip hop culture which are very dominant on British television. On the other hand, it is also possible to view it as a pathology that reinforces the view that black Christians are morally contradictory, ethically untrustworthy or opportunist, and therefore have no real theological value for mainstream Christian culture.

## New position

Despite its ambiguity, the wounded black troubled me as a mode of representation. I wanted to adopt a position of less ambiguity. To this end, I decided that if given the opportunity to make films, I would be unwavering in my commitment to representing myself as 'political black' rather than wounded black. Political black is another way of speaking about an intellectual commitment to an explicit articulation and critique of raced, classed, gendered and homophobic power structures as they intersect with blackness and black communities. Political blackness is 'postmodern blackness', that is to say, it recognises black diversity and multiplicity – there is more than one way of being black and there are diverse responses to racialized oppression. It is however, strategic in that it acknowledges that there are times for a fixed or essentialist viewpoint – in order to produce a critique or defend group interests.[34] Central to my affirmation of political blackness was the foregrounding of my professional role as a black liberation theologian.

Black Liberation Theology is a complex and diverse discipline that has its origins in the fusion of the 1960s Civil Rights and Black Power Movements in America.[35] It is fundamentally concerned with doing theology from black perspectives, whether they are 'raced', classed, gendered or queered, and as such incorporates intersectional analysis.[36] Furthermore, as a theological orientation that seeks to explicitly engage with, deconstruct and liberate *all* people from oppressive power structures, Black Liberation Theology defies the politics of containment and misrecognition. The incarnation of Black Liberation Theology that I develop is the *emancipatory framework*. The emancipatory framework as a contextual black theology draws from black British experience and theology to articulate a vision of God as emancipator from all forms of non-being. The emancipatory framework and its implications for filmmaking are explored in the next chapter.

This new position, beyond the choir and the conflicted Christian body, sits on an intersection of two well-known counter-strategies to media stereotyping of black people.[37]

There are at least three counter-strategies to stereotyping. The first is to reverse stereotypes. This means providing images and narratives where black people occupy dominant positions in visual culture. Ironically, this desire gave birth to the blaxploitation genre. While a complex tradition aimed at empowering black audiences, blaxploitation simply 'reversed stereotypes and inverted the traditional racial binary', so that black became 'good' and white 'bad'.[38] A second strategy to contest racialized representation seeks to provide a diverse range of black images to reveal black diversity and heterogeneity. This may result in the development of 'positive' images as well as affirming blackness. For instance, the independent cinematic productions of black British filmmaker Menelik Shabazz to represent black men as more than studs or criminals, as husbands and successful business people, is one example of this strategy.[39] As a result of offering complex examples and celebrating black representation, this strategy corrects the imbalance of negative types of images of black life in the mainstream. The difficulty with this approach, however, is that while illustrating 'difference' in representation, it may ignore the battle for eradicating racism. In other words, in striving to be different, there is the danger of neglecting the quest for equality.

A third counter-strategy seeks to 'contest representation from within'.[40] It presupposes that representation is a site of struggle or to-and-fro battle over meaning, and that a final victory is never, ever achieved. As a result, this approach does not 'call for new images and perspectives, but instead makes its focus an interrogation of the forms of racial representation at work'. The aim here is to 'out' stereotypes by making them 'work against themselves'.[41] According to Stuart Hall, a good example of this approach is the way that black British comedy has sought to 'expose stereotypes of black people and reveal their hidden depths, as a way of contesting meaning at a given moment in time'.[42]

The counter-strategy or new position implemented in my work incorporates aspects of the second and third camps. It incorporates aspects of the second approach because it seeks to provide an alternative representation of black Christianity, that is, a black liberation theological perspective on the subjects explored in documentary. It may not prioritize the outing of stereotypes but like the third strategy it also recognizes that representation is a fight and that resistance is always momentary and always a part of a wider process of struggle over meaning, and one that is never won outright.

In conclusion, this chapter shows that documentary is more than filming, location and editing; it is also about the positions that filmmakers consciously or unconsciously project onto the work. This is an overlooked aspect of documentary, a neglect that is due in part to the general avoidance of authorial intent in the discipline of cultural studies and its' identification of the location meaning of cultural artefacts. I have personified the importance of the role of the author by describing the evolution of my own position. I began by describing how my chance entry into the world of television broadcasting in 1996 inspired me to get involved in filmmaking. I was challenged by the lack of meaningful representation of black people in general and with a specific concern over *Badass TV*. However, appearing on the show also alerted me to potential racial politics to be navigated. I decided to take a stand and locate myself beyond the confining restraints placed on black presenters and also the stereotypical images of black Christianity, and differentiate my position. My position intersects two modalities of black representation in visual media. It seeks to provide new material to contest representation but only as part of an ongoing struggle that is never won outright. Furthermore, this new position is informed by a distinctive theological orientation or Black Liberation Theology. Black Liberation Theology is not a monolith; it is shaped by contextual and structural realities. Therefore we should think of it as an attempt to combine the particularity of a situation with the universality of the Gospel. My particular brand of Black Liberation Theology emerges from the inimitableness of African-Caribbean diaspora experience in Britain. As a child of Jamaican immigrants, I inherited a rich religious heritage that was forged in the intersection of African and European religions in the slave and colonial world of the Caribbean. The next chapter of this book describes this version of Black Liberation Theology, that is, the emancipatory framework, as a defining leitmotif that underscores my work in documentary film.

# CHAPTER TWO

# Set on, cast out

*The Christian faith provided a language for the meaning of religion, but not all the religious meanings of the black communities were encompassed by the Christian forms of religion.*

CHARLES H. LONG[1]

This chapter introduces the emancipatory framework, the guiding heuristic for my documentary films, and also this book. Central to the emancipatory paradigm is the thesis that colonialism had a detrimental impact on African peoples and that the healing traditions of black faith gesture towards an exorcism with communal post-colonial implications.

As James Perkinson proposes, in many respects colonialism functioned as a kind of religion, replete with a set of beliefs and practices.[2] Often we think of religion as a set of beneficent practices; that is, we associate religion with healing, redemption, security and emotional well-being for its adherents. However, I will discuss religion as a malevolent practice in which the audience it pursues might experience illness, oppression, captivity and displacement. Relating malevolent spirituality to colonialism, I will argue that colonialism can be understood as an *occult practice*. Commonplace examples of malevolent spirituality in which the intention of the religious practitioner is to cause harm are 'casting an evil spell' on an unsuspecting person or placing a 'curse' on one's rival. I want to complicate these facile understandings by contextualizing and personalizing them. Contextually, I appropriate African-derived conceptions of spiritual malevolence that were brought to the Caribbean by African slaves by retrieving duppy narratives, Caribbean versions of ghost stories. Unlike the popular American film *Ghost* and its sequels, the duppy stories are diagnostic and point to social instances of malignancy. On a personal level, I retrieve these stories not from books or interviews with academics, but from my childhood. To legitimate this emphasis on experience, I will explain in this chapter how autoethnography, a scholarly method that takes account of the experiences of the researcher in a research setting, informs my work.

A prevailing response in the Christian tradition to malevolent spirituality and evil oppression has been some form of exorcism in which the oppressive forces are cast out or removed. In contrast to cinematic presentations of exorcism, such as *The Exorcist*, I contextualize and personalize exorcism by placing it in a broader Christian framework of sanctification and healing, and by drawing upon the redemptive practices of the African Caribbean church of my youth. Like my treatment of malevolent spirituality, I gesture towards the communal implications of exorcism, and connect it with colonialism by arguing for the deliverance of the black church in Britain from the legacy of colonial Christianity.

Finally, it is important for me to note the intersection between malevolent spirituality, exorcism and filmmaking. As mentioned in the previous chapter, in contrast to simply researching the subject matter and emphasizing the artistic dimensions of the films I present, I very intentionally adopt a framework that underscores my positioning and particular perspective in film making. The framework is an emancipatory framework that is encoded in my films. In short, the framework identifies and names an experience of oppression, and pinpoints the practices that can, ultimately, overcome the oppression. My analysis of malevolent spirituality is an example of naming oppression, and I refer to this aspect of my framework as 'set on'. Set on in the Jamaican vernacular describes the malevolent actions of an individual or group. In the same manner, my discussion of exorcism is an example of confronting and prevailing over oppression, and I refer to this dimension of the framework as 'cast out'.

Before I get started, a word about methodology. In the previous chapter, I made use of a methodology – positioning – and intend to make use of another reflexive approach, that is, autoethnography. Autoethnography is a complicated academic method whose origins are within anthropology.[3] At its most basic level, it sets out to foreground the *experiences* of the researcher in a research setting and the researcher's feelings, motives and perspectives as the researcher interacts with others and the issues, concepts and theories at hand. This is a highly reflective approach that 'privileges the individual'.[4]

> [A]utoethnography is a form or method of research that involves self-observation and reflexive investigation in the context of ethnographic field work and writing.[5]

By privileging the individual experience, it sets out to produce a version of truth that is missed by traditional research methods. Autoethnogaphy, however, does not completely disregard other research methods but aims to communicate 'hidden experiences and feelings that are often ignored in the dominant version of things'.[6] Autoethnography can take many forms including 'evocative auto/ethnography that seeks to write about personal experience including the emotional response to a given situation'.[7] In contrast, the analytic approach seeks to ground the discipline within 'a research setting, with a commitment to improving theoretical understandings of broader social phenomena'.[8] These two approaches are not, however, always mutually exclusive as autoethnography, like other methods of enquiry, can be worked out as a both/and proposition rather than an either/or stance.[9] It is this combined perspective that informs the use of the research method here. I want to think of autoethnography of a legitimation of the use of experience in any research context – including the researching and the writing of this book. In this case it allows me to appropriate personal experience as a source of meaning. I take seriously the *evocative* dimensions of hearing duppy stories and also the theological aspects of the experience of church-going as a youth. But I also connect these stories to other discourses and *analyses* in order to construct a framework: that is, the emancipatory framework. My intention is to produce a better understanding of an obscure evaluative framework (creolization) in diaspora religious experience. Let me explain.

The two discourses represented in the framework are a combining of African and European Christian thought to frame a critical worldview. But this is not an original thought or the first time that it has happened. Instead, Caribbean peoples of African descent have a long history of creolizing religious ideas from Africa and Europe.[10] Creolizing religion is a piecing together of diverse spiritual and theological elements to construct a new religious perspective.[11] As Charles Long reminds us in the quote at the beginning of this chapter, Christianity was not the only religious tradition in the diaspora.[12] Moreover, it was not untainted by African retentions. This study contributes to scholarly understanding of this African diaspora religious method by revealing a grafting together and combining aspects of African-derived religious traditions and Christian theology. But this is not as straightforward as it may seem. Any form of religious syncretism including creolizing religion, must be responsible syncretism. Responsible syncretism is a concept used in Pentecostal studies to describe legitimate blending of religious ideas.[13] To be responsible, the grafting process must be open, consistent and complementary to scripture and tradition. As we shall see, I believe that these requirements are met with development of the emancipatory framework.

## Emancipatory framework

The emancipatory framework was first developed in my doctoral thesis in the mid-1990s,[14] and here I want to provide a more elaborate version that underscores my filmmaking. The term emancipation has an important resonance in the Caribbean; it is both a legal state and a continuing struggle. As a legal status, emancipation describes the moment slaves were set free from bondage in 1834, although it took another four years for it to be worked into practice in the Caribbean. Emancipation is also a continuing social, cultural and political struggle because, although slavery has ended, the undoing of the slave past and its psychological, cultural and political damage continues for the African diaspora. Thus, the emancipatory framework, gestures towards the continuing struggle for black freedom in the post-slave world. The emancipatory framework includes (1) the experience of oppression and (2) the practices that name and analyse it. Later, in

Chapters Ten to Twelve, I will show how the framework is played out in documentary film. I have named the two central aspects of the framework and the focus and site of struggle as follows:

Set on – malevolent spirituality;

Cast out – Jesus as healer.

## *Set on*

The first feature of the emancipatory framework is malevolent spirituality, and to fashion an understanding of it I draw from the ubiquitous telling and retelling of the duppy story in Caribbean households in Britain. Duppy stories were told to me by my parents and had been passed down from their parents, grandparents and great-grandparents. These stories originate from African slaves transported to the Caribbean during the transatlantic slave trade. African heritage is reflected in the etymology of 'duppy' – said to derive from the Bube (Niger-Congo) *dupe*, meaning ghost.[15] But these were not tales of translucent blobs dressed in white sheets. On the contrary, they were tales of the spirits of the dead and a feature of a complex African cosmology retained and reworked, away from the gaze of the overseer and missionary, by slaves and colonial citizens in Jamaica.[16] Spirits of the dead, which represent one layer of a cosmic hierarchy, were believed to dwell in the place of death until crossing the threshold into the spirit world. It is believed that during this state of limbo, and in the absence of the proper ceremony or ritual by the family of the deceased to ensure the passage of the spirit to the spirit world, duppies roam about at night, frightening the living, or, at the behest of indigenous healers (Obeah-Myal practitioners), being used for malevolent intent.[17] The latter, malevolence, is reflected in the saying 'set duppy pon dem' – meaning to set an evil force on a victim.[18] However, the fear of the duppy is not only of seeing one but also the fear of *being made into* one and as we shall see later in the study of the zombie the *fear* of zombification betrays a more sinister memory of slavery. I learned about these stories during the 1970s, near the time of the national power strikes in Britain. My folks never gave a reason why they told them, but my hunch was that they knew these stories were important and desired to pass them on. As a result, they were relaying important religious-cultural and sociopolitical information.

On a religious-cultural level, the duppy story was the retention of ancestor veneration and benign spirituality coalesced.[19] For instance, in my parents' stories, dead relatives who returned from the grave were greatly revered and, whatever the form, their visitation was always verified by a living witness – someone who had seen the duppy. My father had the best stories, unsurpassed because they were the most creatively narrated and embellished. In his tales, a re-occurring duppy appeared in the form of a dead relative by the name of Gladys Brown. Her materialization was always benign, a reassuring spiritual presence in the midst of chaos and crisis. Jamaican anthropologist Barry Chavannes identifies the purpose of the duppy story in Jamaica when he says that for relatives duppies 'assume protective roles' and communicate with the living in dreams or visitations.[20] But while this first viewpoint may resonate in the Caribbean, it does not have the same force as the second viewpoint, a perspective that was shaped in part by the experience of the Jamaican diaspora in Britain.

What interests me here is the belief in malevolence at the sociopolitical level. At the sociopolitical level, the duppy story was related to power relations.[21] This theme was evident in my mother's tales. My mother's stories were always told and retold in tandem with experiences of colonial and neocolonial subordination. Born in Jamaica in the late 1920s, she was raised towards the end of British colonial rule on the island. She travelled to England in the 1950s as part of the post-war generation of West Indian immigrants to Britain and developed a successful career in nursing. Her duppy stories were informed by Caribbean and British experience. In one of her stories she told of how, when a child, she was walking home late one night along a dusty old road flanked by palm trees, when a duppy suddenly appeared in front of her blocking her way home. Terrified, she immediately changed direction and found an alternative route home. But this was not the full picture. What made her stories equally compelling was that she would either begin or end all her duppy stories by recalling experiences of colonial racial hierarchy, how she had to curtsy to every white woman she met or address young white children with the titles of elders, irrespective of their age or station. She would also speak of land theft or bad business dealings with the colonial authorities and then launch into a duppy story. Sometimes, she prefaced her stories by making use of more present displeasure such as discrimination in her workplace (she was a nurse in the National Health Service), and also of an unprovoked racial slur by an unknown passer-by. I am not sure how unique or ubiquitous this approach was, but what was clear was that within the particularity of *this* re-telling it was *not* well-defined where the duppy story began and the sociopolitical reality ended. As such, her stories pointed to an undoubted relationship in her mind between malevolent spirituality and the colonial/post-colonial experience. That is to say, the duppy story signified malice in the social world and that the social world was inhabited by nefarious spiritual forces.

Her stories had a profound influence on me, not only leaving me with a great sense of fear and mystery – the expressed aim of most duppy stories – but also rendering me incapable of separating the drama and mystery of the duppy story from power relations in colonial Jamaica and post-colonial Britain. By collapsing the supernatural into British colonialism and neocolonialism, she also revealed something mysterious about colonialism/neocolonialism: they had hidden powers. Ironically, it was within this context of African religious retention that my mother, a staunch, conservative Jamaican Christian with a profound expectation of the *parousia* (Christ's second coming) and little regard for the politics of this world, came closest to articulating a political theology – a belief in *structural evil* where evil resides in historical processes and social systems such as British colonialism in the Caribbean and post-war racism(s) in Britain.

I want to work with my mother's conflation of malevolence and the colonial regime to develop an understanding of set on. For my mother, the malevolence within the duppy story merged with talk of the colonial/post-colonial order to reveal a seamless connection between malevolent spirituality and colonial/post-colonial practice(s). For this reason, I want to think of set on as the malevolence of social systems and institutional structures. In this study, it specifically denotes the malicious legacy of colonialism, and in the following chapter I will expand the understanding by drawing on ideas of malevolence from Christian thought and anthropological views of African witchcraft.

## Cast out

The second feature of the emancipatory framework is cast out. Cast out is a theme that emerges from the experience of exorcism in black Pentecostal churches and is intimately related to the image of Jesus, the healer. Growing up, I went to church twice on Sundays and attended prayer meetings midweek. My parents were members of the Pilgrim Holiness Church and my mother was particularly active, founding churches in Wellingborough in Northamptonshire and Coventry in the West Midlands. The Pilgrim Holiness Church derives from an intermingling of Euro-American Evangelicalism and the creolized Christianity of the Caribbean. It was this hybrid version that was transported to Britain by West Indian migrants in the post-war years, and became a feature of the collective known as 'black-led' churches. Back in the early 1970s, worship in the Pilgrim Holiness Church in Britain was a dynamic encounter with the Holy Spirit. Whether in prayer or song, the experience of the presence of the Spirit was the criterion for Christian understanding; by means of the Spirit, all ideas about God were tested and worked through. It was, however, a mixed blessing. On the one hand, we developed a hermeneutic of suspicion towards all god-talk that was not the product of the moving of the Spirit – as we understood it in worship.[22] On the other hand, there was the downside that this episteme was vulnerable to rejecting learning outside of the worship context.

A defining doctrine of the church was sanctification – the experience of increased spiritual awareness and moral fortitude because of the progressive work of the Spirit in the life of the believer. The current Wesleyan Church website sums up this doctrinal understanding:

> We believe that sanctification is that work of the Holy Spirit by which the child of God is separated from sin unto God and is enabled to love God with all the heart and to walk in all His holy commandments blameless. Sanctification is initiated at the moment of justification and regeneration. From that moment there is a gradual or progressive sanctification as the believer walks with God and daily grows in grace and in a more perfect obedience to God. This prepares for the crisis of entire

sanctification which is wrought instantaneously when believers present themselves as living sacrifices, holy and acceptable to God, through faith in Jesus Christ, being effected by the baptism with the Holy Spirit who cleanses the heart from all inbred sin. The crisis of entire sanctification perfects the believer in love and empowers that person for effective service. It is followed by lifelong growth in grace and the knowledge of our Lord and Savior, Jesus Christ. The life of holiness continues through faith in the sanctifying blood of Christ and evidences itself by loving obedience to God's revealed will.[23]

Christology, who Jesus Christ was, is and will be, was intimately related to sanctification in the Pilgrim Holiness Church. Jesus was the 'Son of God' and, as such, was holy. We, in turn, aspired to be holy because it was a sign of our devotion to God and because it was a feature of God's being. As a result, as 'holiness people' we were occupied with the eradication of sin and evil. Redemption was the antidote for sin and Jesus was our saviour. Jesus' work of redemption was ongoing and exhibited in a pronounced interest in healing. Our foregrounding of Jesus as healer may have been the result of the influence of African-Caribbean Christianity in which belief in Jesus as healer was easily adopted by African converts because of the affinity between healing traditions in African religions (which is reflected in African retentions such as the Jamaican Obeah/Myal complex) and the miraculous healings of Jesus.[24]

Every Sunday was a day of healing at the Pilgrim Holiness Church, as believers devoutly approached the altar for special prayer for physical and emotional sickness. As part of the healing ministry, the church practiced exorcism. Exorcism or 'casting out an evil spirit' was both unique and ubiquitous. It was unique in that it was a specific rite to remove an evil presence believed to be harassing or residing within an individual. The unique approach was not practiced regularly or entered into lightly; on the contrary, the act was usually preceded by days or weeks of prayer and fasting. There was, however, lurking beneath the surface, a ubiquitous experience of exorcism. This was a more common but subliminal practice that theologian James Collins terms exorcism/deliverance.[25] Exorcism/deliverance is not 'exorcism light'[26] but is more accessible and 'every Sunday' exorcism was made possible through 'the ministry of a charismatic individual gifted in leadership' or congregation who may administer exorcism of perceived oppressive or possessive spiritual forces through ministry. In practice, this meant people were delivered from oppressive or possessive spirits during the regular Sunday morning service or at special healing services organized by the church.[27]

The second feature of the emancipatory framework, cast out, is informed by black Christian exorcism. Later, in Chapter Four, I will expand its meaning beyond the limitations of the black church tradition so that exorcism/deliverance is not perceived only as an individual matter but also as a social concern. As we shall see, this expanded view of exorcism is exemplified in Jesus' exorcisms in Mark's gospel. Thus, when referring to cast out, I am describing how to remove oppressing forces. Within the contours of this exploration, it refers to the exorcism/deliverance of the black church from the legacy of colonial Christianity.

Now that the framework has been articulated we can return to the question of responsible syncretism and other considerations when applying the emancipatory framework. To recap, the emancipatory framework is a two-fold process, a recognition of malevolent forces in the social world and their overcoming through the healing traditions of the black Church – exorcism. This framework is also a combining of African religious retentions and Christianity. It is a responsible syncretism on two grounds. First, it is responsible because is an open, upfront and explicit presentation of the interaction of two discrete practices. It is not hidden beneath layers of dogma, tradition or church history. As such it is open to criticism, reform and even repudiation. Second, it is trustworthy because it is consistent with the Christian scriptures as it mirrors the oppression-liberation motif and the conflation of spiritual/ social. The oppression-liberation motif in scripture has communal expression in the story of the Exodus in the Old Testament, where God intervenes in human history to free an oppressed people from bondage. The oppression-liberation motif is also witnessed in the healing ministry of Jesus. Jesus frees men and women from afflictions that while expressed in bodily terms have identification with wider social and political realities (Legion, Mark 5). Both incidents convey a merging of the spiritual and social in the biblical world. This syncretism is also aligned with the biblical tradition of borrowing/appropriating of other religious ideas and re-orienting and reworking them in light of Christian thought and practice.

However, while a responsible syncretism, the emancipation framework is not intended as a totalizing theory or universal norm for all time. This is because there is more than one theological pathway to justice. In the diaspora there exist numerous Christian responses to the black predicament. For instance, religious historian Gayraud Wilmore identifies three distinct traditions: survival, elevation and also liberation.[28] Therefore, I offer this framework as one pathway among several. Similarly, the framework is not an attempt to essentialize black experience. That is to say, not all black people or black Christians will automatically identify with this experience or framework, and neither should they be obliged to do so. Instead, the framework moves beyond 'ontological blackness' (attempts to fix black experience as singular or homogeneous) by recognition that the framework emerges out of a black subjectivity. As such, the framework and its implied notions of black experience are but one of many ways of being black.[29] Thought of this way, the emancipatory framework is a strategy to be deployed depending upon the circumstances rather than a norm for all time. It is a strategic choice rather than a mandatory obligation. Finally, this framework should be understood as being cyclical rather than linear in progression. This means that set on and cast out are ongoing, continuous experiences. As a result the starting point may not always be the experience of set on but instead cast out. As a cycle, the accusation that the emancipatory framework and other such liberation motifs make their starting point a negative reality (racism in the social world) rather than positive realities such as the existence of black and white Christian cooperation is redundant.[30]

But is the emancipatory framework Pentecostal theology? Well, much depends on what we understand to be the nub of Pentecostal theology – its distinctive hallmark. As mentioned in the Introduction, my version of Pentecostalism is primarily informed by the theological praxis at Azusa Street. The nexus of glossolalia and new social practices (race, class and gender inclusion) represent the defining dynamic of the fledgling movement. Therefore, in my opinion, authentic Pentecostalism is expressed in a politically inclusive pneumatology (theology of the Spirit). The emancipatory framework is consistent with this understanding of Pentecostalism because it seeks to apply the supernatural power of God in Christ to transform situations blighted by the forces of non-being, such as racism, sexism, classism, homophobia and the continued influence of colonial Christianity. The emancipation framework is not a 'square peg' in the body of Pentecostalism; on the contrary, it is at the very heart of black Pentecostalism.

In conclusion, the emancipatory framework represents a contextual black liberation theology motif arising out of the Caribbean diaspora experience in Britain. On one side, it acknowledges the presence of malevolence in the world, specifically the evil that resides within individuals and structures. On the other side, it embraces the transforming power of Jesus the healer, specifically the exorcizing energy located in certain rites and also the more ubiquitous exorcism/deliverance tradition of black ministry and worship. The framework does not represent an original methodology or combination of elements; instead, it represents a long-established tradition of creolizing religious beliefs and practices in the Caribbean. As such, it proffers the pre-existence of an unconscious liberation framework imbedded within conservative black Christian culture *that should not be overlooked* by those searching for a liberation motif in African-Caribbean Christianity. As we shall see, the emancipatory framework, set on and cast out, shapes and informs my documentary canon and that there are films that identify the set on and others that prescribe the cast out of colonial Christianity. To explain the more nuanced workings of this approach it is necessary to further develop the understanding of the framework. To do so, the following two chapters elaborate the contents of set on and cast out.

# CHAPTER THREE

# Witchcraft

*Give I back I witchdoctor.*

STEEL PULSE[1]

The lyric, 'give I back I witchdoctor' from the song 'Soldiers' (1979) by the Birmingham reggae band *Steel Pulse* has always intrigued me. My curiosity stems from trying to decipher why the singer of the song, David Hines, who is also a committed Rastafarian, aligns himself with African witchcraft, much less call for its reintroduction. One possible answer lies in the context of the song. The track paints a picture of the European military conquest of Africa and the terrible history of colonization and brutality by the former white majority rulers of apartheid South Africa. Colonialism is contrasted with a romantic view of pre-colonial Africa as a land full of levity, environmental equilibrium and harmonious communal co-existence. Therefore, we may conclude that the witchdoctor signifies the civility and nobility of ancient Africa and that the songwriter's request describes a longing for a long lost era. While not wanting to read too much into these five words, we can say that the lyric represents a rare moment in diaspora history where African witchcraft is presented as a constructive way. In the same manner, this chapter also seeks to make use of African witchcraft as a constructive resource by identifying its diagnostic fecundity.

This chapter expands the understanding of the malevolent spirituality of the duppy story and consequently the meaning of colonialism as an occult practice. To recap, the emancipatory framework is fundamental to understanding how to interpret my documentary films. The first part of the emancipatory framework is 'set on' or the malevolent spirituality of British colonialism. This malevolence was expressed in the duppy stories told by my mother, which interwove a real and present sense of the occult (hidden powers) with racial subordination in the Caribbean and Britain. Talk of duppies and malevolent forces has a long history in the Caribbean, and originates in the traditional religions of Africans transported as slaves. However, these traditional beliefs were categorized by the Christian church as superstition, magic and even witchcraft, and were viewed as a threat to the stability of the colonies.[2] I want to challenge the view of the Christian tradition by returning to the origins of witchcraft discourse in Western Christian thought and anthropological reflections on African witchcraft. Ultimately, I believe that more expansive notions of witchcraft can complement and incorporate Christian understandings.

Witchcraft is an incredibly difficult subject to define.

What is witchcraft? Here's what my dictionary says: 'the practice of a witch or witches, especially the use of magic or sorcery; the exercise of supernatural power supposed to be possessed by a person in league with the devil or evil spirits'. That's fine, unless you're the curious type. What do we mean by magic and sorcery? How does one access this supernatural power? Just who are the witches? These questions are difficult and generate questions of their own, expanding the problem, blurring defections.[3]

Is witchcraft being in league with the devil? Sorcery? A religious belief? A social diagnostic? No one is quite sure, and the lack of clarity is due to the plasticity of witchcraft. That is, what is considered witchcraft evolves over time and ideas differ in varying historical and cultural contexts:

We find witchcraft today and in antiquity, in the developing world and in rich nations; it's familiar to young and old, high and low. Some label enemies 'witches,' while others profess or confess witches' skills. There are those who believe, and those who do not (especially those in the West); but everyone recognizes the witch-figure.[4]

Scripture does not provide us with straightforward answers either. This is because it also expresses a degree of ambiguity:

> Not all its magicians were impious sorcerers like the Witch of Endor: some Jewish priests performed magic to demonstrate to rivals the power of Yahweh, and all manner of divination and cursing was condoned if done in His name.[5]

What is being suggested is a contradiction at work. On the one hand magical powers are presented as problematic by those outside of cult of Yahweh, but yet on the other hand, similar practices are legitimate reflections of divine power when inside the cult of Yahweh. Early church history is equally unclear about the precise nature of Christian engagement with non-Christian or traditional indigenous beliefs. Despite St Augustine denouncing witchcraft in *The City of God*, in reality Christianity was relatively tolerant towards it until the thirteenth century.[6] Lack of definitional specificity and historical variation suggest, among other things, that the best way to think of witchcraft is *contextually*.

What we can say with certainty is that witchcraft ideas emerge out of particular contexts and contain specific ideas that are deeply culturally specific. This insider understanding is what anthropologists refer to as *emic* knowledge. Therefore, witchcraft definitions are crafted and constructed by places and spaces informed by particular historical, social, cultural and political forces. For instance, to speak of witchcraft today in Britain is to engage with a controversial discussion associated with *child abuse* as highlighted recently by the British media. The mysterious discovery of the unknown African boy's 'torso in the Thames'[7] and the terrible mistreatment of the African girl Victoria Climbié, reveal a reduction of witchcraft to issues of child abuse.[8] A problem that is all too easily dressed up into a 'moral panic' in the British media.[9] While not seeking to belittle the importance of the particular issue at hand, child disappearance, a useful example of the moral panic surrounding this issue appears in a newspaper piece from *The Guardian*:

> A 'scandalous' number of children as young as four, many of them African, are missing from school rolls in London, it emerged yesterday. The Metropolitan police revealed that

in one two-month period, 300 black boys aged between four and seven vanished from rolls in the capital. Despite extensive investigations, involving police forces across the world, only two of the 300 were traced. Child welfare groups and education chiefs expressed shock at the figure and warned that some of the missing children might become victims of exploitation. Some experts estimate that thousands of children vanish from the system each year. Though it is assumed that most come to no harm, there were calls for the government to bring in regulations to force the authorities to do more to trace all missing children. Hilton Dawson, patron of Africans Unite Against Child Abuse, said: 'It's scandalous. I think the government is hiding from this issue. We need an effective working relationship between schools, social services, the police and immigration. That simply isn't happening.' The depth of the problem was highlighted when police investigated the murder of a young African boy – nicknamed Adam – whose torso was found in the Thames. They asked schools in London to check if any boys aged four to seven had gone missing over the relevant two-month period in 2001. Officers were shocked to be told that 300 had vanished. Of these, 299 had come from Africa.[10]

Consequently, we may define witchcraft in response to the particularity of our situation, the place of malevolence within it. But no definition is exempt from power relationships.

Therefore, in this study, in an effort to contextualize witchcraft, I want to draw on two disciplines to make sense of the malevolence of my mother's duppy stories. I want to construct an understanding of witchcraft that embellishes the duppy story and its concealed meanings. In order to do so, it is essential for me to draw on scholarship that is generated by the disciplines of theology and anthropology to provide a new contextual understanding.

Theology facilitates the interpretation of witchcraft through the categories of sin and evil. However, rather than thinking of evil simply in terms of the nefarious decisions of individuals, I explore social and structural understandings of evil that enable us to recognize the material and sociopolitical dimensions of witchcraft – a practice that is too often 'spiritualized' or depoliticized in popular imagination.

Anthropology, on the other hand, allows me to look at witchcraft not as an end in itself, but as a peephole into the dynamics of obscured, ethereal social and political forces. As such, anthropologists speak of witchcraft as a form of moral discourse – a discourse that is not simply reactionary, but one that diagnoses or interprets social ills. As we shall see, the 'body' is a critical site for both the practice and explanation of witchcraft, for it viscerally implicates social and political bodies.

When appropriately placed in conversation together, theology and anthropology point to witchcraft as evil manifested in social and political forces. This evil is articulated in moral discourse, which creatively engages metaphors to register the presence of these social and political abnormalities. I place this grafted theological and anthropological interpretation into a historical framework. In fact, I use this reading of witchcraft to engage with past centuries in order to understand the history of colonialism in Africa and the West Indies in more complex and socially accurate ways. Furthermore, I appropriate the metaphorical language of cannibalism, which speaks of rapacious consumption, and zombism, which speaks of a 'mindless body' experience, from their glamorized pop-culture environments and place them in this theological-anthropological framework. This hybrid structure allows me to analyse the function and effect of consumptive and death-dealing colonialism upon Africans and their Caribbean counterparts.

## Deliver us from evil

In order for me to parse out the theological perspective (sin and evil), I need to review the 'construction' of witchcraft by the Christian church of medieval Europe. This is because *it is important to acknowledge how witchcraft is determined by theological-political realities that too often deter us from exploring dimensions of witchcraft that enable us to engage with social structures such as colonialism in both religious and social terms.*

Witchcraft as a belief in a witch or sorcerer has various origins in the world and historians have done much to show how in medieval Europe a discourse emerged on witchcraft as false belief or heresy.[11] Witches, primarily women, were believed to be in league with the devil,[12] from whom they gained their magical powers. Witchcraft was anti-religion with its own set of beliefs (satanic) and practices (magic). This type of magic was originally constructed as a 'problem' for the Church in the fifteenth century, when the inquisitor Heinrich Kramer wrote the best-known and most-quoted medieval text the *Malleus Maleficarum*, 'Hammer of Witches', in 1486. What had previously been known as magic, conjure or the creation and use of potions dating back to Greco-Roman times, was now perceived by the church as occult powers or maleficium:

> Prior to the fifteenth century, people spoke in terms of heretics, of maleficium, of monstrous female spirits – the lamiae and strigae, but not of a single composite category 'witch'. By the mid-sixteenth century, however, educated men generally agreed upon the definition of 'witch' and 'witchcraft', definitions that drew upon, but were clearly distinguished from, older categories.[13]

Neither church nor civil court arrived at a strict and ultimate definition of what witchcraft actually was and what it entailed.[14] However, as well as the myths that a witch could be identified as someone able to fly through the air, or have satanic 'orgies' with the devil,[15] there were at least three dubious measures or characteristics of being in league with the devil:

> One was the presence of a least one example of maleficium, an act of harmful magic . . . a major trait of what they were looking for. Another was the witch's intention in performing his or her magical operation, and Roman and canon law especially looked for evidence of this. . . . a third . . . the existence of some kind of pact between the operator of Satan or one of his evil spirits. . . . a private commercial contract.[16]

One central and defining theme that emerges from the attempts to codify witchcraft is church hegemony. The church's domination of the issue allowed it to exert domination over pre-Christian and non-Christian beliefs and practices. Witchcraft accusation was mostly directed at outsiders and deviants and as a result represented the power of the religious and civil authorities to label particular individuals and groups that held heretical views as enemies, as those in league with the devil.

Take for example the case of the Cathars. The Cathars were notorious in Europe from the twelfth to the fourteenth century. They believed that the Catholic Church was evil, as vile as the world itself and that both were to be withdrawn from. The Church responded by accusing the group of satanic acts including 'cannibalism, infanticide, and holding sexual orgies'.[17] In addition, European states continued to persecute witches, mostly women, until the eighteenth century. But, in England, the Witchcraft Act of the early eighteenth century prohibited witch-hunting and indirectly created a space for the pursuit of occult beliefs and spiritualism. The Church continued to oppose both of these interests as forms of witchcraft.[18] In sum, in defining witchcraft, the Church set forth the concept of a witch as an individual in league with Satan, and as one holding beliefs antithetical to the Christian faith. This view has not disappeared with time and revisits us in the form of theologies that continue to define witchcraft as satanic or devil worship.[19] Moreover, the church's construction of witchcraft reveals the symbiosis of witchcraft accusation and power:

> The history of witchcraft illustrates the way that knowledge was not manufactured in a vacuum, but artfully determined by institutions and ideologies. Knowledge was political, and so therefore was witchcraft . . . witchcraft accusations were shaped by material conditions and social relations, both the substance of politics.[20]

Given the relationship between accusation and power, it makes sense to explore witchcraft from other Christian perspectives, including those that emerge from the margins of church history. To do so, I want to draw on another Christian tradition of evil, from Liberation Theology, that I want to rework into an understating of witchcraft.

There are alternative Christian views on the source of evil and non-being that permit us to think of it in social and institutional terms, far beyond the sphere of the individual and the presence of a witch or sorcerer, while still retaining a sense of malevolence and wrongdoing. Naturally this second view resonates with the histories of people who have been on the receiving end of great human atrocities and seek to use theological language to describe what is perceived as a malevolent spiritual presence.[21] To arrive at this second view, it is necessary to work with the descriptive categories of sin and evil. These categories allow us to talk about ruthless actions that result in incredible suffering and harm. I want to arrive at a theological understanding where we can equate witchcraft with evil. To do so, I want to draw on useful insight from constructive theology.

In *Constructive Theology: A Contemporary Approach to Classical Themes*, the authors present a relationship between sin and evil.[22] 'Sin is moral culpability and always carries the potential for enormous suffering', so that sin is experienced as evil. Therefore, 'every sin has the potential for malevolent surplus or evil'.[23] Indeed, for the authors, these categories of sin and evil not only pertain to individual but also corporate wrongdoing, a conceptual move that is defined as 'a journey from classic to liberation reasoning'.[24]

In classic Western theology, sin and evil are 'interior to the sinner'. Much of this is due to the centrality of the story of Adam and Eve in which sin is a result of 'individual human choice and characterized by estrangement from God'.[25] *However, the Bible also points us towards the idea of sin and evil as part of systems that govern social life.* Reflection on this structural idea has led to a revision of the classic model. Paramount here are the words of the apostle Paul in Ephesians 6.12, where evil can be described as power structures:

> For our struggle is not against flesh and blood, but against the rulers, against the authorities, against the powers of this dark world and against the spiritual forces of evil in the heavenly realms. (NIV)

In Liberation Theology, the workings of evil in power relations are made visible.[26] These scholars term evil in structures as 'structural evil'. Cynthia Moe-Lobeda helps us understand structural evil as the relationship between the metaphysical and social arrangements in *Resisting Structural Evil*:

> By structural evil, I do *not* refer to metaphysical forces beyond human agency. To the contrary, while structural evil may be beyond the power of individuals to counter, it is composed

of power arrangements and other factors that are humanly constructed and therefore may be dismantled by other human decisions and collective actions.[27]

Structural evil departs from the personal evil of classical Western thought by accounting for acts of great cruelty and brutality that are 'not the sum total of individual sins, but result from corrupt structures and systems, particularly those that are economic and political'.[28] From this standpoint, evil is more present in the structure of societies and the wider world than within individual moral decisions. This is because unjust 'social forces shape human consciousness and material decisions and these forces once institutionalized and normalized lead to undeserved suffering of innocent people'.[29] In such cases, liberation theologians speak of 'hegemonic forces of evil as structural evil'.[30] As New Testament theologian, Walter Wink, explains, the idea of structural evil emerges from the New Testament world itself. That is to say, the Bible points to the existence of structural evil in the organization of the Roman Empire. Wink notes 'there were Jews and Christians in the first century who perceived the Roman Empire as demonic, but their experience of the system was found in day to day interaction with Roman power, in the form of soldiers, taxes and governors.'[31]

To summarize, the first view of witchcraft describes it in terms of what it accomplishes, that is, evil. Evil or a malevolent surplus is responsible for not only individual iniquities but also problematic social and political relationships that govern the world. There is, however, another view of witchcraft outside of the Christian tradition that allows us to think of witchcraft as a diagnostic tool, and I believe this second view incorporates rather than rejects the Christian interpretation.

## Witchcraft as moral discourse

I also want to consider the contributions of anthropologists of the past century who have sought new ways to theorize witchcraft without resorting to the label of 'superstition'. By so doing, we can begin to view witchcraft not simplistically as an evil 'religious' practice that malevolent Africans performed against each other, but as a set of oppressively evil practices that were performed against Africans to colonize them – practices which were experienced by Africans in both religious and social ways.

It was once thought that the persistence of witchcraft in Africa would disappear with the modernization of the continent, but this has not been the case. Instead, theorists speak of the 'modernity of witchcraft', that is, its ability to reproduce itself within each new historical epoch.[32] This process of adaptation reveals a connection between witchcraft at the local village level and wider geopolitical shifts.[33] This practice of modification also leads theorists to conclude that there are indeed multiple modernities – diverse ways that global cultures have interacted with industrial capitalism outside of Western modernity.[34]

Witchcraft study has undergone a radical revision in the twentieth century and begins in the 1930s with the enquiry of English anthropologist Edward E. Evans-Prichard. After rejecting the existence of the supernatural, Evans-Prichard studied the function of witchcraft among the Azande (of the Congo). Rather than dismissing it as superstition, he concluded that their belief system was rational. Witchcraft explained why things happened, particularly misfortune.[35] After World War II, studies uncovered how witchcraft explained social strife and tensions at the local village level. Prominent among this group of anthropologists was the 'Manchester School' of anthropology (Max Marwick, Victor Turner and Max Gluckman). These scholars provided rigorous analyses and case studies to reveal a range of social strife explanations. For Marwick, witchcraft accusation was part of a 'social strain-gauge', reflecting social change and social control.[36] For Turner, also, witchcraft reflected community tensions, accusations and their resolution as 'social drama'.[37] These 'processual' approaches owed much to Gluckman. Gluckman examined 'multiplex' relationships – people bound together in multiple roles out of which conflicts inevitably ensued. Here also, witchcraft was part of a coherent ideology that bound the village together.[38]

In late modernity, however, a new approach to the study of witchcraft emerged from those interested in the persistence of witchcraft and its adaptation 'in situations where societies were less structured or also experiencing crisis due to the unsettling effects of economic progress or abuse of state power'.[39] This interest led anthropologists to reflect back and reconsider how African witchcraft was adapted to interrogate previous forms of social upheaval, such as colonialism. I will say more about this later. What is clear from modern studies is that rather than being a passenger on the back of modernity, witchcraft is in critical dialogue with it:

> Its changing moral discourses and purifying practices have intervened, diversely, in conquest and colonialism, in state building and stratification, in the advent of markets and the marginalization of local economies.[40]

In these later studies, which lead to more dynamic understandings of witchcraft and its social functions, the purpose of witchcraft discourse is to intervene as a moral discourse, in which the body becomes the focus of attention for wider and ever-changing social and political struggles. Speaking of this dynamic, anthropologists Jean Camaroff and John Camaroff state:

> Its signs work by rooting expansive moral meanings in the naturalizing ground of human bodies. The latter are made to speak disturbingly, viscerally, about ultimate values: about life, death, wealth, power, misappropriation, domination, and so on. Thus procreation and abortion serve as metonyms for social reproduction and its abuse; gluttony and cannibalism signify unnatural consumption and accumulation; the commoditization of vital physical properties and functions is the archetypal image of capitalist exploitation. . . . All this, in turn, underscores a crucial point, one that is confirmed over and over . . . witchcraft is not simply an imaginative 'idiom'. It is chillingly concrete, its micro politics all-too-real.[41]

Moore and Sanders identify one facet of witchcraft as a moral discourse by speaking of it as a process of diagnosing 'illicit accumulation'. Illicit accumulation describes the occult as wealth creation to produce a view on economics in the modern world, particularly, how globalization and its creation of huge disparities of wealth and poverty, and inherent exploitation of the poor, represent illicit forms of exchange. They note:

> A large body of evidence from Africa suggests that witchcraft and other occult practices are intimately bound up with people's

ideas about production exchange and consumption. The flows of information, goods and people characteristic of globalization are experienced as incorporating some and excluding others: a variation that leads to those experiencing its privation to view globalization as introducing a predatory and illicit form of exchange.[42]

Once again the body speaks viscerally of this illicit accumulation:

> Stories of zombies, cannibalism and headhunting are imaginative moral frameworks for making sense of wage labour, consumption, migration, productive regimes, structural adjustment programmes, development policies and the function of markets.[43]

Thus, witchcraft in anthropological thought moves beyond the stilted debate on superstition and seeks to portray African witchcraft as a deeply rational moral discourse seeking to identify the ethical abnormalities that produce occult economies in the contemporary world:

> In this expanded universe of value, some have argued, witchcraft can be seen as indigenously-inflected critiques of modernity(ies), capitalism and globalization, and the inherently problematic relations of production that accompany them.[44]

However, witchcraft and the material realities to which it points are not confined to the contemporary world. *Instead, anthropologists have projected back to propose that this function of witchcraft is historic and applies equally to previous eras and occult economies.* Anthropologist Ralph Austen, for instance, suggests that witchcraft as a moral discourse has a previous incarnation in an earlier form of globalization – as a diagnostic tool to explain the colonial presence and slavery in Africa:

> The conception of witchcraft as ambiguous attribute of power within Africa is often presented in ahistorical terms, as a timeless reflection of the tension between communal values and selfish individualism and anxieties about natural threats to subsistence. Our data on witch beliefs, however, are all either

from the Islamic or European outside world. It is striking that several West African cosmologies link witchcraft with the deployment of victims in a nocturnal and/or distant 'second universe', echoing in more or less explicit terms, the experience of the Atlantic slave trade.[45]

Austen's analysis locates the origin of African witchcraft as a direct response to colonial terror in the form of interpreting and diagnosing its source and impact. This is not a new idea. For instance, Louis White catalogued 'vampire stories' in the nineteenth and twentieth centuries in Africa to reveal a similar connection between the witchcraft idiom of vampires and persistent colonial oppression.[46] Furthermore, religionist Charles Long suggests that we should attribute a religious meaning to witchcraft idioms. Long argues that we should think of the African response (imaginative moral frameworks, zombies, cannibals) as religious idioms that gesture towards 'mysterium tremendum' or overwhelming power that is received negatively.[47] Borrowing 'mysterium tremendum' from theologian Rudolf Otto, he wants us to see the colonial anthropological views of witchcraft as reflecting a sense of an overwhelming force that is not exempt from profound super-rational explanation and meaning. For Long, naming them this way allows us to perceive an otherwise hidden reality, namely, a more profound awareness of colonialism's spiritual logic – as a nefarious supernatural force.[48]

Austen and White give us license to diagnose colonialism as a form of witchcraft, and Long to project a spiritual meaning onto witchcraft idioms. Regarding the latter, Long's appraisal, I want to signal the beginning of thinking about the cannibal and zombie as important themes. I will elaborate on these figures in Chapters Six and Seven. For purposes of this discussion, we can simply say that cannibalism or flesh eating, on one level, expresses fears about the body. For instance, historical analysis has shown how cannibal accusation was 'reciprocal with Africans and Europeans portraying each other as cannibals'.[49] But on another level, for Africans, accusations of witchcraft against Europeans functioned as a description of sociopolitical and spiritual reality – the avaricious and rapacious consumption of African resources and slave bodies. The idiom of witchcraft labelled these consumptive actions as occult practices.[50] The zombie as a witchcraft trope emerges from the slave and colonial experience.[51] It denotes a mindless body, a drone-like experience responding to only to limited external stimuli. While a variety of ideas exist on the precise nature of the causes of zombification, they are all related to unscrupulous spiritual practices. As a result, the zombie describes enslaved, mindless body as a product of nefarious activity.[52] In sum, the cannibal and the zombie are neither abstract nor ethereal but very real and material.

Thus, the anthropological interpretation of witchcraft describes it as a moral diagnostic that seeks to interpret ethical abnormalities in the social world, including the extremes of wealth and poverty. Furthermore, this interpretation also accounts for the emergence of witchcraft idioms such as the cannibal and zombie that can be interpreted socially, politically and spiritually in both colonial and post-colonial African experience.

## Witchcraft, malevolent surplus and moral discourse

It is time to pull these ideas together and define what is meant by witchcraft in this study. As mentioned at the start of this chapter, witchcraft is difficult to define and best understood contextually. I have taken advantage of this opacity and from the location of my own experience and context made use of the disciplines of theology and anthropology. So, I want to think of witchcraft as a belief and diagnostic system. It is a belief system that presupposes the presence of evil in the world. Evil or malevolent surplus is the cause of great acts of violence and terror such as the transatlantic slave trade and the avarice of colonial exploitation. Evil can also be framed in systemic terms and for this reason scholars speak of structural evil. Structural evil provides us with an alternative way of imagining the institutionalized social inequality and economic disadvantage that plagues much of world history. Witchcraft is also a diagnostic system. It provides us with a way of identifying ethical abnormalities in the social world, particularly the structure of occult economies characterized by rapacious and covetous actions that arise not only from individual choices but also from the operation of systems and structures. Fundamental to this study are the optics used to diagnose the malignancy of witchcraft. To this end, I want to foreground the idioms of the cannibal and zombie.

These imaginative terms are neither superfluous nor irrational, but, instead, frameworks for identifying nefarious activities in the social world. As such they lead is to very concrete and material relationships and outcomes.

In conclusion, in this chapter, I have sought to develop the awareness of malevolence recorded in my mother's colonial/neocolonial retelling of the Jamaican duppy stories. Through the grafting of theological and anthropological views of witchcraft we can reframe the duppy story, particularly its sociopolitical version, as an imaginative idiom that functions as an aperture into a religious-cultural malaise: the presence of evil in the world, including a perception of the contamination of social systems and institutions. However, by doing so, I am not claiming that this is the only view of witchcraft or one that is consistent with all other diaspora reflections. Instead, from my location, I have simply sought to position myself in relation to a particular history and make sense of it through the use of specific and relevant tools. Thus, in the spirit of David Hines and *Steel Pulse*, I too view it as a constructive resource.

In closing and anticipating the following chapters, I want to pre-empt a future discussion of witchcraft diagnostic and the way that it allows us to identify the infection of institutions. My view of witchcraft allows us to reframe British colonialism in the Caribbean and the role of the church in the British colonies of the West Indies as forms of witchcraft practice – and these themes will be discussed in more detail in detail in Chapter Five. In the next chapter, however, I will expand on the antidote for witchcraft, the second feature of the emancipatory paradigm, exorcism.

# CHAPTER FOUR

# Exorcism

*He is a miracle working God*
*He is a miracle working God*
*He is a miracle working God*
*He is a miracle working God.*
PENTECOSTAL CHORUS

*With every exorcism, Jesus liberates those who are*
*oppressed and possessed by forces beyond their control.*
*Empire in this material is about both spiritual and*
*geo-political forces . . .*[1]
CHERYL PERO

Healing is the purpose of the second feature of the emancipatory paradigm or 'cast out'. Cast out refers to addressing the named oppression, specifically, the healing tradition of the black church and the role of exorcism. As already mentioned, exorcism is a specific rite and also a general practice, exorcism/deliverance, experienced through the ministry of prayer and worship.[2] Pentecostals are comfortable with the image of Jesus the healer and affection towards this aspect of the life of Jesus is reflected in a multitude of songs and choruses that attest to the miracle-working power of

Jesus in the Bible, and the availability of divine healing for today. No chorus states this reality more succinctly than the repetitive one-line chorus quoted above. In black Pentecostal churches in Britain, healing is mostly confined to physical, psychological and relational (familial) matters, seldom venturing into the social arena. That is to say, black Pentecostals rarely apply the healing motif to political illness or social dysfunction.

The first aim of this chapter is to challenge this Pentecostal 'blind spot' by identifying a tradition of healing and exorcism in the ministry of Jesus that engages with the sociopolitical world. But healing in the form of exorcism is not only marginalized by a socio-political myopia, theological trends have also conspired to obscure the application of exorcism to social ills. From the very outset, the Western Pentecostal movement marginalized exorcism as a resource for believers because of a belief that the indwelling of the Holy Spirit, through the baptism in the Spirit, made receiving exorcism redundant for believers.[3] Exorcism was confined to the needs of non-believers – those more likely to be oppressed or possessed by an unclean spirit. As a result, the second aim of this chapter is to challenge the marginalization of exorcism by re-establishing its centrality as a Pentecostal resource.

I will first survey the evolution of exorcism practices in the biblical tradition, after which I will identify a post-colonial interpretive scheme to tease out the socio-political dynamics of Jesus' exorcism. Post-colonial interpretation emerges out of the world of formerly colonized peoples and foregrounds a hermeneutic sensitive to the presence and also the removal of colonizing forces. When this hermeneutic is applied to the exorcism of Jesus, we encounter an interpretation that addresses colonizing forces in the text. This approach is consistent with contemporary biblical studies which argue that exorcisms reveal more than a religious reality in the first century:

> Reports of controversies in both the Synoptic Gospels and John, as well as extra-biblical evidence, both Jewish and Greco Roman, suggest that exorcisms, like other religious phenomena, were not only understood from what we would call a religious perspective, but were also viewed as socio-political acts.[4]

I will end by providing a post-colonial reading of one of Jesus' most important exorcisms, the healing of the Gerasene demoniac in Mark 5.1–10.

## Exorcism in the Bible

I want to begin by briefly surveying biblical exorcism but centre on the exorcisms of Jesus. Exorcism presupposes the presence of evil spirits or demonic forces. Intriguingly, spirit possession or the 'overcoming by, or negotiation of, an external force', is responded to in different ways across time and cultures.[5] In the Old Testament, spirit possession and oppression is evaluated negatively and remedy involves attempts to expel the occupying spirit. However, the Bible provides very little information about the presence of demonic oppression or possession and the need for exorcism until the New Testament,[6] however, the Old Testament provides an important intersection of exorcism with power relations and culture.

The closest resemblance to spiritual 'oppression' in the Old Testament is found in references to 'lying spirits' (1 Kings 22.19–24), a 'spirit of jealousy' (Numbers 5.14–15) and the spirit of 'whoredom' (Hosea 5.4). However, these spirits 'do *not* possess individuals but instead remain as evil presences'. For instance, the evil spirits that plague Saul in 1 Samuel (16.14–17) 'do not enter his body, but reveal a "transfer of spirits", where the Spirit of the Lord leaves and an evil spirit troubles him'.[7]

> **14** Now the Spirit of the Lord had departed from Saul, and an evil [a] spirit from the Lord tormented him. **15** Saul's attendants said to him, 'See, an evil spirit from God is tormenting you. **16** Let our lord command his servants here to search for someone who can play the lyre. He will play when the evil spirit from God comes on you, and you will feel better.' **17** So Saul said to his attendants, 'Find someone who plays well and bring him to me.' (1 Samuel 16.14–17, NIV)

Exorcism is not outside of power relations. On the one hand, those mediating the spirit world are generally condemned (Exodus 22.18). On the other hand, practices resembling exorcism are permitted inside the cult of Yahweh, as witnessed in the dual between Moses and Aaron and the Pharaoh's magicians in the book of Exodus:

> 8 The Lord said to Moses and Aaron, 9 'When Pharaoh says to you, "Perform a miracle," then say to Aaron, "Take your staff and throw it down before Pharaoh," and it will become a snake.' 10 So Moses and Aaron went to Pharaoh and did just as the Lord commanded. Aaron threw his staff down in front of Pharaoh and his officials, and it became a snake. 11 Pharaoh then summoned wise men and sorcerers, and the Egyptian magicians also did the same things by their secret arts: 12 Each one threw down his staff and it became a snake. But Aaron's staff swallowed up their staffs. 13 Yet Pharaoh's heart became hard and he would not listen to them, just as the Lord had said.
>
> 14 Then the Lord said to Moses, 'Pharaoh's heart is unyielding; he refuses to let the people go. 15 Go to Pharaoh in the morning as he goes out to the river. Confront him on the bank of the Nile, and take in your hand the staff that was changed into a snake. 16 Then say to him, "The Lord, the God of the Hebrews, has sent me to say to you: Let my people go, so that they may worship me in the wilderness. But until now you have not listened. 17 This is what the Lord says: By this you will know that I am the Lord: With the staff that is in my hand I will strike the water of the Nile, and it will be changed into blood. 18 The fish in the Nile will die, and the river will stink; the Egyptians will not be able to drink its water."' 19 The Lord said to Moses, 'Tell Aaron, "Take your staff and stretch out your hand over the waters of Egypt – over the streams and canals, over the ponds and all the reservoirs – and they will turn to blood." Blood will be everywhere in Egypt, even in vessels[a] of wood and stone.' 20 Moses and Aaron did just as the Lord had commanded. He raised his staff in the presence of Pharaoh and his officials and struck the water of the Nile, and all the water was changed into blood. 21 The fish in the Nile died, and the river smelled so bad that the Egyptians could not drink its water. Blood was everywhere in Egypt. 22 But the Egyptian magicians did the same things by their secret arts, and Pharaoh's heart became hard; he would not listen to Moses and Aaron, just as the Lord

had said. **23** Instead, he turned and went into his palace, and did not take even this to heart. (Exodus 7.8–19, NIV)

Exorcism also intersects cultural practice in the closest associations with exorcism in the Old Testament, in the narratives of David.[8] David is presented as performing works associated with exorcism, which incorporate cultural expression. As we shall see later, culture is inscribed with a specific understanding of exorcism. Here David removes an externally tormenting spiritual entity through the medium of culture by playing a harp:

> Whenever the spirit from God came upon Saul, David would take his harp and play. Then relief would come to Saul; he would feel better, and the evil spirit would leave him. (1 Samuel 16.23 NIV)

Finally, Solomon is also given a place among the exorcists. In the Septuagint's Wisdom of Solomon, a sacred writing in the Jewish tradition that is not found in the canonical books of the Protestant Bible, we are told that Solomon gives thanks to God for the power he has been given to . . . 'know the spirits', although he also expresses ambivalence regarding this power, and is critical of those who perform magic.[9] It is God alone who has the power to rebuke evil. For instance, in Zechariah 3.10, God rebukes Satan. Thus, despite very little evidence of a specific and universal practice we can call exorcism, the Old Testament reveals practices to remove the external spiritual entities that torment the body.

Exorcism in the New Testament appears as a relatively clearly distinct practice, which emerges out of the inter-testamental period, with four differences from the Old Testament.[10] First, there is the emergence of human mediators who have various powers including exorcism. Second, the influence of a philosophy of ethical dualism[11] leads to the belief in indwelling evil or demonic possession as a sign of evil presence. Hence, in the ancient world, evil spirits were thought to affect a person by causing illness, encouraging sin or through *possession*.[12] Third, the New Testament is less concerned with Old Testament issues of witchcraft or the cause of demonic activity than with the 'destructive nature of the demon and what it does to a person's body and social existence'.[13] Finally, exorcism in the New Testament is discursive, reflecting the interests of the New Testament writer. Therefore, with every exorcism there is a simultaneous exploration of several issues. For example, as we shall see later, the exorcism of Legion in Mark is also a coded critique of the Roman Empire.[14]

In the New Testament, exorcism is described in a variety of ways, although the word 'exorcism' only appears once (Acts 19.13) in the form, 'to exorcize', which refers to the removal of evil spirits. This utterance suggests that a demon could be exorcized by what a person said or did. Furthermore, the synoptic writers make use of a range of terms to designate exorcism.[15] Separate verbs are used to distinguish exorcism from healing, although the two often overlap. The most common terms indicating exorcism are to 'remove' (Mark 1.25–8) and 'cast out' (Mark 1.34). Both terms point to the relocation of the possessing element.

> 25 And Jesus rebuked him, saying, 'Hold thy peace, and come out of him.' 26 And when the unclean spirit had torn him, and cried with a loud voice, he came out of him. 27 And they were all amazed, insomuch that they questioned among themselves, saying, 'What thing is this? what new doctrine is this? for with authority commandeth he even the unclean spirits, and they do obey him.' 28 And immediately his fame spread abroad throughout all the region round about Galilee. (Mark 1.25–8, KJV)

> And he healed many that were sick of divers diseases, and cast out many devils; and suffered not the devils to speak, because they knew him. (Mark 1.34, KJV)

Also present is the idea of 'releasing and binding'. For instance, in Luke 13.10–17 Jesus releases the woman from her debilitating condition. Another example is the binding of the 'strong man' or Satan (Mark 3.27; Matthew 12.29).

> No man can enter into a strong man's house, and spoil his goods, except he will first bind the strong man; and then he will spoil his house. (Mark 3.27, KJV)

> Or else how can one enter into a strong man's house, and spoil his goods, except he first bind the strong man? and then he will spoil his house. (Matthew 12.29, KJV)

There are other terms such as 'to silence' (Mark 4.39) and 'to overpower' (Luke 11.22).

> **39** He got up, rebuked the wind and said to the waves, 'Quiet! Be still!' Then the wind died down and it was completely calm. (Mark 4.39, NIV)

> **21** When a strong man, fully armed, guards his own house, his possessions are safe. **22** But when someone stronger attacks and overpowers him, he takes away the armor in which the man trusted and divides up his plunder. (Luke 11.21–2, NIV)

Intriguingly, demons are only given a degree of influence. Nonetheless, they are portrayed as mischievous, antagonistic, the source of illness (Mark 9.17), cause of self-harm (Luke 11.26) and evil (Luke 11.26). Thus, in the New Testament exorcism implies the driving out of evil forces and spirits by the actions, rituals or performance of an individual.[16]

The exorcisms of Jesus are one of the most under-investigated areas of Jesus' ministry,[17] and what we do know about Jesus' exorcisms comes primarily from the synoptic Gospels, particularly Mark. Although there is not a great deal of comparative material available to contextualize Jesus' exorcisms, New Testament scholar Howard Clark Kee notes that Jesus as exorcist represents a role compatible with rabbinic Judaism.[18] In contrast, anthropological studies take a broader religious view. For instance, Amanda Witmer places Jesus' exorcisms within a wider comparative framework to reveal similarities with shaman traditions:

> . . . Jesus was known in the earliest traditions as a spirit-filled exorcist and that his baptism by John and his vision of the spirit of God entering into him at the beginning of his public mission, bore striking similarities to the experiences of prophets reported in the Hebrew Bible and to those of shaman-healers across cultures.[19]

What is key for Jesus is that exorcism is a sign of divine power, the harmonious relationship between the exorcist and God, and a sign of the reign of God to come.[20] For instance, when asked to justify

His method, Jesus says that He casts out demons by the 'Spirit (or finger) of God':

> 25 And Jesus knew their thoughts, and said unto them, Every kingdom divided against itself is brought to desolation; and every city or house divided against itself shall not stand: 26 And if Satan cast out Satan, he is divided against himself; how shall then his kingdom stand? 27 And if I by Beelzebub cast out devils, by whom do your children cast them out? therefore they shall be your judges. 28 But if I cast out devils by the Spirit of God, then the kingdom of God is come unto you. (Matthew 12.25–8, KJV)

Thus, even though it may have appeared that He was acting on His own, Jesus was clearly identifying the source of His power and authority. Conversely, we may assume that to fail at exorcizing suggests wrong relationship with God or lack of faith, as in the case of the sons of Sceva in Acts 19.[21] Exorcism as a sign of God's power continues into the early Christian mission. To reveal the power of the Gospel, miraculous occurrences take place, including exorcism. Indeed, for Luke-Acts, exorcism offers a critique of occult practices:

> 11 And God wrought special miracles by the hands of Paul: 12 So that from his body were brought unto the sick handkerchiefs or aprons, and the diseases departed from them, and the evil spirits went out of them. 13 Then certain of the vagabond Jews, exorcists, took upon them to call over them which had evil spirits the name of the Lord Jesus, saying, We adjure you by Jesus whom Paul preacheth. 14 And there were seven sons of one Sceva, a Jew, and chief of the priests, which did so. 15 And the evil spirit answered and said, Jesus I know, and Paul I know; but who are ye? 16 And the man in whom the evil spirit was leaped on them, and overcame them, and prevailed against them, so that they fled out of that house naked and wounded. 17 And this was known to all the Jews and Greeks also dwelling at Ephesus; and fear fell on them all, and the name of the Lord Jesus was magnified. 18 And many that believed came, and confessed, and shewed their deeds. 19 Many of them also which used curious arts brought their books together, and burned them before all

men: and they counted the price of them, and found it fifty thousand pieces of silver. 20 So mightly grew the word of God and prevailed. (Acts 19.11–20 KJV)

Exorcism is also a pedagogical moment to pronounce the Lordship of Christ (Acts 16.18–40), as in the case of the exorcism of the slave girl (16.16).[22]

However, despite these references, the reader is provided with few intimate details of how to discern its use. What *is* noted in the New Testament is that the dismissal or removal of evil spirits can be executed through agents of God, and that it is always a sign of God's superiority to Satan.

## Interpreting exorcism

How we view exorcism in today's world depends very much on hermeneutics, the practice of interpreting and applying biblical interpretation to particular contexts. There are at least four competing pathways. First, we can reject exorcism and other miracles as symptomatic of a pre-scientific age, which has no empirical basis, then or now. But this view fails to acknowledge the supernatural and its role in the lives of many believers. Conversely, we can accept exorcism as a past and present reality predicated on the belief in demonic forces and influences in the world.[23] Thus, demonic possession cannot be totally dismissed or relegated to the level of the symbolic. This second view has no place for reductionist scientific explanation. A middle pathway exists whereby rather than rejecting exorcism, we can reinterpret the texts through contemporary social, cultural thought or medical explanation. As a result, exorcism is taken seriously but given new significance or contemporary resonance.[24] This middle position does not mean we reject the miraculous dimension of exorcism but simply aim to re-interpret its core meaning for today.[25] Finally, there is a psychological perspective in which the belief in possession can be interpreted as a form of mental illness.[26] This view is related to the first category but the focus is on psychological explanation. Therefore, the assertion of demons is only real in the mind of the one possessed, and the most sensible view is to understand these stories as mental-health narratives.[27]

The approach in this study occupies the third pathway and relies upon a creative tension between the need to explain exorcism for today, without denying that for many people, including black Pentecostals, exorcism is a legitimate belief in and response to evil forces in the world.[28] What this means in practice is accepting a priori that the New Testament exorcisms are a reliable source of information about the life and ministry of Jesus. My approach also posits a belief in a supernatural spirit world, the presence of malevolent forces and exorcism as a legitimate practice, while also seeking to explain exorcism in contemporary language. In this case, interpretation of exorcism is guided by *post-colonial interpretation*. As such, exorcism, while making use of supernatural categories, is very much concerned with addressing social oppression(s) intimately related to colonialism and empires.

# Post-colonial interpretation

Post-colonial readings of the bible emerge from post-colonial studies.[29] Post-colonial studies seek to reveal continuity of thought and action from the colonial to the post-colonial period, and as such recognize 'postcolonialism' as an endurance of themes and practices. Consequently, the term 'post-colonialism' refers to the period immediately after the end of the empire, while postcolonialism examines the cultural and social impact of colonialism. These two themes are interwoven in a complex and varied field of analysis and investigation:

> 'Post-colonialism/postcolonialism' is now used in wide and diverse ways to include the study and analysis of European territorial conquests, the various institutions of European territorial conquests, the various institutions of European colonialism, the discursive operations of empire, the subtleties of subject construction in colonial discourse and the resistance of those subjects, and, most importantly perhaps, the differing responses to such incursions and their contemporary colonial legacies in both pre-and post-independence nations and communities.[30]

Postcolonial biblical studies make the academic interrogation of the biblical text their primary focus in order to identify discursive interests of empires transcoded into interpretations of the Bible.[31] But postcolonial hermeneutics move beyond identifying these interests by developing alternative readings based on the history and experience of colonized peoples and their descendants.

We can distil postcolonial hermeneutics into two stages. These are, [i] to '. . . uncover colonial designs in both biblical texts and their interpretation, and endeavor to [ii] read the text from such postcolonial concerns as identity, hybridity and diaspora'.[32] The first stage seeks to identify colonial interests not only within the biblical text itself – how power relations shape and inform the narratives and theologies of the ancient world – but also within the interpretive scheme of the interpreter. To identify these themes, postcolonial biblical scholars deploy a range of tools including ideological criticism[33] – which makes its locus 'the world of the text and the context of the interpreter, namely acknowledging one's positionality and politics'.[34] Hence, postcolonial interpretation is a highly reflexive methodology. It seeks to transform practice. In the second stage postcolonial biblical readings are interpreted from newer positions of former colonized peoples. This postcolonial contextuality has resulted in a plethora of positions in diaspora communities that give priority to the specificity of their own circumstances, 'based on the experience of 'race', gender, sexuality and ecology'.[35] My interest here is diaspora, that is, how postcolonial reading challenges the religious identity of black Pentecostals in Britain. Armed with this new postcolonial sensibility, let us return to exorcism in the biblical text. As a case study, I will explore postcolonial readings of the Gerasene exorcism, not as an isolated incident but as one that is paradigmatic of Jesus' exorcism in the Gospel of Mark (5.1–10).[36]

## Gerasene demoniac

Jesus performs four exorcisms in the Gospel of Mark and all are performed in relation to the sociopolitical context.[37] My presupposition here is that Mark's Gospel places the exorcisms of Jesus strategically in opposition to Roman rule, although this view is disputed among Markan scholars.[38] On the one hand there are scholars who believe Jesus' exorcism was different from the Pharisees. That is to say, for Jesus, religion and politics were united in his engagement with demon possession to produce a healing tradition that was also a critique of Roman rule. Paul Hollenbach puts it this way:

> Jesus' interpretation constituted a radical transformation of the values held by the Pharisees. They were conservatives who focused narrowly on doing God's will in everyday life. This permitted them to escape confronting directly the terrifying social conditions and issues of their day. They were ready to pay not only taxes but total allegiance to Caesar in exchange for maintaining their privileged place in Galilean society. They were willing, naturally, to practice a kind of genteel medicine that included intermittent exorcising. But to focus on exorcising (as well as other kinds of healing) as a major form of action was not within their purview, probably because they recognized, even if they refused to face up to, the connection between the illness of their time and the unjust colonial social system of which they were an integral privileged part.[39]

Hollenbach believes that the demonic and social conditions are irrefutably interconnected, so that exorcism is a confrontation of power – a view shared by John Dominic Crossan and Richard Horsley.[40] Moreover, Amanda Witner's anthropological and sociological analysis of Jesus' exorcisms leads her to conclude that it is only within the sociopolitical context of the time that we can parse out their political meaning:

> Jesus' role as a Galilean exorcist, then, was deeply rooted in the socio-political and cultural context of his time and region, and possession by unclean spirits and his exorcisms were not only personal or psychological experiences, but reflected and commented on social and political issues. . . . the religious, social and political were deeply interconnected in first-century Galilee and that many of those who experienced spirit possession were in some way reflecting on and contributing to a broader discourse on the problematic nature of living under foreign rule and the effects of this on all levels of life. . . .[41]

Conversely, other scholars argue that there is little evidence of the Pharisees' privileged position and power group dynamic, and little evidence of Jesus' direct opposition to Roman rule played out in exorcism.[42] Naturally, postcolonial interpretations side with the first school of thought and the story of the Gerasene demoniac has particular importance.

1 They went across the lake to the region of the Gerasenes. 2 When Jesus got out of the boat, a man with an impure spirit came from the tombs to meet him. 3 This man lived in the tombs, and no one could bind him anymore, not even with a chain. 4 For he had often been chained hand and foot, but he tore the chains apart and broke the irons on his feet. No one was strong enough to subdue him. 5 Night and day among the tombs and in the hills he would cry out and cut himself with stones. 6 When he saw Jesus from a distance, he ran and fell on his knees in front of him. 7 He shouted at the top of his voice, 'What do you want with me, Jesus, Son of the Most High God? In God's name don't torture me!' 8 For Jesus had said to him, 'Come out of this man, you impure spirit!' 9 Then Jesus asked him, 'What is your name?' 'My name is Legion', he replied, 'for we are many.' 10 And he begged Jesus again and again not to send them out of the area. (NIV)

Historical critical analysis suggests that the story could reflect a historical event that occurred in the Decapolis region,[43] 'somewhere on the eastern side of the Sea of Galilee, although the precise location remains undetermined'. Scholars have also suggested that while there are good grounds for the historicity of the story, 'additional elements, such as the appearance of the pigs (vs 12–13) may have been included later'.[44]

The colonial context of the story is evident from the outset as the story takes place in a region where cities were protected by the tenth legion.[45] Hence, it cannot be separated from the colonial backdrop where Rome and its power are interwoven into the narrative. However, scholars differ on just how much influence the imperial backdrop has on the narrative, ranging from those who suggest 'little vestiges of empire in Mark',[46] to others who intimate that the empire is omnipresent.[47] I am interested in pursuing the latter, the presence of empire, and moreover an anti-colonial consciousness within the text. There are two basic postcolonial readings that emerge from the text, one individual, and the other social.

The individual postcolonial interpretation of exorcism is evident in the work of R. S. Sugirtharajah.[48] Here the focus is the specific case of the demoniac and his personal place in the Roman Empire. A clue to this relationship lies within the recruitment practices of the Empire. Sugirtharajah begins with the fact that the Romans recruited colonial subjects to their army. He cites the historian Josephus who informs us of Jewish recruitment by writing about Jewish guards at the funeral of Herod.[49] Therefore, Sugirtharajah surmises that Legion may well have been 'a potential recruit whose mind was deranged by the presence of the Roman army stationed in that area and the possibility of his expatriation'.[50] Hence, his name 'Legion' reflects the source of his trouble. A legion was the largest unit of a Roman army consisting of 4,000–6,000 men. Witmer concludes that there is 'no clear historical evidence that would disqualify a link between the presence in the area of troops and demon possession'. Therefore it is possible to assume that the Roman presence was understood as demon possession.[51] In the individual reading, the healing is a return to sanity:

> The healing of the Demoniac was bringing back sanity to a person who had been mentally unsettled by the colonial presence and the prospect of severe military duty outside of his own country.[52]

This idea, the demoniac as one who is traumatized and unsettled by the presence of the occupier, is given modern impetus by postcolonial psychologist, Frantz Fanon. In *The Wretched of the Earth*, Fanon catalogues the mental disorders caused by French colonialism in Algeria, all of which has led scholars to reinvestigate the meaning of mental illness, such as the uncontrollable psychotic outbursts similar to the demoniac in Mark,[53] as psychotic responses to the presence of the Roman empire.

This first postcolonial reading allows us to retain a vision of possession as individual affliction but also demands that we rightly identify the source of the demonic and its place within a wider domination system.[54] That is to say, that the cause of individual demonic oppression may reside within the social world and particular systems and practices. This leads to the second reading.

The second or social postcolonial reading of Jesus' exorcism of Legion is one in which the demoniac is representative of a wider struggle against the forces of evil of which it is a sign. New Testament scholar Richard Horsley suggests that the best way to understand this tension is 'through a violent Manichaeism'.[55] In this case, it is the 'two-tiered world of colonial occupation, characterized by a violent oppression, that is removed only by violent struggle'.[56] He continues by arguing that in order to make sense of the situation, the people reflected on their faith and arrived at an explanation of their plight:

> The problem was not simply the Roman armies. Superhuman evil forces – Belial or The Spirit of Darkness . . . Satan in the Gospels – had seized control of history. But God was ultimately in control and would finally at a certain time . . . intervene . . . to defeat the oppressive empire and restore the people to sovereignty and life under God's rule.[57]

Against this backdrop, the exorcisms of Jesus in Mark's Gospel reflect the encoding of a superhuman struggle in the text.[58] It is a battle between God and Satan as a political struggle 'where demonic possession symbolizes the Roman occupation of the land and exorcism their expulsion'. Evidence for this reading is fecund in the passage, particularly the military symbolism.[59] For instance, 'the demon's self-identification as "Legion" is telling since a military presence was omnipresent. Also, throughout the passage, exorcism is described in military terms resonant with the expulsion of an armed force'.[60] For example, the term *aposeile* (v. 10) means, 'to dispatch'.[61] Thus for Horsley, the episode represents a clear move by Jesus to identify the real cause of distress, that is, Roman presence. In this macro reading, exorcism is an index of a wider struggle against evil beyond the sphere of the individual. It allows us to interpret exorcism as an engagement with the external structures of colonialism wherever they are found – in social arrangements, unjust laws or the continued influence of past empires.

Combined, these postcolonial readings reveal three things. First, the text is the site of a power struggle where the religious is interwoven with the social and political. As Pero states in the quote at the start of the chapter, theology, politics and empire are interwoven in Jesus' healings. In this case, the healing of the demoniac is intimately related to the power struggle between the occupying forces of Rome and subjugated Palestinian Jews.

Second, that the text reveals an anti-colonial sentiment, namely a critique of the occupying forces and the desire of the people to have them removed from the country. Finally, the text speaks into the present – it challenges oppression by unmasking the brutality of occupying forces on the individual and society and identifying the way of Jesus as distinctively anti-colonial.

# Exorcism and the emancipatory framework

For black Pentecostals, the Gerasene exorcism reveals the undeniable connection between healing, exorcism and sociopolitical action. That is to say, healing encompasses problematic political predicaments. Jesus' interweaving of the healing with the social and political in Mark's Gospel affirms the resourcefulness of this practice for today and thereby contests the myopic and limited approach adopted by many black Pentecostals in Britain. Exorcism is a legitimate practice for believers and has use for today.

As part of the emancipatory framework, these postcolonial readings of Jesus' exorcisms define the meaning of cast out. To cast out is to remove an occupying or harassing malevolent spiritual force from the physical body and also social world. It is in opposition to bewitchment in so much as it directly confronts and overcomes the spiritual malevolence diagnosed in witchcraft.

In conclusion, exorcism in the Bible, while by no means static in meaning, appears in the Gospel of Mark with political implications. The exorcisms of Jesus are political acts demonstrating the expulsion of the occupying colonial force out of the mind and body of Israel. This interpretation not only facilitates a religious critique of empire but also allows me to view exorcism as a sociopolitical reality, whereby to exorcize is to engage in struggle against witchcraft, that is, structural evil. This chapter concludes the description of the emancipatory framework and the next task is to explore the focus of the framework, colonial Christianity and its continued influence on contemporary black British Pentecostalism.

# CHAPTER FIVE

# Bewitchment of empire

*In fact, in a very real sense the Church was just another branch of royal government and another means of political control over the colonists.*

ISAAC DOOKHAN[1]

As I have shown in previous chapters, witchcraft is a belief in evil that can be diagnosed through African witchcraft idioms to reveal a way of speaking about inappropriate consumption or the rapacious and avaricious behaviour of individuals and societies. Such behaviour, whether war, mass rape or brutal and crippling economic policies, represents a 'surplus of sin' experienced as evil. Furthermore, we can identify witchcraft practice through the bodily idioms of the cannibal and zombie. These idioms reveal concrete social and political activities in the world. Understanding witchcraft this way, allows us to return to the historical past, armed with new tools for unlocking the meaning of history, particularly the histories of subjugated peoples. In this case, it is the use of witchcraft to unlock otherwise hidden meanings of the histories of colonial oppression in the New World during the age of European expansion that is the locus of inquiry.

A witchcraft critique of the origins of Christianity in the Caribbean is essential for identifying the origins of the bewitchment of black Pentecostalism. This is because Caribbean Christianity is the soil out of which black Pentecostalism in Britain grew and drew its basic nutrients. Caribbean Christianity is a complex and diverse tradition of thought and action and traditions are positioned in different ways in relation to the colonial past. For instance, there are Christian traditions that have sought to interrogate the colonial past to eradicate any lingering negative effects and to reconcile unresolved issues. For example, since 2007, the Baptist Union in Britain has engaged in a serious evaluation of its complex colonial history, including apology for its support of Britain's slave trade and colonial enterprise in the West Indies. However, other Christian traditions have not embraced the Baptist model, and instead remain ignorant and oblivious to the role of the slave and colonial past on the development of their theological ideas. With no scholarly reflections on the subject and little interest or reference in its preaching and teaching I propose that we place black Pentecostalism in Britain in this second camp.

In this chapter, I want to diagnose the church's role in Western expansion in the New World as complicit with witchcraft. Western expansion began with explorers and travellers and grew into state-sponsored exploitation of the resources of newly encountered peoples. This history can be evaluated through various fields, disciplines and perspectives. In this case, the focus is history and locus of interest is Christianity. Christianity plays a complex and contradictory role in the age of empire, and encompasses the work of a multitude of individuals and major denominations spanning numerous continents and cultures. However, I want to identify a tragic process in Christianity, that is, the drift from compromise to complicity. Church *compromise* with evil can take various forms:

> It partakes of structural evil if it rejects something good (legalism) or accepts something bad (compromise). Protracted indecision (out of ignorance, lack of discernment or cowardice) . . .[2]

Church *complicity*, however, is active involvement; it is co-conspiratorial and collaborative.[3] Borrowing from legal studies where complicity is associated with illegal acts, I want to work with a form of complicity known as 'lawful complicity'.[4] 'Lawful complicity' permits us to examine acts that while technically lawful in the particularity of a given context are nonetheless aggressive and brutal in impact. Lawful complicity also conveys a sense of agency where the co-conspirators decide on the nature of their participation.[5] Examining the complicity of the church opens up a new field of analysis, whereby we can reframe its Christian mission as co-conspiratorial with the empire's occult practice. I will focus on two moments of the drift from compromise to complicity. These moments are the early Catholic acquiescence to African slavery in the colonization of the Americas (1492–1565), and the Protestant Christian institutionalization of ignorance among slaves in Barbados in the early eighteenth century (1710–1834). *Combined, these two moments represent a holistic process: a subjugation of the body (cannibalism) and then the mind (zombism).*

## Catholic cannibalism

The Catholic Church was entangled in the adventure to find new lands and people from the outset. Indeed, the late medieval era was an age of Christian hegemony, and as African American theologian Willie Jennings states, the discovery of new lands and new peoples was as much theological as it was social or economic.[6] A religious pragmatism folded into economic opportunity, uniting church and profit. Pope Alexander VI blessed the first voyage of Christopher Columbus in 1492 and required him to find lands, gold and spread the Gospel to heathen nations.[7] The Pope's conversion/capitalism binary is mirrored in Columbus' assessment of the people he encountered. In a letter to his Catholic sovereigns he writes:

> Most powerful sovereigns: all of Christendom should hold great celebrations, and especially God's Church, for the finding of such a multitude of such friendly peoples, which with very little effort will be converted to our Holy Faith, and so many lands filled with so many goods, very necessary to us in which all Christians will have comfort and profits.[8]

Christian mission and commerce, however, were not the only presuppositions shaping Spanish attitudes towards discovery. One outcome of the conquest of Granada was the development in Spain of an aggressive, imperial faith intolerant of the non-believer.

When the Spanish of the Reconquest reached the Indies, they carried with them their habits of war, and they forced the Tainos of the Island of Espanola to submit to their authority in the same fashion which they had brought the Moors of Granada to their knees.[9]

Thus, the ruling elite was primed for Holy War: defeating the infidel in the name of the Christian God,[10] and this potent mix of intolerant religion and striving for profit could only spell disaster for encountered peoples. Nevertheless, all was not lost for those on the receiving end of empire, as there was a thin protective veil separating them from the rapacious and avaricious Spanish; this protective veil was the Catholic Church. The Pope as the arbiter of international relations was required to provide legal and religious regulation including the protection and education of newly encountered peoples. After all, as the representative of God on earth and as the head of Christendom, he was endowed with ecclesiastical power over all of humanity. Thus, in 1493, when Pope Alexander VI granted the Spanish sovereigns, Ferdinand and Isabella, possession of the Indies, he also demanded responsibility for the conversion of these heathen peoples.[11] But even in the age of church supremacy the Pope was not omnipotent and there were political and geographical limits to what the church could realistically achieve. Ultimately, the pursuit of wealth with the Church's blessing could only have one result: in the face of unfathomable material wealth, a *compromise* of godly intent.

## Destruction of the Indies

The tragic unfolding of events begins in 1492 when Columbus arrives in Hispaniola (La Española), which today which consists of the Dominican Republic and Haiti. The arrival of the people from the sea marks the beginning of the 'spell' for the inhabitants, the Tainos, a group within the Arawak peoples. The island was quickly carved up into governable regions and thousands of the Tainos were enslaved and forced to toil in a system of land distribution and Indian enslavement known as the *encomienda*. The *encomienda* (literally 'recommendations') required the Indians to work for the colonialists with no guarantee of manumission. Enslavement was however not only an economic principle but also the summation of theological rationale, for the full humanity of the Indians was in question. Like that of other non-Christian peoples who, from the vantage point of a perceived superior culture that was foaming at the mouth with coercive violence, the Tainos were a sub human species.[12] As Columbus scholar Tzvetan Todorov argues, Columbus had no inkling of the full humanity of the Indians:

> . . . Columbus's behavior implies that he does not grant the Indians the right to have their own will, that he judges them, in short, as living objects. It is as such that, in his naturalist's enthusiasm, he always wants to take specimens of all kinds back to Spain: trees, birds, animals and Indians; the notion of asking their opinion is foreign to him.[13]

A major text in this field that describes the conquest and colonization is *A Short Account of the Destruction of the Indies* (1542, published 1552) by the priest Bartolomé de Las Casas (1484–1566). This record gives voice to the immense cruelty and unfathomable horror that characterized the Spanish conquest. Las Casas was ordained as a priest in the Americas in 1507 and became *encomendero* – assigned to natives in Cuba to teach them the faith as well as extract profit from their labour. A turning point in his life came in 1513 after the massacre of the Caonoa in Cuba. At this point, Las Casas began to see the colonial enterprise as cold-hearted – and that '. . . the devil got into them (Spanish)'.[14] He said soon after, 'Everything perpetrated on the Indians in these Indies was unjust and tyrannical'.[15] In response and as an act of repentance, he decided to free his Indian slaves and crusade on their behalf. He was less willing to relinquish ownership of his African slave, for he still possessed one in 1544.[16]

Las Casas paints graphic, disturbing images of the marauding Spanish in Hispaniola as part of a process to win native rights (but at a cost). In one account, Las Casas describes the wholesale slaughter of native people:

> As we have said, the island of Hispaniola was the first to witness the arrival of Europeans and the first to suffer the wholesale slaughter of its people and the devastation and depopulation of the land. It all began with the Europeans taking native women and children both as servants and to satisfy their own base appetites; then, not content with what the local people offered

them of their own free will (and all offered as much as they could spare), they started taking for themselves the food the natives contrived to produce . . . Some of them started to conceal what food they had, others decided to send their women and children into hiding, and yet others took to the hills to get away from the brutal and ruthless cruelty that was being inflicted on them. The Christians punched them, boxed their ears and flogged them in order to track down the local leaders, and the whole shameful process came to a head when one of the European commanders raped the wife of the paramount chief of the entire island.[17]

As is so often the case with marauding armies of conquest, devoid of moral responsibility, a perverse joviality and sickening one-up-man-ship characterizes the slaughter of innocent people and Las Casas captures this aspect of the Spanish orgy of violence:

They hacked them to pieces, slicing open their bellies with their swords as though they were so many sheep herded into a pen. They even laid wagers on whether they could manage to slice a man in two at a stroke, or cut an individual's head from his body or disembowel him with a single blow of their axes. They grabbed suckling infants by the feet and, ripping them from their mother's breasts dashed them headlong against the rocks . . . The way they normally dealt with the native leaders and nobles was to tie them to a kind of griddle consisting of sticks resting on pitchforks driven into the ground and then grill them over a slow fire, with the result that they howled in agony and despair as they died a lingering death.[18]

Notwithstanding Las Casas' desire to shock, the colonizers' descent into a normalized brutality was, to quote Francophone post-colonialist Aime Cesaire, a process of de-civilization – an arousal of their own basic instincts, avarice and abhorrence of the black 'Other'.[19]

## Collusion with the empire

Yet, on one level, the Catholic Church was a source of restraint. Evangelism provided a platform to curb excesses. Vitally important to this cause was the role of the priests who travelled with Columbus on his return to the island in 1493. Not all priests remained, but those that did witnessed the transformation of a peaceful fledgling colony into a vicious commercial enterprise. Several priests, including Las Casas, alarmed by the ill-treatment of the Indians, their enslavement and degradation, began to petition the authorities for more missionaries and better conditions rights for these human beasts of burden.[20] Churchmen who defended the Indians argued that the papal bulls did not give Spain the right to exploit and kill the natives but only to preach the Gospel. Furthermore, they argued that the Indians were capable of religious instruction and therefore should not be categorized as enemies of Christ and subjected to the sword.

On another level, the Catholic Church also compromised with the conquest and subjugation. That is to say, its arguments to support the native people were made inside of empire. A Christian imperialism guided the reforming priests. As church historian Daniel Castro puts it in his reflection on the politics of Las Casas, Las Casas and the priests defending the Indians were 'another face of empire'.[21] They wanted to convert the Indians to the colonizer's religion and their disagreement with the state was a question of the nature of engagement: 'they wanted a non-violent conversion and an ecclesiastical imperialism' in contrast to the 'violence and hegemony of the state'.[22] Todorov explains this church project as a form of *colonialist ideology* differing from the *enslavement ideology* of the state:

> One thing is sure: Las Casas does not want to put an end to the annexation of the Indies, he merely wants this to be effected by priests rather than by soldiers. This is the content of his letter to the council of the Indies of January 20, 1531: the conquistadors must be 'expelled from these countries and replaced by persons fearing God, of good conscience and great prudence'.[23]

Nonetheless, from the location of the oppressed, whether colonizer or priest, both were equally adept at producing 'cultural genocide'.[24]

The church also colluded. There are several competing historical moments vying for the point of collusion, including the nature of the church's initial involvement, the Pope's blessing and the commodification of the Indians. Note, Las Casas captures the commodification of the native bodies when he tells of the colonizers referring to them as 'pieces'.[25] All are important points for consideration. However, I want to opt for a perspective that takes into account African subjugation and this critical moment appears when the church makes one group of subjugated people more expendable than another. The tipping-point is the declaration that Africans are more replaceable than the Indians.

The defining moment of Catholic Church collusion with colonial violence is made when Africans are declared more expendable. This tragic event takes place in 1516 when, to preserve the Tainos in La Hispaniola, Las Casas suggests that Africans be imported. In a letter to the Crown he proposed, 'If we could each get licenses to bring a few dozen Negro slaves from Spain or Africa' he suggested, 'it would go better with the Indians'.[26] He thought Africans were able to bear the burden of servitude better than the Indians.[27] After all, growing up in Seville, Las Casas had witnessed African slaves at work in a context of relative restraint and good treatment, and had no knowledge of the industrial slavery being introduced on the Portuguese and Spanish colonies.[28] Las Casas would later change his mind on this subject and come to view African slavery as equally tyrannical as the Indian experience.[29] But the fact that he still owned an African slave until 1544 gestures towards him having a more abstruse attitude towards African manumission.

I want to think of the Catholic complicity as a form of cannibalism. The decision to enslave the Africans and subject them to the terror of slavery is a commodification of black flesh. The commodities were 'negroes' who were, as historian Markus Rediker notes, manufactured from African substance in the 'factories' of the slave ships.[30] Made into commodities, they were *consumed* – 'pieces' for the industrial slave machine, a consumption which the church legitimated and also participated in.

## Protestant zombies

The second moment is also a step beyond compromise, and a conscious decision on the church's part to be complicit with slavery, but this time in the British Empire. After the Catholic monopoly in the New World was broken in part by nationalist and religious wars in the sixteenth and seventeenth centuries, Spanish control of access to new territories was severely weakened. This vulnerable position allowed the British to establish colonies in the Caribbean, such as Jamaica (1655), in the first half of the seventeenth century.

Akin to its Catholic counterpart, the Church of England also wished to participate in the fulfilment of the Great Commission, the biblical mandate to spread the Christian Gospel across the globe, and initially the New World offered evangelistic opportunities, exclusively among the slave-owning class.[31] Early missions in the West Indies were spasmodic and unorganized. This was due in part to the chaotic nature of colonization and the instability in England during the Civil War (1642–55). Early missions to the West Indies were dominated by non-conformist groups, such as the Puritans and Quakers. However, with the transformation of the West Indies through sugar production and direct royal governance in 1660, the Church of England, through the auspices of the Society for the Propagation of the Gospel (SPG), was able to exert ecclesiastical authority.

The Church of England overseas was under the care of the Bishop of London until the second decade of the nineteenth century, and attempts to administer it in earnest began with Archbishop Henry Compton in 1676.[32] However, it was not until the Islands had suitable civil arrangements that a more systematic process could begin. Barbados was the pioneering island. 'With no indigenous people to subdue, the civil administration was established with relative ease'.[33] Jamaica was soon to follow with the island's capture in 1655 and the cessation of hostilities with the Spanish with the signing of the treaty of Madrid in 1667; the door was open for missionary activity – but among the white colonialists. On islands, distance, terrain and the availability of financial resources impinged on a parish's ability to achieve its religious goals. Moreover, most of the vestries performed more administrative and civil work than ecclesiastical. Therefore, from the outset, 'mutuality defined the relationship' between church and the fledgling colonial government.[34]

# Legitimating slavery

The importation of African slaves into British colonies such as Barbados and Jamaica raised the question of how to meet their spiritual needs. Not everyone, however, was open to the idea of the evangelization of slaves. There was personal and economically motivated opposition from the planter class. For some, slavery provided the opportunity to satisfy their lust for sexual and sadistic pleasure and they rejected church interference.[35] For others, there was a general fear that 'Christian slaves' would be legally free and, therefore, inhibit the pursuit of profit and property in the slaveholding West Indies.[36] Voicing opposition was not the only form of protest. Planters opposed to evangelism among slaves would either deny access to their slaves or only allow them to be baptized when near to death.[37] So what was the church to do? Confrontation and opposition was not an option, as during the course of seventeenth century the church had learned to live with the enslavement of Africans. So, naturally, the Church of England sought compromise with the evangelism of slaves. According to historian Richard Hunte, the issue was first raised in Barbados in the middle of the seventeenth century, and resolved after the Lords' Committee on Trade and Plantations urged the Governor to make clear the position on slavery and Christianity. The Governor's reply elucidates the church's stand:

> And for the propagation, and Increase of ye Christians faith and Religion, you shall make it your special care, that all Negro Slaves, and servants remaining in the said colonies be instructed in the Principle of the same Religion (Church of England). And that such who shall arrive at a competent knowledge therein, be admitted to the Sacrament of Baptism. And that it be declared by Law in the respective Colonies that such Baptism shall not at all be extended to their Enfranchisement or Manumission.[38]

The British legislature lent support to this theological rationale by passing laws in 1696 and 1729 which made Christian conversion and the enslavement of Africans compatible,[39] although many still doubted whether slaves were capable of meaningful conversion.[40] With slavery compatible with religion, it was left to the colonies to determine the amount of missionary influence. In some cases, religious groups were barred from instructing slaves. Such was the case of the Quakers in Barbados.[41] In other colonies such as Jamaica, despite the urging and goodwill from England, little effort was made to convert slaves.[42] Without doubt, a major obstacle was self-inflicted – the quality and number of priests sent to minster was questionable. Fewer than 50 were resident across the region by 1800,[43] and historians point out that most were men seeking to increase their own wealth and influence rather than spreading the Gospel.[44] Thus, while priests were free to work among the planter class and possibly instruct slaves, the Church of England influence was, in reality, muted:

> The Church of England was the established church, but its hold on hearts and intellects was tenuous indeed. It was not a mission church, and it was unsympathetic to missionaries . . . The first bishop was appointed in 1825. But the majority of Anglican clergy were involved in slave management until emancipation, and the planters were their friends and patrons, part of the same social world.[45]

Not every churchperson agreed with the status quo, as there were also those in the field who revolted against colonial complicity. For example, the Anglican churchman and missionary Morgan Goodwyn (1640–86), who inspired the formation of the Society for the Propagation of the Gospel in Foreign Parts, was driven out of Virginia and faced severe opposition in Barbados on account of preaching that planters should Christianize their slaves. Based on the belief in the humanity of Africans, he wrote:

> [A]ll men have an equal right to religion . . . that negroes are men and therefore are invested with the same right . . . that being thus qualified and invested to deprive them of this right is the highest injustice.[46]

However, his predecessors were more reluctant to upset colonial society and were comfortable working with it rather than against it.

# Church of England complicity

There are various contenders for the fight for the defining moment when church compromise turns into complicity. A major contender is the formation of the Colonial Christian Union in the mid-1820s. The Colonial Christian Union was a group of clergy and planters united in their desire to maintain slavery. The Union included the notorious Anglican slavery apologist George Wilson Bridges.[47] However, I content that, because of its unique status of a church run slave plantation that the victory has to go to the Codrington Estate in Barbados.

It all begins with Christopher Codrington (1668–1710), Governor of the Leyward Islands and plantation owner. He desired to see good clergy in the West Indies instead of the ineffective clergy the region had attracted. Good clergy would be committed to evangelizing slaves and would take seriously their own vows of obedience.[48] As an example and possibly for personal atonement, Codrington bequeathed his estate in Barbados to the Society for the Propagation of the Gospel (SPG) upon his death in 1710. He had no objection to slavery, but sensed the benefits of Christianity should extend to all, including slaves. He stipulated that the land be used to establish a college. The plantation remained intact but provision was made to evangelize the slaves. These were grand aims, but, unfortunately, within the business of slave agriculture, they proved unworkable. Let me explain.

To ensure that the estate was a viable business, the SPG was forced to comply with the profit-making aspects of slavery. Africans on the plantation were dying from malnutrition and disease; therefore, the Society had to rely on the slave trade to maintain the estate's viability. Christian education was also difficult. By 1726, no slaves had been converted and the college was more interested in educating white children. Ironically, as one historian puts it, the only reading and letters that slaves were exposed to were S-O-C-I-E-T-Y, branded onto their bodies by the SPG until 1733.[49] In theory, slaves on the estate were given a basic Christian education and allowed to attend school. In practice, however, to maintain the status quo, priests obeyed two unwritten rules of mission.

The first unwritten rule of mission was to maintain an ideology of black inferiority. Black inferiority was the prevailing discourse

of the day, and the SPG grew to be generally compliant with it.[50]
Public worship reinforced inferiority, with blacks seated at the back
or in separate parts of churches during worship. Christian rituals
also played an important role in securing black subordination.
As Nicholas Beasley demonstrates in his study of Anglicanism
in the American and West Indian colonies, whites sought to
control liturgical and ritual space to ensure that blacks were
either omitted from it or marginalized within it. When omission
was not possible, whites withdrew their religion into the private
sphere (homes) to ensure that their black slaves had no presence
among them. Ideologically, this practice served to preserve a white
English cultural identity and moreover, ensure that worship space
maintained black inferiority:

> . . . the translation of English religious culture to the plantation
> colonies held together European cultural identity and articulated
> a profound set of desires for the ordering of colonial experience.
> In the familiar structures, repetitions, and drama of Christian
> worship, white residents of the plantation colonies reproduced
> sacred moments from their collective English and European past,
> erasing the difference and distance that separated them from
> the mother country. . . . By rendering their Christian ritual life
> largely free of the presence of Africans and their descendants,
> white worshippers were able to deny the social reality of life in
> the plantation colonies, thus eliding the difference and distance
> that separated them from the metropole. That denial was often
> pursued in the setting of parish churches constructed at public
> expense . . . sacred space in the British plantation colonies
> . . . especially seating in it was essential to colonist's efforts to
> remind themselves of their Englishness. Working within their
> understanding of the parish community, colonists fashioned
> liturgical spaces that created community for whites and offered
> only a low place in their hierarchy to free persons of color and a
> few slaves. . . . Even as whites sought to dominate public life by
> controlling ritual space and time, they also largely withdrew to
> private places for the initiatory rites of marriage and baptism . . .
> Europeans readily embraced higher expenses for these rites in
> order to have them celebrated at home. When celebrated mostly
> in domestic spaces, these rites served to legitimate the sexuality
> and reproduction of Europeans. Removed from the public

discourse of the parish church, baptism and marriage were largely unavailable to the enslaved. While free persons of color were often baptized and married in Christian rites, most were obliged to celebrate these rites in the more public venues that whites had largely abandoned for those purposes. By removing baptism to the domestic sphere, whites sought to evacuate it of the spiritual egalitarianism inherent in the rite and reserved its celebration of legitimate reproduction to themselves. Similarly, the celebration of marriage at home symbolized the manner in which that rite was privatized, giving Europeans ideological room to develop a long-running discourse on the supposed illegitimacy of the marital and reproductive habits of enslaved Africans and their descendants. . . .[51]

Black inferiority was further marked by the permanent threat of physical violence. For instance, the Codrington estate never renounced the use of the whip as punishment.[52]

The second unwritten rule of mission was a Christian solipsism, the institutionalization of ignorance through Christian miss-education.[53] Planters feared theologically literate slaves, believing that knowledge of God would make them less inclined to hard work and following instruction. Slaves were kept ignorant of the emancipatory content of the Gospel and very little effort was made to teach them to understand the richness of the Bible. Indeed, the church abandoned Codrington's wishes to teach the slaves to read and write. Instead, slaves were taught to obey the instructions of their priests and were dissuaded from thinking that they had the ability, or should desire, to understand for themselves. To secure obedience, the church taught from Bible passages that referred to slaves being obedient to their masters (Colossians 3.22), and undergirded a divine hierarchy in which blacks were ordained to be beasts of burden (Genesis 9.20–7). The combination of inadequate education and teaching obedience were the basis of a Christian-motivated slave false consciousness. However, as Hillary Beckles makes clear in his *History of Barbados*, not all churches shared this vision of slave life. Non-conformist missionaries were keen to educate slaves and challenge the Church of England hegemony.[54] But even these attempts to empower slaves were inside of empire, and, as Caribbean historian Isaac Dookhan tells us, well within the boundaries of the ideological legitimation of the slave system:

By inculcating a sense of moral obligation in the slaves, they sought to promote the subordination of the slaves in the society. By giving a religious bias to education, by preaching the virtues of industry, honesty and obedience, and by keeping the standard of education low, the denominations sought to make the slaves better laborers and at the same time unable to contemplate more worthwhile alternatives than plantation labour.[55]

Summarizing the spiritual failure of the Church of England enterprise in Barbados, historian Jeffery Cox moves beyond ideological legitimation and towards complicity:

The SPG ran their plantation from the first like any other West Indian plantation. The record throughout the eighteenth century is one of neglect of the working conditions of the slaves, the sale of 'surplus slaves' by plantation managers, demographic decline in the population of the plantation, and resort to the whip as punishment. Managers had great difficulty keeping the number at 200 as specified in the bequest and often requested permission, which was granted, to sell 'surplus slaves'. The SPG committee only ordered a hospital to be built for slaves in 1792, and this order was ignored. As late as the 1820s, when the SPG attempted to abolish the whip, they received a report that this was impossible and the slaves would be uncooperative. (While catechists were provided for religious instruction of the SPG's slaves, (but) they were provided irregularly and those who were sent often reported back their work was impossible either because the slaves were unteachable or because teaching them to read would be useless to the slaves and possibly dangerous politically.) Some slaves were baptized. One catechist reported in 1740, the first such report, that sixty-five were baptized, but that they could not attend worship because the plantation was short of labour. In an estate under their direct control the SPG sent agents who did little to baptize slaves, almost nothing to educate them, and nothing at all to promote Christian marriage. Instead of providing them with the ministries of a confessional church, the SPG allowed them to be whipped when they were working and sold when they could no longer work.[56]

I want to think of the Christian practice at the Codrington estate in terms of witchcraft, as a form of *zombification*. To recap, the zombie is an enslaved, mindless body, and on one level all slaves on the Codrington estate were zombies, that is, enslaved people. Nevertheless, there was another level of zombification at work on the Codrington estate: Christian zombification. A useful way of interpreting the process of making African slaves into Christian zombies is through the analysis of slave ontology by sociologist Orlando Patterson.[57]

Patterson thinks of slavery as a form of 'social death' in which religion plays a seminal role by providing the symbolic rituals of black inferiority. Religious conversion maintained the master-slave relationship because baptism was entered into without full entry in the human family, and as religious sanction for obedience to an unjust order.[58] In other words, the Christian practice maintains the subjugation of the slave and thereby creates an enslaved Christian body with limited Christian knowledge, that is, a Christian zombie. The Christian zombie was not an attractive option to slaves and it is of little surprise that the majority of slaves on the plantation rejected this option and furthermore chose religion as a focal point for their resistance to slavery.[59]

In summary, there are many ways of thinking about the role of European Christianity within the European expansion into the New World. Until the high waters of the abolitionist movement, Christianity was sunk deep beneath the miry clay of colonialism as co-conspirator with imperialism. The brutal subjugation of newly encountered peoples, the theft of their land and destruction of their livelihood, were acts of unfathomable wickedness that we can describe as evil. Furthermore, the diagnostic tools of the cannibal and zombie allow us to not only reframe the colonial enterprise but also the role of the church within it. I have suggested that the church was party to both the cannibalism and zombification of empire, that is, a consumption of newly encountered peoples. Indeed, we may even surmise that these themes help us to begin to understand the full horror of the colonial enterprise, mostly hidden from view by layers of historical revision by Western scholars. Thus, the coming of the West on African and African bodies was a 'religious experience', a malevolent spiritual force of great magnitude or *mysterium tremendum* to which the church was party.[60] The critical questions that concern us next are whether these forms of devouring continue into the present, and if Christian religion is still complicit with it?

# CHAPTER SIX

# Memory cannibalism

As suggested previously, for Africans on the continent and in the Caribbean the coming of the West can be conceived as a religious experience, a witchcraft that I interpret through the lenses of the devouring tropes of the cannibal and zombie. Furthermore, I show that colonial Christianity is not outside of this analysis but complicit with colonialism's witchery. I want to complete the discussion of witchcraft by exploring continuity of influence. Influence suggests a strong and even direct relationship but it is meant in a particular way, that is, to express the power of meaning. Continuity of influence describes a continuity of *meaning*, that is to say, how the core ideas of the cannibal and zombie in the colonial period find new meaning in different contexts. This shift allows the cannibal and zombie to be projected onto other discourses, including discourses of economics, political economy and worship.[1] In this chapter, I will analyse how the idiom of cannibalism, in a particular form (memory cannibalism), detrimentally impacts black Pentecostalism's political witness in the present. To arrive at the contemporary influence, I will work through an archaeology of cannibal accusation, beginning with slaves and ending with a cannibal experience of post-colonial subjects in contemporary Britain.[2] In the following chapter, I will explore the continued influence of the zombie idiom, but this time, through a comparative analysis between zombism and black Pentecostalism. Comparative analysis, while a complex method, facilitates an assessment of agreements,[3] that is, in this case, what features of the zombie are unwittingly reconfigured in black Pentecostal contexts. While neither archaeology nor comparative analysis can provide a definitive scientific, historical continuity, both have discursive importance; that is, they help to shape how we think about black Pentecostalism in the present.

## An archaeology of cannibal accusation

The West's devouring of African substance in the transatlantic slave trade fails to disappear with emancipation or the independence of former colonies in the Caribbean. Instead, a record of the practice of illicit accumulation is detailed in literature, music and religion.[4] What is recorded are alterations and reconfigurations of illicit accumulation that are sometimes explicit but mostly hidden beneath layers of metaphor. Take, for example, the Jamaican term, 'nyam'. It is a term used in everyday Jamaican patois to describe gluttony. It is, however, more than greed as it also registers the idea of complete devouring – and this second meaning may well register a historical memory of aspects of colonial exploitation.[5] Cannibal culture matters because, as I will show in the final part of this chapter, the persistence of cannibal culture continues to stalk black Pentecostalism in Britain.

This chapter has three parts. The first part explores cannibal accusation in the slave context, how the enslaved and their abolitionist supporters made use of cannibal imagery to describe their perceptions of captivity and exploitation. The second part explores the continued influence of cannibal imagery in the post-colonial Caribbean, specifically cannibalism as a metaphor for the machinations of the post-colonial state. The third part of the chapter examines a contemporary contextual devouring and focuses our attention on the church as an agent of cannibalism. I want to show how devouring continues in the Caribbean diaspora in Britain; but in this case, it is intimately related to church relationships and the devouring of the memory of slavery, or what I will term 'memory cannibalism'. To explain this last point of connection in the cannibal archaeology, I will use as a case study the Westminster Abbey Service to commemorate the Abolition of the Transatlantic Slave Trade in Britain on 27 March 2007.

# White cannibalism

Slave narratives played an important role in highlighting the horrors of the slave trade and also lending support to the abolitionist movement in Britain.[6] However, a lesser-exposed feature of the slave narratives and abolitionist discourse is their use of cannibal imagery to mask the savagery of the slave trade. Slaves and also their friends and allies in the anti-slavery movement fashioned images of white cannibalism to capture the essence of their experience and also challenge the myth of Western civility. Beginning with the slaves, two narratives evoke cannibal imagery. These are *The Interesting Narrative of the Life of Olaudah Equiano or Gustavus Vasssa* (1789) and *A History of Mary Prince* (1831).

Olaudah was born in the Igbo region of what is now southern Nigeria, and *The Interesting Narrative* contrasts a simple and dignified view of the people of Africa on the woe and brutality of slavery. The British were at the time of Olaudah's birth the dominant slaving power, having gained advantage over the Spanish and Portuguese traders. Out of these contrasting experiences, he reflects on cannibalism. The first mention is satirical – a subversive play on European travellers' tales. Speaking of the customs of his homeland, Olaudah describes cannibalism as a threat to naughty youngsters:

> We had a saying among us to any one of a cross temper, 'that if they were to be eaten, they should be eaten with bitter herbs'.[7]

However, the second example is more serious and draws a parallel with the fear of slavery. When Equiano was captured, he believed that the occupants of the slave ship would eat him:

> When I was carried on board I was immediately handled, and tossed up, to see if I were sound, by some of the crew; and I was now persuaded that I had gotten into a world of bad spirits, and that they were going to kill me. When I looked around the ship too, and saw a large furnace of copper boiling, and a multitude of black people of every description chained together, every one of their countenances expressing dejection and sorrow, I no longer doubted of my fate, and quite overpowered with

horror and anguish, I fell motionless on the deck and fainted. When some of those who brought me on board, and had been receiving their pay; they talked to me in order to cheer me, but all in vain. I asked them if we were not to be eaten by those white men with horrible looks, red faces and long hair? They told me I was not.[8]

The fear of being eaten by whites does not leave him and surfaces again when he reaches Barbados:

... merchants and planters ... made us jump, and pointed to the land, signifying we were to go there. We thought by this we should be eaten by these ugly men, as they appeared to us ... [A]t last the white people got some old slaves from the land to pacify us. They told us we were not to be eaten, but to work.[9]

But what was the fear expressed in the language of devouring? The narrative goes on to expose the horrors of the trade including his eyewitness accounts of torture and theft by those he sarcastically terms 'Christians'. Thus within the context of the time, the fear of being eaten by slavers is a metaphor for slavery and a contestation of the slave system.

Another reversal of accusation from the location of the slave appears in *A History of Mary Prince*. Prince was born into slavery in 1788, with both of her parents enslaved in Bermuda. Prince and her mother were sold as household servants. Mary was sold again when she was 12 to a Captain John Ingham by whom she was severely mistreated.[10] As punishment, she was sent to work in the salt mines of Grand Turk. She returned to Bermuda in 1810 and was sold to work in Antigua as a domestic slave. In 1826, she married Daniel Jones, a freed slave, for which again she was sternly punished by her owner. Her owner took Prince to London in 1828 to work as a domestic servant. Since slavery was illegal in Britain, she was eventually thrown out by her owners and left destitute. She found shelter with Moravian Christians and was given employment by the abolitionist Thomas Pringle,[11] who arranged for her biography to be written and eventually published in 1831.

Prince describes the experience of being sold at 12 so that her master could raise funds in order to remarry. The imagery used to describe the experience is profound:

The black morning at length came; it came too soon for my poor mother and us. While she was putting on us the new osnaburghs in which we were to be sold, she said, in a sorrowful voice, (I shall never forget it!) 'See I am shrouding my poor children; what a task for a mother!' – She then called Miss Betsey to take leave of us. 'I am going to carry my little chickens to market', (these were her very words,). . . .[12]

The metaphorical language (black slaves as animals) has a variety of potential meanings. It may evoke endearment and as well a deep sorrow, that Mary says was expressed by the owner upon having to sell her prized assets. However, what I want to propose here is that the imagery also signifies the idea of black flesh as a source of 'food' for the industrial slave machine. This sense of slavery as devouring reappears in Prince's narrative when strangers at the slave auction examine her sibling and herself:

I was soon surrounded by strange men, who examined and handled me in the same manner that a butcher would a calf or lamb he was about to purchase, and who talked about my shape and size in like words – as if I could no more understand their meaning than the dumb beasts.[13]

However, what was the devouring she feared? Upon her arrival at her new owner's estate, she is warned by other slaves of the harshness of the master and the cruelty of his household. Relentless floggings, beatings and other forms of ill treatment befall her. Thus, in the concluding paragraph of her autobiography, Prince identifies broken bodies and continual torture as a central component of slavery's racial terror – an image aptly summarized in an account of an eighteenth-century slave speaking in response to his master's offer of freedom. The slave replies, 'Master you eated me when I was meat now you must pick me when I am bone.'[14]

The image of slavery as cannibalism was not lost on the anti-slavery movement in Britain where anti-slavery activists mobilized the cannibal idiom. All of this suggests an alternative entry point of cannibal discourse into the lexicon of slavery and its perceived modus operandi. In this case, sugar became an extension of the slave's body; this connection enables us to compare consumption with cannibalism. For example, in 1791 abolitionist Thomas

Cooper called for abstinence from sugar on the moral grounds that a boycott would weaken the slave economy and assist with the abolition of the slave system. He compares sugar consumption to cannibalism by quoting a French writer who says that each sugar lump is 'stained with spots of blood'.[15] Similarly, William Fox in his famous 1791 'Address To the People of Great Britain, on the Propriety of Abstaining from West Indian Sugar and Rum' continues the analogy of sugar consumption as cannibalism. He declares that sugar is 'steeped in the blood of our fellow creatures' and that each pound of sugar consumed is equivalent to two ounces of human flesh.[16]

In sum, during the slave trade, cannibal imagery is projected onto the slave system. Its capture and objectification of Africans as commodities to be 'used' in the industrial slave system signifies a devouring of black flesh or cannibalism. In this case, the core idea of the cannibal, or flesh-eater, is retained and reworked to interpret the genocide of millions of Africans.

## Babylon system cannibal

The independence of former colonies in the West Indies in the mid-twentieth century does not result in an end to cannibal discourse. Instead, it is recontextualized to identify the workings of the new state, specifically, the post-colonial context of Jamaica. This second stage of devouring implicates the post-colonial state and furthermore identifies the church as co-devourer. This is not a completely new idea, for we have seen already that Equiano implicates 'Christians' in the devouring of Africans. He feared being eaten, but was not. However, a more specific critique emerges in post-colonial Jamaica where the church is part of the bloodsucking Babylon system. In 1970s Jamaica, the image of cannibalism was projected onto the Jamaican government and other leading institutions. Rather than emanating from literary works or biographies, these cries of the oppressed emerged in popular music culture. The criticism targeted the fact that colonialism left intact its capitalist infrastructure and hierarchies of economic power. Thus, post-colonial societies, while free from European political control, remained locked into capitalist exploitation. In the Jamaican case, despite gaining independence in 1962, material wealth remained in the hands of the former colonial plutocracy.[17] The economic wealth from tourism and the mineral extraction of bauxite failed to 'trickle down' to the rural or urban poor.[18] Reflecting on this predicament, Bob Marley, the renowned reggae artist, introduces the notion of the Babylon system.

In Marley's 'Babylon System' from the 1979 *Survival* album, state cannibalism emerges as a multi-headed hydra. The hermeneutical presupposition in the 'Babylon System' is that the black poor in Jamaica are the modern day Israelites captive in the Jamaican Babylon. Babylon in the Bible refers to the historic experience of Israelites exiled in Babylon by King Nebuchadnezzar in 586 BCE until their release by Cyrus the Great in 539 BCE. In Marley's appropriation, 'Babylon' signifies the post-colonial state's rapacious devouring of the flesh of the black poor.

The track begins with defiance; the poor must 'refuse' to follow the dictates of those in power. But what is it that they must resist? Marley speaks of an educational system that wants to educate the masses to be subservient labourers for the capitalist system. This process of 'equal opportunities' is false consciousness. Rather than granting real freedom and liberty, the place of the poor is to be new fodder for the exploitative economic system or 'winepress'. Marley demands real freedom, not the false consciousness of equal opportunities.

Marley then elaborates on the forces behind the oppression, the Babylon system, which he describes as a vampire that sucks the blood of children and the suffering poor. Intriguingly, Marley's critique of the post-colonial economic system finds identification with Marx's critique of capitalism as a vampire sucking the blood of workers and eating their produce:

> Capital is dead labor, which, vampire-like, lives only by sucking living labor, and lives the more, the more labor it sucks.[19]

The church is an agent of the post-colonial state, one of the two pillars of Babylon – the other being the university. But how does Marley explain Christian complicity? He does so by identifying a theological problem wherein theology becomes ideology or an obfuscation of the real causes of distress.

The collusion of the church is expressed in the narration of a fictional confrontation in an earlier work, 'Get up Stand Up', from the 1973 *Burnin* album. Here, Marley rejects the Christian promise of a future in heaven in return for toil on earth. This dismissal of heavenly longing reflects the problem of an otherworldly eschatology and, inadvertently, Marley identifies a tension in the New Testament that remains problematic today.[20] Eschatology has tended to veer between three basic positions: futurist, inaugurated and realized.[21] The futurist position asserts that the Kingdom of God is fundamentally a future event and will in time break into human history. The inaugurated, in contrast, asserts that the Kingdom of God has arrived but is not fully realized – 'the now' and 'not yet' of Christian eschatology. The final position, the realized, asserts that the Kingdom of God has been realized in the coming of Jesus.[22] Marley's critique is of a perceived futurist position, which he believes is insufficient to transform the world.

For Marley, the church in Babylon is a part of the state's cannibalism because of its ideological role; it obfuscates reality, nurturing obsession with the life to come instead of pursuing a this-worldly struggle for freedom and justice. As a result, the church legitimates passivity in this life and inadvertently becomes part of the political problem confronting the oppressed. This is not a new accusation levied against Christianity or an idea that that has gone unchallenged inside of Christian scholarship. Much of twentieth century Western theology has devoted time and energy to determining the ethical outcomes of transcendence in theology and church.[23] What is important here, however, is that this critique of the church as a feature of state cannibalism can be extended beyond post-colonial Jamaica into the domestic neocolonial context of contemporary Britain – and this is the final linkage. While Marley focused on the problem of theology (eschatology) in relation to cannibalism, I want to identify how 'memory' is the new 'flesh' to be devoured in neocolonial cannibal discourse.

## Memory cannibalism

I want to propose that a very contemporary form of flesh-eating emerges over the struggle to control memory: that is, how and what we remember from our collective history, particularly the history of slavery. Moreover, the churches in England are a party to this devouring. Colonial history is contentious in contemporary Britain where, at one pole, revisionist historians have sought to re-imagine the British Empire as a mixed blessing for colonized people, while at the other end of the pole subversive historians seek to identify the devastating impact of empire and the hidden struggles of indigenous people to rid themselves of British rule.[24] This study falls into the latter camp. To evaluate the role of the church in this struggle over the memory of slavery, I will combine two viewpoints, one from post-colonial theory and the other from Christian theology, to articulate a view of cannibalism as *an eating of memory or memory cannibalism*.

The first theme is 'epistemic violence'. Within postcolonial studies, Gayatri Chakravorty Spivak borrows the term 'epistemic violence' from Michel Foucault to describe an imperial construction of archives, which seeks to control memory and thereby safeguard the power of interpreting history.[25] Control is not only power over 'others' but also harm because this control of knowledge informs political arrangements and how 'others' are represented. Epistemic violence is therefore the pain and suffering inflicted by those who control historical records, which impact how we remember the past.

The second viewpoint is 'loss of memory'. This is a theme that emerges in the theology of Johann Baptist Metz. In *The Emergent Church: The Future of Christianity in a Postbourgeois World*, Metz reflects on memory, specifically the memory of the Holocaust. He argues that the modern world is characterized by a loss of memory, particularly the memory of suffering.[26] For Metz, historical memory has power and its loss renders us less able to cope with the onslaught of 'market place' values and world-views of the wider society.[27] 'Market capitalism not only regulates economic realms but also impinges on social relationships and political and spiritual life. One result is that, everything now appears to be exchangeable and interchangeable, even interpersonal relationships and our life commitments'.[28] Loss of memory or 'massive forgetfulness'[29] paves the way for fatalism and apathy.[30] In response, Metz calls for a new moral imagination that must ensure the 'memory of suffering accumulated in history'.[31] Because the memory of suffering has the potential to uncover falsehoods of evolutionary thinking by exposing the 'senseless suffering inflicted upon people in the name of human progress', it is a 'dangerous memory'. Metz elaborates on these 'dangerous memories' as:

> . . . memories which make demands on us. There are memories in which earlier experiences break through to the centre point of our lives and reveal new and dangerous insights for the present. They illuminate for a few moments and with a harsh and steady light the questionable nature of things we have apparently come to terms with and show up the banality of our supposed 'realism'. They break through the canon of the prevailing structures of plausibility and have certain subversive features. Such memories are like dangerous and incalculable visitations from the past. They are memories that we have to take into account, memories, as it were, with a future content.[32]

Memory cannibalism, as I use the term, is an aggregate of aspects of Spivak's political struggle over archives and Metz's loss of dangerous memories. *Memory cannibalism is the process of controlling archives so as to render 'dangerous memories' ineffective.* This process is achieved not by completely dismissing or forgetting the past (as was the case with Metz) but entails *policing* how the past is perceived in the present so that certain memories are nullified. Thus, memory cannibalism seeks to edit out or 'consume' aspects of the past and thereby deliberately or unwittingly *inflicts harm* by denying status, autonomy and well-being to 'others' in the present.

## Bicentennial food

In the final part of this chapter, I want to suggest that memory cannibalism is present in the ecumenical exchanges at the heart of the Bicentennial of the Abolition of the British Transatlantic Slave Trade in 2007.

The year, 2007, commemorated the nineteenth-century abolitionist movement and the abolition of the transatlantic slave trade in Britain in 1807. In view of the fact that slavery did not end in the Caribbean until 1834, and was then followed by a form of indentured labour until 1838, this anniversary was always going to sit uneasily in the struggle for slavery's memory and recompense. This proved to be the case a year before the commemoration when a heated debate ensued regarding how best to reflect on slave history from a variety of contemporary situations. Another controversy centred on whether the nation should apologize for profiting from the slave trade. Black community groups and mainstream civic organizations were provided with funding for a myriad of exhibitions, educational tours and other commemorative acts. In the end, the British government expressed 'deep regret', although some of the cities with slave trading in their past went further and provided municipal government-led apologies (the cities of Liverpool and London). Bristol, however, a city steeped in slavery, much to the annoyance of the organizers and activists of the bicentennial events, flatly refused to offer any meaningful statement of apology or serious regret.

A major event in the commemoration was a high-profile worship service attended by the British establishment and led by the Archbishop of Canterbury, Dr Rowan Williams at Westminster Abbey in London. The event will be remembered for Pan Africanist Toyin Agbetu's dramatic, solitary protest in front of Queen Elizabeth II and then Prime Minister Tony Blair. About 45 minutes into the commemoration, Toyin began screaming at the top of his voice, while the Queen, Prince Philip, Tony and Cherie Blair and the Archbishop of Canterbury looked on dumbfounded. Agbetu's protest began just as the Archbishop had finished his main address and the service moved to 'confession and absolution'. At this point, Agbetu yelled, 'You should be ashamed. We should not be here. This is an insult to us. I want all the Christians who are Africans to walk out of here with me!' No one got up and followed him.

A year after the event, I interviewed three attendees about their responses to the 'outrage'. One couple, Christian pastors from Birmingham, stated that they were embarrassed by what had happened and accordingly 'fixed their faces like stone' to reflect shame and disgust. Another woman who worked for a major charity spoke of an internal conflict. She wanted to get up and follow Agbetu, but lacked the moral courage to do so. Others were not surprised by the intervention and had anticipated that something would happen. One of the members of the black church who was involved in organizing the event spoke of a litany of tensions on both sides of the divide. 'Something was bound to happen', he said, because of the lack of a meaningful expression of black culture during the service.

I watched the events unfolding on the BBC World Service in a hotel room in Accra, Ghana, where I was filming *The Great African Scandal* documentary: a film about the underside of globalization. My first thought was whether Agbetu would get out of the building alive! After all, in a terrorist-conscious age, as we know from the tragic case of mistaken identity that led armed police to shoot dead an innocent man, Jean Charles De Menezes, on his way to work in London two years prior, the police might shoot a suspect merely for looking like a terrorist, let alone behaving like one. The hesitation of the security guards was eased somewhat when Mr Agbetu yelled, 'I have no weapon! I have no weapon!'[33] Speaking in language reminiscent of Marley's Babylon system, Agbetu declared the motivation behind his protest:

> I don't believe it was right for us to have remained in a venue in which the British monarchy, government and church – all leading institutions of African enslavement during the Maafa [African Holocaust] – collectively refused to atone for their sins.[34]

Agbetu was ejected from the Abbey, arrested and after a lengthy investigation faced no legal charge. However, speaking to him a year after the event, he remained adamant that his cause was just. He also relayed to me the mental stress he had suffered as a result of making the complaint. For me, what is important about Agbetu's protest is how it signals recognition of continued devouring – which was the real offence.

So how did the eating take place at the Abbey? There were two stages. It began with control of memory, in this context the attendees and the nation at large lacked the opportunity to reflect wholeheartedly on the pain and suffering of the slaves, and the organizers of the service missed an opportunity to nurture a sense of recompense or justice. The service was arranged by Churches Together in Britain and Ireland, an ecumenical organization charged with fostering church unity. There was much debate and discussion about the content of the liturgy and format of the service. A balance needed to be struck. It was important to be respectful of the suffering of slaves, but also to praise the work of the white British abolitionists – who represented a very different side of the same abolition. However, some of the black Christian organizers became increasingly dismayed by a perceived lack of focus and interest on the suffering of slaves. For this disaffected group, the lack of generosity was evidenced by the unwillingness of the Westminster Abbey leadership to permit a strong African cultural presence at the service in the form of a traditional African drumming troupe. There was, however, some reference to pain and suffering in the service, including a moving musical reflection on Psalm 69. One of the disaffected group inadvertently described how the policing of memory had taken place when he told me, 'We were in their house (Anglican abbey), and had to play by their rules'. In other words, the service was dominated by an Anglican Church perspective and in so doing represented a control of slavery's memory.

The second stage was a muting of dangerous memories so that slave history was represented as white salvation of black suffering. Indeed, this was very much the normative approach to the whole year in which a selective historical amnesia failed to grasp the depth of Britain's slave past, the suffering of slaves or the relationship between slavery and contemporary racism(s). For instance, 1807 meant very little to Africans in the 'West Indies'. After all, it took an additional 30 years before any semblance of freedom emerged – a freedom that was paid for with the death of hundreds of slaves who took up arms against their captors in the slave revolts of the third decade of the nineteenth century. Their bloodshed is remembered in the title of Richard Harts' study of Jamaican history, *The Slaves Who Abolished Slavery*.[35] Thus, the dangerous memories of suffering, slavery and racism(s), and the blacks who abolished slavery were omitted not only from the service but from the mainstream reflections on the year. Moreover, harm was inflicted.

## Non-prophetic ministry

My analysis of memory cannibalism leads me to discuss its effect on black Pentecostalism. While this solitary service cannot be held responsible for a complex Pentecostal prehistory, as a showcase event, I assert that it served to reinforce prior black Pentecostal experience of subservience in the face of Western Christian theopolitics. After all, a large and prestigious Pentecostal delegation was present at the Abbey service. Moreover, distinguished black Pentecostals participated in the planning of the service, which demonstrates that black Pentecostals were involved and complicit.

Was harm really inflicted? Well, we could dismiss any negative association and view the event as an ecumenical gathering in which all parties reflected on the past. Or we might read it as an event marred by an unfortunate outburst from a megalomaniac Black Nationalist activist. But neither of these explanations do justice to the deeper levels of meaning at work in the service.

On one level, the service was a continuation of the meaning of slavery's cannibalism that not only 'eats' memory but also *solidifies black Pentecostal non-prophetic ministry*. Non-prophetic ministry is the denial of the political role of the black church, and its inability to speak truth to power and struggle for justice.[36] It has resonance with the apolitical tradition within global Pentecostalism, a tradition that 'retains a millennial focus on the coming of the Kingdom of God in place of political engagement'.[37] In other words, eating the memory of slavery extinguishes this dangerous memory and encourages otherworldly pursuits. On another level, the service was an example of black Pentecostals colluding with their own oppression, or victim complicity. By agreeing to a liturgy that orchestrated memory cannibalism, Pentecostals were, by their presence and participation, party to the devouring.

So the harm is this: the Abbey's memory cannibalism affects black Pentecostalism by policing slave history so as to sanitize dangerous memories and reinforce the persistence of non-prophetic ministry.

In summary, I have explored the use of cannibal language to describe the continuation of inappropriate devouring of black flesh. The idiom first appears with the history of slavery as enslaved people accused slavers of cannibalism – a morbid diagnosis of the slave condition. Instead of diminishing with abolition, the use of cannibal imagery to reflect illicit exchange has continued in new contexts and is used to describe the devouring of the post-colonial state in the Caribbean. In mid-twentieth century, it is the grandchildren of slavery, sucked dry by post-colonial capitalism and unfair wage labour, who use the idiom. Moreover, the church is complicit. On the one hand it is a part of the Babylon system and on the other creates false consciousness in the form of otherworldly eschatology. In the early twenty-first century, the Church of England has not ceased devouring; indeed, eating has taken a new form in the shape of memory cannibalism. The consequence for black Pentecostalism is the prolongation of its political impotence in the form of non-prophetic ministry.

# CHAPTER SEVEN

# Zombie worship

'When you go to church leave your brain at the door.' I have often wondered why people say this about attending church services, especially black Pentecostal churches. The statement suggests that church life and rational thought are incompatible. For many years, I countered this perception in relation to black worship by defending the way that Pentecostals worshiped in an unencumbered way that was not restricted by wordy liturgies and predictable routines. Worshipping, as black Pentecostals do, in 'Spirit and truth' is super-rational and therefore it is not confined by reason. However, while not wishing to completely rule out this earlier analysis of black Pentecostal worship, I have come to understand that there is a place for critical thought within the worship space. Critical thought can appear in sermons, liturgies and prayers and its role is to facilitate a more complex understanding of the work of God in the world and usher in a deeper faith. However, there is a double-standard at work in the ministries of several high-profile black Pentecostal leaders in Britain, which I believe belies a more sinister history. Although these leaders have eschewed serious theological training and react negatively to persons in their congregations with theological credentials, they nonetheless crave the scholarly recognition associated with a BA or PhD in theology. This desire for academic respectability has led many pastors to procure honorary doctorates from dubious academic institutions while professing to be 'trained' in theology.

I believe this improbity points to something sinister lurking in the background: an unresolved relationship between black British Pentecostals and academic theological education. As I have argued in Chapter Five, the lack of resolution has its roots in colonial Christianity and the fissure between faith and reason implicit in the missionary mis-education of slaves. Furthermore, I believe this unresolved tension in the history of black Pentecostalism has a modern counterpart in worship in the form of a zombie worship experience.

This chapter explores malevolent spirituality in relation to black Pentecostalism in the form of the zombie. As mentioned in Chapter Two, the zombie existed in history as an enslaved, mindless body, and so to speak of zombies is coded language for the illicit exchange of human flesh. Similarly, in new significatory contexts today, the figure of the zombie continues to reveal a diagnostic capability, identifying occult economies that arise from the exploitation of others.

In this chapter, I want to do two things. First, I want to further develop this diagnostic understanding of the zombie, by drawing on Haitian history. The zombie tradition emerges in Haiti from Africans slaves within the cauldron of French industrial slavery. These lesser beings in the French colony fashioned a sophisticated religious tradition out of the material from the Old and New World. This religious tradition came to global prominence in the early twentieth century during the short-lived American occupation of the island and, in my analysis, its emergence signals the presence of a contemporary occult economy – the American occupation. Second, I will appropriate *this* zombie tradition but place it in comparative analysis with the contemporary world, specifically black Pentecostalism. My aim is to demonstrate how black Pentecostal worship can result in the formation of, what I term as, a 'Christian zombie': a mindless body in worship. Concretely, I argue that popular forms of Pentecostal worship unwittingly fashion passive and compliant Christians who marginalize critical thinking and theological scholarship by privileging affective ways of knowing God and validating truth. Moreover, this marginalization of academic theological education has comparative identification with colonial Christianity's mission to create subservient Christian slaves.

# *Vodou*: A Short History

Contrary to its popularization in Hollywood films[1] such as *I am Legend*, the zombie originates neither from outer space nor from lethal pathogens – but instead out of Haitian *vodou*. To explore the meaning of the zombie we must first crawl back through French colonialism and slavery to the origins of vodou on the island.[2] In 1492, Columbus landed on an island the Arawak people referred to as Haiti or 'Land of Mountains', which Columbus duly named and claimed for Spain as Hispaniola (Española). As was noted in Chapter Three, the Spanish set about extracting wealth by forced enslavement of the indigenous people. Through a potent mixture of brutality and disease, most of the inhabitants were wiped out. Bartolomé de Las Casas petitioned the Spanish crown to send African labour to the colonies as an alternative workforce, and cheap, efficient African slave labour began to arrive wholesale in 1517.

Hispaniola was not immune to European national rivalries and the west of the island became increasingly difficult to administer due in part to raids by French pirates. Over time, the French gained control over the west, and by 1675 former pirates or *boucaniers* had turned their attention to agricultural development in the new colony. Spain did not have the resources to challenge the French incursion and opted for peaceful co-existence, enshrined in the Treaty of Ryswick 1697. The treaty ceded possession of the west of the island to the French and Saint-Domingue was established.

Both the Spanish and the French shared a desire to extract profit from slavery but they differed in their approach to religious instruction. While the Spanish provided their slaves some religious teaching and encouraged missionary work, the French were initially less interested, thus inadvertently providing 'space' for the religions of captured Africans to develop in this new but troubled soil. Therefore, by the time the French decided to evangelize, African religions carried by slaves were unofficially established.

As the number of Africans increased in the colony, some effort was made to begin active conversion to Christianity (the Catholic Church). For instance, The Code Noir (1683), the articles of slave regulation in the colonies, condoned forced Christian baptism but banned African religious practices.[3] Further regulations prohibiting the slaves to meet were imposed in 1758 and 1777 to enforce the Christianization of slaves, including the death penalty for slaves who met surreptitiously without the presence of a priest and the outlawing of the use of drums and the selling or buying of religious items.[4] Whatever the benefits to be had by converting to the slavemaster's religion, African slaves were reluctant to abandon their beliefs and rituals. Instead, they sought to rework their traditions in light of slavery's racial terror. The early Catholic mission eventually unofficially acknowledged the presence of these African religions, but in its early years vodou practitioners were careful to camouflage their retention of African-based practice. Scholars suggest that it is through this secrecy that Catholic signs and symbols were used as cover for African ideas.[5] For instance, Catholic saints masked vodou deities or *lwas*. The main lwa, Legma, the gatekeeper between worlds, became associated with Christ and St. Peter.[6] After the Haitian rebellion in 1791 and the quest by former slaves to establish independence, a friction between Rome and the fledgling republic of Haiti made it difficult for the church to challenge vodou due to few priests being sent to the island. By the time the tension was eventually resolved in 1860 with the appointment of clergy, vodou was normative in Haitian culture. The battle lines were drawn: vodou presented a problem for the Catholic church, which came to associate vodou practices with the satanic.[7]

The term vodou probably originates in the Fon language of Dahomey, a pre-colonial kingdom of Benin and parts of Nigeria and Togo, where it means 'an invisible force' or 'spirit'.[8] Dahomey provided slaves for the New World from diverse tribes that shared many core beliefs. In West Africa, each group had its own vodou – ancestral guardians and deities often tied to specific dynasties. 'Groups would congregate to venerate the ancestors, offer sacrifices and receive messages from the vodou, usually through possession of the body'. In Saint-Domingue, the French colony that is now modern-day Haiti, the vodou were no longer tied to African soil and nobilities and, therefore, became 'part of a general family of spirits or *nanchon*'.[9] Vodou is therefore a generic term covering a range of beliefs and practices, and several divisions or branches, although these traditions are complex and the distinctions and boundaries never clear-cut.

The largest division of vodou is Rada. While some debate exists on the origins of the term, many commentators suggest that it comes from the Dahomey holy city of Allada.[10] Within this religious cosmos exist a number of lwas or deities, beliefs and rituals. Vodou, in the form of Rada, involves service to the lwas in order to ensure 'the energies of the universe, which are believed to reside in Africa (Ginen), and are harmonized with human life'.[11] The aim of the vodou is to 'maintain balance between these forces and human life by tapping into the sources to ensure well-being by grounding the self, family and community in meaningful existence'.[12] There are several energies within the vodou cosmology. First, there is the Bondye (supreme power), then the manifestations of Bondye – the lwas or *mysteres* (of which there are many). Next, the ancestors or *les mortes* and other spirits, and finally, humans. These deities, while metaphysical, are given concrete physical manifestation in nature, such as Damballah (rainbow/snake) and Agwe (sea).[13]

The cruel environment of French industrial slavery led to the creation of other divisions of vodou, primarily to make sense of the brutality of subjugation. As a result, the Petro (Pethro) rituals and deities emerged. These lwas or deities were more aggressive in their approach to problem-solving. For example, 'while Rada rituals used water, Petro made use of rum'.[14] Petro deities are not always separate from the Rada deities but focused on alternative intents. Thus Petro lwas permit devotees to access deities depending on their need, revealing 'a pragmatic relationship between the deities and humans'.[15] Given the focus of Petro, it should be of no surprise that it is the Petro traditions that are central to the Haitian revolution, where slaves drove the French masters off the island:

In order to produce greater unity among the rebels . . . he [Boukman] conducted an impressive ceremony during the night of August 14, 1791. After an enormous crowd had assembled a violent storm arose, and in the midst of thunder and lightning an old Negro woman appeared, danced wildly, sang, and brandished a huge cutlass over her head. Finally, the silenced and fascinated crowd saw her plunge the cutlass into the throat of a black hog. The slaves drank the animal's blood and swore they would execute Boukman's orders. . . .[16]

In addition to the Rada and Petro deities, there are 'lesser' spirits devoted to specific tasks. These are weaker spirits associated with the Congo *nanchon*.[17] They are renowned for cheerfulness and good nature and have the responsibility of returning Haitians back to Africa. There are also malevolent spirits, or *Baka*, who do the bidding of the lwas and are at the service of human magicians. 'The ancestors are also important within this cosmology because they are the link between the two worlds; they remind devotees of the connection between this life and the next, Haiti and Ginen'.[18]

Humans comprise the next level of existence. The human being is said to have two souls, or 'little angels', housed within the self. These are the *ti-bon-anj* (the little good angel) responsible for ethical conduct and personality and also the *gwo-bon-anj* (the big good angel) responsible for memory, intelligence or the soul.[19] Vodou rites and practices are essentially focused on enabling an individual to develop their gwo-bon-anj and live a good and responsible existence. Malevolence, however, may feature in the life of the souls. If the ti-bon-anj is not cared for after death through proper rituals by devotees, it may 'feed off the body and become *Baka*', and be used by magicians or sorcerers for malevolent intent.[20] During ceremonies involving spirit possession the gwo-bon-anj leaves the body, and at this point the devotee is vulnerable to corrupt conjurers who may block its return and thus leave the body a zombie.[21]

# The zombie

The zombie, an enslaved, mindless body, represents malevolence in an otherwise holistic and harmonious religious system. How one becomes a zombie has a supernatural explanation, which belies a more concrete and all-too-real experience of slavery and subjugation on the island. The supernatural explanation asserts that deceitful spiritual practitioners can turn a person into a zombie. In vodou, the body is a vessel for communication with the deity and this is achieved through spirit possession. Possession occurs when an lwa temporarily displaces the soul (big good angel) of a devotee and becomes the force in the body. This allows the lwa to communicate clearly and exercise their authority over the individual.[22] During ceremonies involving spirit possession, the devotee is vulnerable to unscrupulous conjurers who may block the return of the human's soul, rescind intelligence and personality and, thus, leave the body a mindless husk or zombie.[23] Without the soul, and its attendant characteristics, the conjurer can enslave the body. But this is not the full picture because beneath the surface the zombie is a symbol of a much longer and enduring history on the island. Let me explain.

The idea of a zombie, a mindless body, within a context inscribed with the brutalization of black bodies can also be read as memory of slavery's malevolence. Within this interpretation, the zombie signifies the existential reality of slavery, that is, to be a soulless being in a world of pain and suffering. As anthropologist Mimi Sheller notes, in attempting to capture a sense of the zombie in Haiti's past, one only needs to imagine the powerless, dejected and soulless bodies of slaves on French colonial plantations as human drones devoid of personality.[24]

The phantasm of the zombie – a soulless husk deprived of freedom – is the ultimate sign of loss and dispossession.[25]

The idea of a zombie as a slave was rekindled during the American occupation of the island in the 1920s.[26] Some debate exists on the success of the American occupation as infrastructure and political improvements took place but at the expense of Haitian dignity; for instance, forced labour was used on several of the American-led infrastructure projects. The return of slavery, under the pretext of development and stability, revived a sense of zombification among Haitians:

In Haiti, memories of servitude are transposed into a new idiom that both reproduces and dismantles a twentieth century history of forced labor and denigration that became particularly acute during the American occupation of Haiti.[27]

In sum, the zombie represents a malevolent dimension of vodou. It is the product of dishonest religious practitioners, which can also be viewed as a coded memory of rapacious French colonialism, and contemporary forms of illicit accumulation in the island's troubled history. It is the second feature, coded memory of slavery, that informs my thinking in this study.

The question we now must ask is where *black Pentecostalism is positioned in relation to zombification*? To find out, we must evaluate black Pentecostalism in light of zombie discourse and illuminate two features. The first feature highlights the site of zombification, the moment at which the black Christian body becomes a Christian zombie. The second feature identifies its beneficiary; that is, it asks who profits from this enslavement? By way of response to both these questions, I will describe the worship at an apostolic Pentecostal church in the Midlands, and then parse the zombification and its malevolence.

# New Church

New Church is the fictional name of a Midlands church I attended as a full participant for 24 months. The purpose of my involvement was to explore the dynamics of neo-Pentecostalism, which I will explain below. It soon became clear to me, however, that there was a distinctive attitude towards theological education that resonated with my theory of zombification – and it is this latter theme on which I want to reflect. I attended the 10:30 a.m. worship service at New Church,[28] where a great effort is made to ensure that the best vocalists, equipment and musicians are resourced to produce dynamic worship. Therefore, it should be of no surprise that the church is renowned for worship ministry across the city.

## *Context*

New Church is neo-Pentecostal. Neo-Pentecostalism signals a theological shift in emphasis from divine judgment towards 'abundant life' or a life of economic prosperity, health and well-being in the present. Consequently, believers are encouraged to accommodate themselves to the wider culture and society, instead of completely rejecting it.[29] Accommodation does not mean capitulation; rather, it entails a relaxation of dress codes, an affirmation of the pursuit of wealth or prosperity doctrine and approval rather than disdain towards patronage of the leisure industry (cinema, theatre, etc.). Indeed, at New Church, business innovation and self-help are major themes preached regularly from the pulpit.

New Church is a 'family church' in terms of leadership. The leadership is a small elite with strong familial ties. Further, this group determines the direction of ministry and mission. In theory, this means that the pastors appoint and support individuals that they believe are both talented and 'called' to ministry. In practice, however, the pastors' children head up key ministries, including the music ministry. These strong familial ties did not appear to cause friction or discontent within the congregation. On the contrary, there was a sense of acceptance that pastors will call upon their family members to support their ministry. Typical of this view was the response I received when I asked one member of the congregation what he thought about the family emphasis in the leadership team. In reply, he reminded me of a biblical fact by asking, 'Weren't Jesus and John in a family ministry?'

## *Worship*

Worship is a communal event characterized by a divine-human encounter. It is a public ritual marked by profound interactions, 'both visual and subliminal, between worshippers and those leading worship'. As such, it is a 'shared social practice that has the power to shape orientation, perspective and behaviour'.[30] I wanted to know how worship produces episteme, or ways of knowing, because the absence of the 'mind' is central to identifying a zombie body in worship.

The worship at New Church consisted of three overlapping stages. First, there was a general 'Call to Worship' and the reciting of 'The Declaration', the mission statement of the church. Next, there was a time of praise and worship, where the ministry team led the congregation in singing choruses and praise and worship songs. Finally, there was the sermon and altar call where believers seeking to respond to the sermon amassed at the altar for additional prayer and support. On average, the service lasted just under three hours with the sermon consuming most of the time, nearly 40–50 minutes.

The high point of the service at New Church was the praise and worship session.[31] Rooted in Caribbean Pentecostalism, worship at New Church retains the tradition of worship as eudemonic or providing well-being.[32] Transformation, pleasure and fulfilment lie at the heart of worship and, for this reason, believers speak of worship as being 'good' or 'bad' based on its ability to 'reach', 'touch' or 'bless'. The praise and worship segment was the most participatory, collaborative and engaged moment in the service and, as a result, when quizzed after service, respondents were more likely to comment on the quality of the worship in reply to the question, 'What did you like most about the service?' Four themes cut through the worship at New Church: spirituality,[33] ethics,[34] power relations[35] and episteme. It is, however, episteme that concerns me here.

## Episteme

New Church contained its own ways of knowing – all of which were consistent with the ways of knowing at work in much of Pentecostalism.[36] The most prominent feature, I want to call 'body knowledge'. This expectation is registered in services when the worship leaders appeal to the congregation to be 'open to the Spirit' and 'hear from God'. These phrases are also code-switches for transition from an upbeat, high-tempo worship to a slower-paced but deeply intimate worship. The result is an intensification of focus and change in the mood of the congregation.

There are at least two aspects to body knowledge. The first is the *affective* source of knowing. Believers expect to 'feel' the Spirit in their bodies and allow the Spirit to enlighten them in the faith. Here, expressive, emotional physicality (crying, laughing, shaking and moving) is a pathway to divine knowledge. The *affective* is gendered in apostolic Pentecostal churches with men and women responding differently to the moving of the Spirit.[37] The second dimension of this body knowledge concerns the collective bodies in worship, that is, group *validation*. Group validation is a collective working out of what is truth and therefore useful for the group. It is the Spirit leading everyone into truth (John 16.13). Thus, when a believer tells of a life experience in a sermon, testimony or song (narrative ways of knowing), the members of the congregation validate its truthfulness and usefulness by their bodily response. Shouts of 'amen', the raising and waving of arms, nods of the head or spontaneous clapping legitimate the validity of what has been preached, testified or sung. Conversely, the absence of acknowledgement from the congregation generally indicates group displeasure, suspicion and rejection of what has been heard. These two features of the episteme, the affective and group validation in worship are potentially revolutionary. Both have the capacity to democratize theological inquiry by providing an alternative means of validating truth claims in radical contrast to the critical thinking of mainstream theology:

> Pentecostalism is revolutionary because it offers alternatives to 'literary' theology and defrosts frozen thinking . . . it allows for a process of democratization of language by dismantling privilege of the abstract, rational and propositional systems.[38]

However, body knowledge episteme, while potentially revolutionary and meaningful, fails to acknowledge a deeper historic and problematic undercurrent, which is the inability of black Pentecostals to combine the affective with critical thinking, which as I have suggested at the beginning of this chapter, leads to unethical practices amongst some clergy. Pentecostal educator Cheryl Bridges Johns describes this tension as a division between an 'oral-affective' (spoken action theology) mode, and a 'critical cognitive' (critical thinking) mode.[39] This tension was played out at New Church, where running concurrent with the body knowledge episteme was an official mistrust of critical thinking. Either by discarding the importance of academic theology or mocking the accents of educated people, the pastors would exhort the congregation of the dangers of 'thinking too much' or 'analysing all the time'. That is to say, there was an anti-critical thinking sentiment that descended into anti-intellectualism.

Furthermore, there was very little interest in formal university theological education among the leadership and their entourage. For instance, once after a sermon by a junior minster that, while powerful and dynamic, was structured in an unorganized manner, I sought to offer advice and support. I suggested to the junior minister, 'Would you consider studying the structure of sermons if it meant that it would be easier for people to follow your train of thought?' His response was a resounding, 'No, Brother!' Now his reaction could have been, in part, a response to his perception of me as the university lecturer applying perceived academic standards to the work of the Spirit in the context of the church. Even so, it was a definitive rejection of critical thinking via academic learning as a route for improving communication. As a result of the worship experience and attitude towards theological education there were signs of a Christian zombie, that is, a mindless body in worship. But there was something else at work. Those seeking to challenge body knowledge were seduced or 'policed' by a new, all-encompassing motif arising out of the neo-Pentecostalism.

There was, however, some resistance to the status quo from a small, critically minded group within the church. This small group of mainly well-educated professionals wanted to embrace academic theological education. While affirming the tradition of body knowledge, they also believed it could be enhanced rather than destroyed by engagement with academic theological education. However, this quest to unify two different ways of knowing was undermined by the domination of body knowledge in worship. The role of this critical group was vital to understanding how worship functioned as zombification. I came to understand that what I term, 'aspirational' worship, appeased this critical group and inadvertently created the Christian zombie.

## *Aspirational Worship*

At New Church, the standoff between an opposition to and affirmation of critical thinking and theological education is resolved by aspirational worship. Aspiration as a type of worship experience collapses worship into social ambition and social mobility. This process took place in two specific points in the worship service. It was foregrounded at the beginning of worship at New Church with a communal call to faith termed 'the Declaration'. The Declaration affirmed divine favour, material blessing and divine protection from disease, sickness and demonic attack. Second, sermons, testimonies and informal conversations constantly conflated divine blessing and career progression and economic development. For instance, one of the more business-oriented leaders gave a testimony in which he said:

> God has been good to me this week. I was praying to Him to ask Him how I could make another £100,000 this year. The year is still young (March) and I know God is going to continue to work His miracles in my life. . . .

The almost vulgar openness to discuss and even flaunt wealth, a tradition that is greeted with some dislike in British culture and churches, can be explained in part by the social location of the congregation. The image of God as benevolent provider was a result of the sociopolitical context. Much of black (African-Caribbean) Birmingham is 'economically disadvantaged' with high rates of unemployment, usually double that of the national average. In addition, this group often experiences exclusion in the workplace and social life.[40] Therefore, an emphasis on economic advancement, in a context of discrimination, is a legitimate pastoral concern. However, the social location is only part of the explanation. There is something else at play: a shift from worship as empowerment to worship as aspiration.

Pentecostal worship has traditionally navigated the difficult social realities of inner-city, black, British life through empowering worship. As Roswith Gerloff notes, empowering worship provides spiritual resources to cope with, overcome and transform reality.[41] It is communally orientated and focused on the black church as a benevolent community.[42] In contrast, aspirational worship is highly individualized. It seeks to advance the individual (outside of group troubles). It is concerned with identity, but in relation to social mobility rather than ethnicity. Aspirational worship is a feature of neo-Pentecostalism, and its drive for the material empowerment of believers.[43] Material resources by themselves are not problematic (education, financial and family stability and employment opportunities), but become tricky when the desire descends into rampant materialism. What I am suggesting here is that at New Church, through aspirational worship, a shift takes place from self-giving to self-seeking. A useful way of explaining the dynamic of aspirational worship on the individual is through the concepts of the liminal and the individualization of religion.

According to social anthropologist Victor Turner, the liminal is the place where the past is suspended and the present not yet begun. In these moments of 'subversive flicker', people are able to imagine themselves in a different way.[44] The liminal applies to worship. Subversive flicker can be a revolutionary moment. Take, for example, the evidence from early Pentecostal worship where worship was an opportunity for working-class and working-poor blacks in the American post-war 'apartheid' to imagine themselves as equal with all Americans in the eyes of God, and therefore worthy of respect by their fellow citizens.[45] But building an egalitarian, benevolent community was not present in the context of New

Church. Instead, through dynamic music ministry, individuals were encouraged unconsciously to imagine themselves as individual recipients of God's abundant blessing. The shift in emphasis is seductive, inviting believers to become Christian consumers rather than social transformers. I contend this new emphasis radically reduces the capacity to agitate for a benevolent community, and undermines an appreciation of academic theological education – a desire that was present in the critical group.

Aspirational worship is also related to the 'turn towards the self in contemporary religion'. According to Heelas and Woodhead, 'the turn' is a move away from life 'lived in terms of external or objective roles, duties, and obligations, towards life lived by reference to one's own subjective experiences (relational as much as individualistic)'.[46] So the subjective turn moves one away from 'life as', or duty to others, towards 'subjective-life' or life 'lived in deep connection with the unique experiences of my self-in-relation'.[47] Applied to the context of worship at New Church, aspirational worship facilitates the turn towards the self by legitimating the believer's focus on his or her own passions, desires, aspirations and dreams. But it is not a *complete* 360-degree turning away from communal responsibility, for there still remains some sense of communality and group responsibility in order to function as a 'church'. It is instead a partial or limited turn, which allows worshipers to feel at ease with the new emphasis on the self.

A personal footnote is helpful here. As I participated in the worship, my sense of the transcendent was informed by the wider material discourse of testimonies, exhortations for tithes and offerings and sermon topics. Therefore, I found myself responding to what I needed in my life rather than thinking horizontally of others, the wider world or whether this sort of worship was indeed reflective of meaningful Pentecostal theology. It is in these moments that the tension between the pew and the pulpit is resolved: aspiration appeases the pew and maintains the domination of the oral-affective theology of the pulpit. Aspirational worship is a spiritual sedative for those who seek a place for academic theology in worship at New Church.

# Zombie worship and academic-theology phobia

To compare worship with Haitian zombification can only take place in a limited way but it is nonetheless meaningful. This limitation is because of the historical, cultural and religious distance and differences between these two religious traditions. But we can make a conceptual comparison that has deeper political implications. Zombification at New Church takes place in the worship experience, through the tacit, exclusive acceptance of body knowledge. This zombie-like existence is reinforced by aspirational worship, which pacifies those who might agitate for critical thinking and academic theology as an addition to the other ways of knowing. Thus, in worship, a Christian zombie is produced. It is a 'mindless body' that registers a negation of academic theological education.

Who gains from this state of affairs? Apart from maintaining the status quo of power relations between clergy and congregation at New Church, there was another, hidden, beneficiary in the form of colonial Christianity. As mentioned in Chapter Five, colonial Christianity in the Caribbean placed little emphasis on the meaningful education of slaves, in the belief that Christian knowledge might lead to insubordination and impertinence. In this way, Christianity performed the 'ritual' justification for the slave's subjugation. Ironically, at New Church, the imperial design of colonial Christianity to create docile, uncritical and compliant believers is unwittingly given credence by the black British descendants of slaves. In this modern case, however, one is free in Christ but in the worship space is not able to think critically and academically about the meaning of God in the world – a reality that I will refer to hereafter as academic-theology phobia.

## Conclusion

In this chapter, I have argued that black Pentecostal worship is a zombie experience. The zombie in Haiti is both a spiritual and sociopolitical reality. In the sociopolitical sense it is a reminder of slavery's dehumanization of black bodies and the creation of docile, complicit slaves for use in French industrial slavery. Thought of this way, the zombie is an exploited, mindless body. I have argued that black Pentecostal worship is a zombie reality because it reproduces a zombie-like experience. In the case of worship, black Pentecostals are encouraged to disconnect critical thinking and academic theology in order to worship God. However, this practice, while being an affirmation of the super-rationality of worship, also reflects an unresolved tension at the heart of black Pentecostal worship: the tension between affective and critical modes of worship. This tension, I have argued, is resolved by the leadership through aspirational worship. Aspirational worship is individualized, self-oriented worship, which indirectly nullifies critical thinking and creates an environment for a black Christian zombie, that is, a mindless body experience in worship.

The last two chapters have examined 'set on', the continued influence of colonial theology in black Pentecostalism in the forms of non-prophetic ministry and academic-theology phobia. The influence of colonial Christianity on contemporary black British Pentecostalism cannot be charted in terms of direct historical continuity; that is, there is no simple overarching cause and effect relationship that we can draw between the past and present. Rather, there is a continuity of influence that permits us to rethink the meaning of particular action, behaviour and belief among black Pentecostals today. But set on is only one side of the emancipatory paradigm. There exists a tradition of resistance ('cast out') that I have framed as 'exorcism'. The next section, 'cast out' begins the turn towards exorcism by converting the emancipatory framework into a documentary film practice.

# CHAPTER EIGHT

# Signs and wonders

*The domains of 'preferred readings' have the whole social order embedded in them as a set of meanings, practices and beliefs.*

STUART HALL[1]

In my Introduction, I used the example of a young Christian brother who appreciated and interpreted the various meanings I wanted to convey in a television documentary that I had presented. I was fortunate. Many times audiences do not 'get' the intended meaning that the television producer or filmmaker wants to get across. (Just think about how your own take on a movie may have nothing in common with the review offered by the professional movie critic.) The gap between the filmmaker's intended meaning and the audience's received meaning is captured by the practice of encoding/decoding. Encoding/decoding refers to the process by which those who produce meaning (such as filmmakers) encode or inscribe cultural products with intended meanings that can then be decoded or interpreted by receivers as 'preferred readings'. However this process has very few guarantees, as there is interference between the two moments of communication.[2] In other words, I may inscribe my intended meanings, but it is not a certainty that the audience will decode it in the way that I envisioned. There are incidents, in contrast to the example I cited in the Introduction, where viewers do not accept my intended meaning. For instance, my intended meaning for the documentary 'Who Wrote the Bible?' was to affirm the importance of critical study of the Bible. However, after the film was broadcast, I was shopping in Birmingham city centre and received a very different interpretation from a sales assistant. The assistant, an early 20-something, student type, young African-Caribbean male, was serving me in the HMV record shop, where I was buying a CD. He recognized me from the documentary and said that he liked the film, and moreover, it had made crystal clear to him that there was no value in reading the Bible anymore. Although I knew nothing of his life or the context from which he was viewing, I was nonetheless shocked at his contrary reading or 'oppositional position', and became resigned to the reality of distortion between the message and its reception, what is often referred to as the over-determined or nature of encoding/decoding.[3] It is the process of encoding/decoding that enables me to convert my emancipatory framework into documentary film, although there is no guarantee that viewers will discern my intended message.

Of course encoding/decoding is not limited to the world of filmmaking. This process is also found in Pentecostalism, whereby theological beliefs are encoded in cultural products in ways that transform the understanding and purpose of those very objects. In an effort to reveal a more *nuanced* understanding of encoding/decoding, with particular relevance to filmmaking, I will use methods and resources that are internal to Pentecostalism. This is because, naturally, as a black Pentecostal seeking to engage primarily but not exclusively with black Pentecostals, it is important to show that my method, rather than being separate from black Pentecostalism is, instead, very much a part of it. By doing so, I hope that black Pentecostals will be drawn into the world of encoding/decoding, appreciate the levels of meaning at work in cultural products in the church and appreciate my appropriation of this black Pentecostal technique.

The aims of this chapter are threefold. First, I will illustrate how the encoding/decoding process occurs in Pentecostal churches by examining the doctrine of sanctification. As part and parcel of functioning as a biblical and doctrinal belief, sanctification refers to the practice of conveying divine meaning and purpose on persons and objects that, on the surface, are not looked upon as 'holy'. In my research, cultural products such as music, attire and décor are imbued with theological meaning. But my intention in using this illustration from black Pentecostalism is to arrive at a method for converting the emancipatory framework into a visual practice, and this is the second aim. The third aim is to place the method (encoding/decoding) within a religious context. This is because, the act of endowing material culture with religious meaning for the purpose of healing or the transformation of culture is reflected in another practice that I appropriate, namely conjure. Both the concepts of sanctifying and conjuring allow me to convey how I encode religious meanings in my films, which have transformational resonances, in the *hope* but not certainty that viewers will interpret my emancipatory intentions.

## Sanctification

The term sanctification derives from the Hebrew word *qdš* and the Greek word *hagiazo*, which mean 'to make holy'.[4] Sometimes translated as 'sanctify', or 'holy', sanctification is applied to people, places and occasions, for all three can be set apart for divine use and empowerment (Isaiah 65.5; 66.17).[5] I refer to this aspect as the setting apart of persons and things for divine purposes, or *conferring* sanctification, as the 'is sanctified perspective'. Sanctification is also something to strive for. Hence, in the New Testament, the apostle Paul prays that the Thessalonians will be sanctified fully in Spirit, soul and body (1 Thessalonians 4.3–4). I term this the 'becoming sanctified perspective'. There is some dispute among Pentecostal theologians as to whether sanctification is instantaneous with regeneration or a staged process.[6] In Western Pentecostal history, there have been times when sanctification has been taken to an extreme in order to develop doctrines of moral perfection.[7] However, sanctification is generally understood by most Pentecostals, in Wesleyan terms, as a work of grace and intent of heart rather than complete faultlessness.[8]

Sanctification is not only a theological category but is also the centre of a cultural practice where it is inscribed in church culture. To illustrate this process, I want to make use of examples from three black Pentecostal church cultures. These are music/broadcast equipment, attire and décor.

## Music/Broadcast equipment

The use of broadcast equipment has emerged out of music ministry – the organized direction of a congregation into worship and encounter with God through various dimensions of music. Music ministry is an important, if not the central, component of black Pentecostal worship. If there is one thing that Pentecostals are known for, it is the loudness of their music! For example, as I write, a legal case is in progress in Birmingham concerning the level of noise that is appropriate for Pentecostal worship without disturbing the peace of those living near the church in question.[9] But there is more to Pentecostal music ministry than decibels. Music ministry is also a sophisticated audio-visual, theological aesthetic incorporating 'popular'[10] and 'sonic faith'.[11] While sanctification is often explored in music composition and aesthetics, less attention has focused on the sanctification of the equipment.

Modern music and broadcasting equipment are an important hallmark of these congregations. The first generation of black Pentecostals in Britain led the way and created openness to music technology by importing the Hammond organ from the United States, and utilizing electric guitars and drum kits in their music ministry. An emphasis on staying 'up to date' and developing an *audio-visual* ministry has become a feature in the twenty-first century, with musicians and vocalists performing with state of the art gear. For instance, as part of my research I attended at small Pentecostal church in Derby. The size of the sanctuary was no more than 50–60 meters in length and 20–30 meters in width. As such, the building could not accommodate more than 100 people. The pastor had recently remodelled the sanctuary to incorporate a dedicated production suit, to facilitate the work of a technician committed to managing the audio-visual equipment, such as mixing boards, filming equipment and monitors. The church was furnished with dedicated microphones in the pulpit and above the seating of the choir, as well as large TV monitors on either side of the pulpit. The monitors were used to display hymns and relay the events taking place on the pulpit if they were out of view during specific services, such as baptismal or child dedication services, when an increase in those attending may obscure the view of the front of the building for those at the back. Although, given the smallness of the sanctuary and the limited number of regular attendees, the secondary use of the monitors, in response to visual obstructions, was rare! What is important in this case is the audio-visual enhancement of the music ministry and also the introduction of broadcast equipment. In short, the historical openness to music technology makes relatively easy the embracing of broadcasting equipment and to create, what I term, a 'megachurch aesthetic'.

The megachurch aesthetic describes the interior of a megachurch, a congregation with a membership of thousands.[12] These churches have become more visible in Britain as a result of the rise of televangelism in America through the auspices of satellite and cable television, which have exposed more megachurches to an international audience. Megachurches provide a unique Sunday morning experience for the worshipper, in which choreographed choirs, celebrity preachers and guest soloists regularly grace the pulpit. There are many unique cultural and theological themes associated with the megachurch,[13] but what is most important here is the use of high-tech equipment such as monitors, cameras, amplification units and mixing desks.[14] The use of such equipment in the British context has led to a technologization of place. The sanctuaries of these churches are transformed into high-tech performance venues with large screens at the front of the sanctuary, and elaborate mixing boards and mini-television studios to control what is seen on the screens and heard internally and externally.

Intriguingly, in the UK context the megachurch aesthetic transcends the megachurch and has become a feature of smaller churches with fewer members. For instance, as mentioned above, I have witnessed small- to medium-size churches making use of large plasma screen televisions and expensive multimedia technology for Sunday morning worship. In these cases, the contemporary musical and broadcasting technology *is sanctified*, that is, set apart for divine use. This conferral of holiness or sanctification (the 'is') can be explicit or implicit. Explicit conferral results in specific rites or prayers to commission materials for use within the church. It is not uncommon for Pentecostal churches to hold special services when they dedicate newly purchased items for the church. Implicit conferral is a less formal recognition that once the church has made use of an product it is de facto redeemed and reclaimed, and therefore it *becomes* 'God's property'.

## *Attire*

Attire is another way that black Pentecostals inscribe sanctification on church culture. By attire I am referring to the dress codes operating within a church context. Pentecostal dress codes vary and are bifurcated on grounds of age and also, more importantly, theological orientation. In black Pentecostal worship, the black Christian body is a canvas on which theological ideas are painted. This practice is analysed by Pentecostal historian Anthea Butler in her study of the Church of God in Christ (COGIC) in North America, where attire expresses theological orientation within a given historical moment.[15] The choice of attire as a means of expressing one's theological perspective, particularly sanctification, is however controversial, for Butler also suggests that the wearing of certain clothes may reflect perspectives that run contrary to the theology of the church, especially when attire becomes a performance or an ostentatious display.[16]

Butler's viewpoint, the dividing line between sanctification and showiness (worldliness) in dress codes, complements my own experience in Britain. For instance, when I was growing up in the Wesleyan Holiness Church in Britain in the early 1970s, attire was analogous with a theology of holiness. To show that we were sanctified, that is, had set apart our lives for divine use, we dressed up (Sunday best) but also dressed simply to display our devotion to God and to ensure that we did not take on the of the showiness of the 'world'. We took inspiration from biblical texts that encouraged modesty (1 Timothy 2.9–10; 1 Peter 3.3–4) and gendered attire (Deuteronomy 22.5). Ironically, for mature men, simple dress was the wearing of suits that were popular in the 1950s and 1960s, which at one point of time were fashionable in the secular world. This time delay in fashion acceptability was also extended to female dress, but with additional restrictions. In the 1970s and 1980s, as a sign of modesty, women were not permitted to wear trousers in church and had to cover their heads at all times during the service.

Today, black Pentecostal attire is expressed in diverse ways and reflects differences in theological perspectives. Conveying sanctification remains a salient issue but representation has been transformed by new theological alignments. It is, however, a fluid practice and I have observed in black Pentecostalism an 'attire-sanctification spectrum'. At one end is the 'well-dressed perspective'. Here, good grooming, fine formal clothing and sophistication convey separateness from the world. It is a 'give of your best to the Master' perspective where honouring God is expressed with formal attire. As Butler suggests, this view may succumb to materialism and excess, as 'well-dressed' might also be a code for flamboyance. At the other pole is a rejection of formality, so that casual clothing, such as sportswear, is understood to convey holiness. It is a 'rend your heart not your garment' perspective that nonetheless elevates morality through attire. Either way, formal or casual, what you wear in black Pentecostal churches is a visual sign of the *is sanctified* life.

## Décor

I turn now to the subject of décor. Décor refers here to the internal design and furnishing of church buildings. It is important to note that, with few exceptions, most black Pentecostal churches were purchased from Anglican, Methodist or Baptist congregations in the 1960s and 1970s when existing congregations had died out or were 'scared out' after the migrants moved into the inner city. Therefore, the style of the physical buildings, many of which were Victorian, was predetermined. Even so, black Pentecostals have not left these buildings completely intact and have developed a distinctive approach to church interiors, which I want to explain by comparing them to the décor of the traditional African-Caribbean 'front room'. Again, my purpose here is to illustrate how the practice of encoding is not limited to filmmaking, but encompasses religious practices.

As cultural theorist and artist Michael McMillan shows in his exhibition, 'The West Indian Front Room' (2006), the first generation of immigrants from the West Indies adorned the front rooms of their homes with deeper meanings in mind than were obvious from a quick glance.[17] He goes on to explain how, beneath the surface, these rooms were an exercise in taste and expression of identity. In terms of taste, the front room was a place to 'deposit nice things purchased from shops or on visits to holiday destinations, usually British seaside resorts'.[18] Some of these items, however, were homemade and reflected years of artistic endeavour. Take, for example, the crocheted covers for the back and arms of the prized 'best' sofas and chairs. Walls were adorned with pictures of biblical figures, wall ornaments, personal photographs and certificates of achievement. Also important was cleanliness and order; these things were not supposed to be used but were on 'display'. In terms of identity, the front room was an exercise in diaspora identity formation. For example, pictures on walls or shelving of men and women in their new work clothing from various industries, such as nursing, transport and manufacturing (that were often sent back home), as well as family portraits from local photographic studios, signalled the transition to a new life in Britain, and also confirmed that these immigrants were 'here to stay'.[19]

In radical contrast, the same people who adorned their front rooms were less willing to beautify their places of worship. In first-generation churches the interiors were austere. Despite having the opportunity to adorn, embellish and transform the interiors, very little effort was made to add colourful images or create a sense of home. There was little sense of journey, progress or cultural struggles over belonging. Instead, insides were plain, with few, if any, pictures or paintings in the sanctuary. This was not a result of financial restriction. Even with the monetary capacity to build new churches with the assistance of architects and designers, leaders and congregations remained unyielding in their commitment to maintaining simplicity and functionality over style and creativity. There are theological influences that contribute to this aesthetic. In addition to the protestant and evangelical traditions of avoiding fussiness and distraction in church interiors,[20] there are also contextual ideas at work, specifically, a theology of place.

A theology of place is a useful way of interpreting the décor of black Pentecostal churches. It demarcates the relationship between God, people and location,[21] but it is not a static concept as it undergoes an evolution in the biblical text.[22] It is geographically specific in Old Testament topography in locations such as the Garden of Eden or Jerusalem. However, there is a progression of thought to a more fluid and dynamic theology of place in the New Testament. Inspired by the incarnation (John 1.1–8) and Pentecost event (Acts 2), place remains important. Nonetheless, it is the Spirit's presence that mediates the meeting of God and people, anywhere, anyplace and anytime. It is this fluid idea that informs these churches.[23] In other words, the city of Jerusalem is re-imagined as a 'New

Jerusalem', which for black Pentecostals is found 'where two and three are gathered in My name . . .' (Matthew 18.20). What this means in practice is that the Spirit is present wherever believers are gathered and moreover that décor should facilitate the mediation of the Spirit and take precedence over artistic considerations. The sanctuary as a reflection of a theology of place is therefore fashioned to 'edify' or 'build up' the people of God. While some may choose to use specific visual imagery to encourage or educate believers to focus on particular biblical themes, and as we shall see later, this book calls for such an approach, the theology of place in contemporary black Pentecostalism suggests otherwise. Instead, to facilitate the presence of the Spirit, buildings and interiors are decorated as simply as possible. In this way, décor reflects a view of sanctification as both conferral (holy ground) and striving (edify) – and as such must be devoid of 'visual noise'. The lack of visual noise, however, is somewhat compensated for by a surplus of the sonic.

These cultural products – music/broadcast equipment, décor and dress – are all inscribed with sanctification and consequently their usage is transformed by black Pentecostal appropriation. The process of converting a theological concept into cultural practice is integral to my work as a theologian and filmmaker, because I, too, encode meanings. To clarify this black Pentecostal method of conversion and show how it relates to converting the emancipatory framework, I will elaborate the nature of encoding/decoding as a black Pentecostal practice.

## Encoding/decoding

Encoding/decoding are features of a wider communication system known as 'signification'. Signification is a system that helps to explain how meaning is conferred upon particular 'signs' or objects, and therefore fills the gap between the object and the perception of it. The original idea emerges from the work of Swiss linguist Ferdinand de Saussure. Saussure provides the basic components for the system, namely that signs have two parts: a signifier (sound, object or image) and a signified (concept). A sign can be anything that stands for something else but the relationship has to be learned. In the case of black Pentecostalism, the signifier (music/broadcast equipment, dress, décor) is signified (sanctified). Signs, however, are never outside of a social and material reality, as signs do not operate autonomous from the concreteness of the world. For instance, a gun (signifier) is a weapon and fires bullets! Therefore the signifier/signified has material consequences.

Roland Barthes' clarification is most instructive. Barthes describes two levels of meaning in an image or object that can equally apply to cultural products such as music/broadcast equipment, attire and décor. These are the denotative and connotative meanings.[24] Images and objects can *denote* literal truths or descriptive value. But they are also open to interpretation depending on the viewpoint of the onlooker; that is, they also *connote* meaning. Scholars debate just how much difference there is between denotation and connotation, with some suggesting that all signs are connotative; but the distinction is necessary for analytical value.[25] Applying Barthes to black Pentecostal music/broadcast equipment, attire and décor, we could say that in addition to being denotative (buildings, equipment, place of worship), they also are connotative (sanctified). That is to say, the adherents interpret these cultural forms in the context of church life in a particular way. However, connotative meaning also depends on where the onlookers situate themselves in relation to what they are viewing or experiencing. Therefore, there can be more than one way of interpreting what is seen or heard. The subjective nature of interpretation leads to the idea of polysemy, that images always carry multiple meanings.[26] Accepting this ambiguity in connotative meaning, we might prematurely conclude that within black Pentecostalism the doctrine of sanctification is connoted in cultural products, but these products have many meanings that change over time and depend on the position of the viewer. The position of the viewer is another way of speaking about the various ways that a viewer might decode the meaning.

However, it would be rash to come to this conclusion so quickly because we must take into account the specificity of signifying within black Pentecostalism – as reflected in the sanctification theme in music/broadcast equipment, attire and décor. In these cases, there was a deliberate attempt to secure a particular theological understanding. In other words, we need to find a way of ensuring that sufficient weight is given to the 'intended theological meanings' and the conventions established to promote their dominance. The signifying system that contains this emphasis is 'encoding'. 'Even so, encoding is never a "neat fit" because . . . the receiver might not get the intended message'.[27] In other words, the communication of meaning is never guaranteed.

*Thus, encoding describes the method for converting the emancipation framework into documentary film.* It allows me to inscribe meaning but never be completely sure if viewers will accept my intended meaning. Alas, there are no guarantees. What this means is that signifiers (music/broadcast equipment, etc) are interpreted according to rules. In the case of sanctification, for example, the rules were conventions established by church doctrine. Furthermore, in the absence of these rules or conventions, the connection is lost and the signifier loses its preferred reading.[28] Again, using the example of sanctification, without learning the theology of the church, music/broadcast equipment, attire and décor lose their distinct theological meanings.

As we shall see later, encoding takes place in the documentary narrative. The narrative within individual films is full of symbols, denoting deeper levels of meaning at work. In other words the narrative is a site of signifiers at play.[29]

# Conjure

Encoding documentary with religious meanings, particularly bewitchment and exorcism, calls for a new interpretation of the religious documentary. This is because this mode of encoding presupposes that culture carries a spiritual potential that might engender a religious experience. The idea of culture charged with the Spirit (enchanted) is one side of a Pentecostal theology of culture. James K. A. Smith describes it this way:

> . . . Pentecostal spirituality is marked by a deep sense of the Spirit's immanence. While it might not be articulated as such, implicit in the prayers of pentecostals is a richly pneumatological understanding of creation that affirms the Spirit's continued presence and activity in what we could call the 'given' or physical layer of creation – 'nature' as well as the Spirit's operation in the 'made' or human layer of creation – 'culture'.[30]

However, while recognizing that culture is enchanted with the Spirit's presence, Pentecostals are also aware of the mis-enchantment of the world by 'other spirits':

> Pentecostal praxis is sometimes almost overwhelmed by a concern with spiritual warfare and the demonic that fines expression in ministries of 'deliverance' and liberation. There is a deep sense that multiple modes of oppression – from illness to poverty – are in some way the work of forces that are not just 'natural'.[31]

The 'enchantment/mis-enchantment' theology of culture opens up a new way of thinking about the encounter with culture as a religious experience. In other words culture carries the potential to mediate the *numinous*. The numinous is the *experience* that underlies all religions and originates from a concept derived from the work of Rudolf Otto. The numinous has three components. First, *Mysterium* is the experience of something different to everyday life or the 'wholly other'. Second, and as mentioned in our reflection on witchcraft in Chapter Three, religious philosopher Charles H. Long makes use of another of these components, by appropriating Otto's idea of *mysterium tremendum*. Mysterium tremendum describes the sense of terror evoked by the presence of an overpowering religious force. In the case of Long, mysterium tremendum designates the experience of slavery and colonialism as an overpowering religious force. But the numinous can also express a third experience, that of an entirely opposite religious experience of mercy and grace or attraction despite the fear and awe, that is, *fascinans*.

If we correlate aspects of enchantment with the numinous and apply it to the religious documentary then we can theorize that documentary film, as a cultural product inscribed with religious categories, carries the potential for a religious experience of the numinous, which in the specificity of this study gestures towards the experience of colonial Christianity as mysterium tremendum and the experience of exorcism as fascinans. To capture this spiritual dynamic in religious documentary, I want to contour a new modality that carries with it a sense of evoking the Spirit in culture, that is, *conjure*. However, conjure in African diaspora cultures, seeks to arouse the Spirit for discrete ends – which I will also incorporate into this new modality.

I want to propose that religious encoding moves encoding beyond the boundaries of cultural studies into a new Pentecostal theology of culture, in which culture is perceived to have a spiritual dynamic. To conceptualize this religious encoding of culture and frame it as a new form of religious documentary, I want to draw on the notion of conjure.

Conjure is an evocative term that is usually connected with magic and mystery. Such monikers fail to do justice to what is a more general idea of appealing to the spirit world, often with the assistance of religious imagery or products. Conjure is an appeal to the spirit world for intervention and *transformation* of earthly existence and may involve the mediating use of cultural products, that is, conjuring culture. Conjure is universal and a feature of all religions that utilize icons, religious objects, imagery, attire or paintings – including Christianity.[32] But here I want to develop a more refined understanding of conjure by drawing from topographies of conjure in black Atlantic cultures, where conjure is a source of individual and sociopolitical healing.

Conjure as a source of individual healing emerges from the black Christian tradition. According to African American scholar of religion Theophus Smith conjure traditions in the black Atlantic were transported by African slaves as religious practices, and at the heart of conjure is *pharmacosm* – healing or harm, but in this case, I focus on healing.[33] This view is given a Pentecostal identification by Yvonne Chireau's study of conjure in black religion. She asserts that black Pentecostalism incorporates conjure techniques into its healing practices through the use of oils and the laying on of hands in prayer.[34] In these instances, material objects (Bible, oil) are given a spiritual quality or symbolize divine presence/power in the healing process.[35]

There also exists a sociopolitical tradition in the black Atlantic where social activists conjure words and ideas to transform imaginations and political realities. This second feature has a long history in the African diaspora and is not necessarily disassociated from religious traditions.[36] In this second case, conjure is enacted through spoken words, rhetoric and ideas professed and presented by preachers, activists and politicians aimed at transforming the status quo. We may think of the ways in which the language and ideas in the speeches of Marcus Garvey, the preaching of

Malcolm X, the ideas of Kwame Ture or the writings of bell hooks, Patricia Hill Collins, Jacquelyn Grant, Anthony Pinn, Paul Gilroy and Randall Bailey seek to challenge and transform political relationships, especially the destruction of oppressive forces that impinge on well-being and flourishing of black communities. In this sense, all discourse is also a site of conjure – a theme I will build upon in the next chapter on documentary. The sociopolitical tradition seeks to conjure healing but the healing is that of social and political strife.

Conjure as the new understanding of the religious documentary describes the encoding of distinct religious meaning on cultural products for the sake of healing. Specifically, it is inscribing the emancipatory framework on documentary film to heal black Pentecostalism from its colonial bewitchment. As a religious-cultural activity, where culture is enchanted, this mode proffers, but cannot guarantee, the numinous. Within the specificity of this study, the numinous relates to the fear, dread and awe experienced by the continued colonial presence and, conversely, the experience of grace and mercy in the practice of exorcism.

In conclusion, in this chapter I have demonstrated how I translate the emancipatory framework into a visual practice, specifically, documentary filmmaking. By making use of the example of Pentecostal sanctification, I identify a modality that is known in the language of cultural studies as 'encoding/decoding'. However, cultural studies fails to do justice to the religious aspects of encoding, namely a desire for spiritual transformation. To capture this religious nuance, I describe the method as 'conjure' – the religious encoding of cultural products for the purpose of healing. While capturing the religious features of encoding/decoding, however, conjure is nonetheless subject to the limitations of all communication systems, namely the inability to guarantee the intended meaning.

# CHAPTER NINE

# Poetic justice

*. . . what is fitting to documentary and what is not change over time.*

BILL NICHOLS[1]

'How do you feel about what you have seen here today?' The producer was asking me to respond to the day we were spending in a small village in central Ghana. I was filming a sequence for the film *The Great African Scandal*, a film on multinational corporations' malfeasance in Ghana. Adjacent to the village was a large pit containing contaminated gold mining waste that the villagers blamed for polluting the local water table. 'Give me a few minutes to get my thoughts together', I replied. I wanted to get my reflections out at one time and to do so I required a few minutes to process the events of the day. That day, I had experienced the underside of globalization – the effects of economic liberalization policies. In this case, I observed how large international corporations, unfettered by northern European regulations, extracted mineral wealth from the developing country with questionable regard for the cost to the environment. Moreover, there was devastating impact on local people, most of whom were some of the poorest people on the planet. I had a brainwave. I would use the word 'nigger' to symbolize how the gold company was treating the local people. My use of the word was not just for impact, but also a cipher connecting this latest incarnation of Western economic exploitation and British colonialism in Ghana. I returned to the camera and said:

> You know what, when I heard the people's stories . . . I thought to myself, 'This is . . . they are being treated like niggers'. That is the only way you can describe how these African people have been treated. You cannot say to me that these people are considered to be human beings with feelings, emotions, values and having something worth living for. Because the way they are being treated here, I have not got words for it. The only word that you can use [to describe how they are being treated] is that they are being made to live and be like niggers – people who are less than human.

Connecting these two economic discourses was an example of conjuring in the documentary narrative. Simultaneously, I was able to address the local situation but also my subliminal concern of encoding bewitchment – British colonial avarice as an overwhelming religious force, which among other things dehumanized African people.

In Chapter One, I explored documentary from the perspective of the author in order to identify the motives and positioning of my work. In this chapter, I will focus on the technical side of documentary as a film genre. The reason for doing so is to identify the location of conjure in the documentary aesthetic. *Conjure takes place in the documentary narrative at a subliminal level.* Therefore, as we shall see later, the documentary narrative is always double-voiced. This practice may come as a shock to some readers because when most people watch or think about a documentary film they generally associate it with a form of truth-telling or a representational mode of filmmaking that reflects the historical and social world rather than a religious practice bent on challenging colonial residue. Whether one is watching the BBC's *Panorama* or a documentary movie such as Al Gore's *An Inconvenient Truth*, we expect the film to communicate facts and themes as they actually occurred in the real world. But this is a romantic view of documentary because, in reality, it is a much more complex and messy genre. Like all filmmaking, documentary films are also subject to layers of editing and interference. As a result, it is possible to think of documentary as both *record* (reflecting the social world) and *signifying practice* (interpretation). It is the latter, signifying, that is the arena for conjuring films. In order to identify how conjure works in documentary, I will briefly trace the origins of documentary, the tension at its core and how conjure is imbedded in the poetic mode of documentary.

## What is documentary?

According to Bill Nichols, 'every film is a documentary'. This is because, 'even the most whimsical of fictions gives evidence of the culture that produced it and reproduces the likeness of the people who perform within it'. He continues by identifying two types of films, the second being more commonly associated with documentary film.

> In fact, we could say that there are two kinds of film: (1) documentaries of wish-fulfilment and (2) documentaries of social representation. Each type tells a story, but the stories, or narratives, are of different sorts. Documentaries of wish-fulfilment are what we would normally call fictions. These films give tangible expression to our wishes and dreams, our nightmares and dreads. They make the stuff of the imagination concrete – visible and audible. They give a sense of what we wish, or fear, reality itself might be or become. Such films convey truths if we decide they do. They are films whose truths, insights and perspectives we may adopt as our own or reject. They offer words for us to explore and contemplate, or we may simply revel in the pleasure of moving from the world around us to these other worlds of infinite possibility. Documentaries of social representation are what we typically call non-fiction. These films give tangible representation to aspects of the world we already inhabit and share. They make the stuff of social reality visible and audible in a distinctive way, according to the acts of selection and arrangement carried by a filmmaker. They give a sense of what we understand reality itself to have been, of what it is now or what it may become. These films also convey truths if we decide they do. We must assess their claims and assertions, their perspectives and arguments in relation to the world as we know it and decide whether they are worthy of our belief. Documentaries of social representation offer us new views of our common world to explore and understand.[2]

As Nichols notes above, the fiction film is a documentary of wish-fulfilment and the non-fiction film a documentary of social representation. But this is just one of many definitions of documentary. There are many descriptions of documentary, such as 'art of record' and 'reality capture', all of which reveal a connection between the form and the historical world.[3] A useful way of understanding documentary, however, lies with its intended audience, as political documentary theorist Michael Chanon describes it:

> One of the crucial differences is that . . . documentary addresses the viewer primarily as a citizen member of a civil society, putative participant in the public sphere.[4]

Thought of this way, documentary has a social function: to identify themes, subjects and concerns in the social world that have real and substantial merit for discussion in the public square(s). Despite its association with real life, documentary is not 'real' in the sense that it is an unadulterated capturing of real-life events and happenings. Instead, documentary makes use of editing practices that give rise to a lived tension between the 'real' or actuality, and the 'reel' or editing practices.

The tension at the heart of documentary arises with the emergence of the form in the West. Documentary film begins in the occidental tradition with American Robert Flaherty's *Nanook of the North*, a short North American film shot in Canada in 1922.[5] Flaherty's objective was similar to that of sightseers intending to take home a evidence of their holiday. On this occasion, he wanted to show the Eskimos he met on his explorations. In the process, he inadvertently developed a novel form of filmmaking. His second film, *Moana* (1926), caught the attention of John Grierson, a Scottish man visiting America who coined the term 'documentary value' in an article in *The New York Sun* (8 February 1926) to describe the new form of filmmaking. Later Grierson would develop his understanding of the documentary to label it as 'the creative treatment of actuality'.[6]

This definition, 'the creative treatment of actuality', and the tension it represents continued to inform documentary theory for most of the century. For instance, documentary theorist Paul Ward states that the 'creative treatment of actuality' underscores 'the

central anxiety within debates on the definition of documentary . . .'.[7]
Similarly, in clarifying this predicament, Stella Bruzzi describes the
relationship as a tension:

> Documentary is predicated upon a dialectical relationship
> between aspiration and potential, that the text itself reveals the
> tension between the documentary pursuit of the most authentic
> mode of factual representation and the impossibility of this
> aim.[8]

Consequently for Bruzzi, documentary is fundamentally a
'representational mode of filmmaking' that has 'at its core the
notion of film as a record'.[9]

To clarify the location(s) of the tension in the documentary,
Etienne Souriau's interrelated three-level analysis of filming helps.
First there is the 'afilmic' or the reality that exists independently
of the camera; it is what would have happened if the camera were
absent. Next is the 'profilmic'. It describes what is found in front of
the camera and is filmed. 'These include such occurrences in front
of the lens . . . as location shooting, following the action, and having
the presenter talk directly into the camera from the scene of events'.[10]
Finally there is the 'filmic' or what the film becomes as a result of
the editorial and aesthetic decisions that are made.[11] *Interference
or interpretation starts well before the studio edits because human
agency impacts how the (afilmic) world is referenced through
the lenses of the camera (profilmic), and the edit of the producer
and others in the cutting-room (filmic).*[12] On reflection, I learned
very early that taking a camera and microphone into any social
situation disrupts the natural flow of events, course of conversation
and original intention of contributors. So 'real life' does not always
mean 'real' in the sense that this is what would have happened if
the camera were not there. Instead, documentaries record events,
but the process is shot through with levels of interference and
interpretation.[13]

A useful example from my work occurred when I interviewed
Richard Land in Atlanta for *Who Wrote the Bible* (Channel 4,
2004). Land was at that time one of the religious advisors to then
US president George W. Bush. During the pre-interview chat, he
instructed me that he wanted to be interviewed in a particular pose
with the right side of his face to camera (afilmic distortion). Also,

I had prepared guide questions (about 20) that I put to Land in a variety of ways to tease out meaningful answers. The cameraman, Vaughn Matthews, began filming before the interview, during a moving sermon Land had given to a conservative, pro-Republican church congregation about America's involvement in the second Gulf War (profilmic). However, this theme was just one part of a 40-minute sermon covering a range of religious subjects related to an impending election. When the interview was cut, edited and aired as part of a two-hour film, the one-hour interview was reduced to three minutes. The sequence began with Land preaching in support of the Iraq war. Next, the camera cut to the presidential cuff-links he was wearing to give a sense of presidential authority and connection. Out of the 20 questions he answered, two were used to illustrate his views on how to interpret the New Testament, including a stirring one-liner, 'God said it, that seals it, I believe it'. Underlying the whole interview was music composed to convey a sense of unease and danger (filmic reality).

Thus, what the viewer sees on screen is in part an edited reconstruction of a real-life event. But this does not mean that there is no 'truth to the encounter'. Instead, documentary represents a particular kind of truth-telling. Documentary filmmaking is best understood as the way that '. . . a lawyer may represent a client's interests: they put the case for a particular view or interpretation of evidence before us'.[14] This means that viewers are situated as '. . . witnesses rather than as vicarious would-be participants'.[15] As a result, the viewer must not only 'look at' but also 'look through' or understand the nature of representation at work in documentary.[16]

Filmmakers negotiate this tension at the heart of the documentary by choosing to locate themselves somewhere on a spectrum of documentary filmmaking practice. At one end of the spectrum is empiricist realism.[17] Here, filmmakers desire to keep documentary representation as pure as possible. In practice, this means adapting rules to 'ensure nothing is staged and as little interference takes places as is possible'.[18] This approach gives rise to the observational documentary or the 'fly on the wall' method that seeks a unpolluted representation of what takes place. The difficulty here is that while the filmmaker will not intervene during filming, filmed material is always shaped and edited at the profilmic and filmic levels. In the opposing camp are those who argue that it is impossible to make a documentary in the pure sense because documentary is more than pointing a camera; it also involves layers of editing and production that make capturing a pure afilmic world problematic. This second camp or 'ideological school' focuses on the signifying aspects of documentary film; namely, that while intimately related to the social world, documentary also signifies the handicraft of those involved in editing it. These two approaches are not mutually exclusive or unrelated. In the middle of the spectrum are those attempting to balance the two poles. In the centre, documentary is both/and – it is record and signifying system.[19] It is a record because it films events occurring in the social world, and it is a signifying practice because of the profilmic and filmic realities. Encoding the emancipatory framework veers towards the signifying end of documentary and encoding is made possible by using a particular documentary mode.

## Documentary modes

Documentary theorists have invested a great deal of time and energy identifying the basic types of documentary and how they have morphed into new and hybrid forms. Bill Nichols has done most to catalogue documentary types. In *Representing Reality* (1991) he identifies four modes:

> A very cursory history of documentary representation might run like this: expository documentary (Grierson and Flaherty, among others) arose from a dissatisfaction with the distracting, entertainment qualities of the fiction film. Voice-of-God commentary and poetic perspectives sought to disclose information about the historical world itself and to see that world afresh, even if these views came to seem romantic or didactic. Observational documentary (Leacock-Pennebaker, Fredrick Wiseman) arose from the availability of more mobile, synchronous recording equipment and a dissatisfaction with the moralizing quality of expository documentary. An observational mode of representation allowed the filmmaker to record unobtrusively what people did when they were not explicitly addressing the camera. But the observational mode limited the filmmaker to the present moment and required a disciplined detachment from the events themselves. Interactive

documentary (Rouch, de Antonia and Connie Field) arose from the availability of the same more mobile equipment and a desire to make the filmmaker's perspective more evident. Interactive documentarists wanted to engage with individuals more directly while not reverting to classic exposition. Interview styles and interventionist tactics arose, allowing the filmmaker to participate more actively in present events. The filmmaker could also recount past events by means of witnesses and experts whom the viewer could also see. Archival footage of past events became appended to these commentaries to avoid the hazards of reenactment and the monolithic claims of voice-of-God commentary. Reflexive documentary (Dziga Vertov, Jill Godmilow and Raul Ruiz) arose from a desire to make the conventions of representation themselves more apparent and to challenge the impression of reality which the other three modes normally conveyed unproblematically. It is the most self-aware mode; it uses many of the same devices as other documentaries but sets them on edge so that the viewer's attention is drawn to the device as well as the effect.[20]

He adds another later in *Blurred Boundaries*:

Films suggesting this alternative mode, which may be called performative documentary . . . What such films have in common is a deflection of documentary from what has been its most common purpose – the development of strategies for persuasive argumentation about the historical world.[21]

While these modes are presented as separate approaches, in reality they represent various techniques that filmmakers deploy strategically within a film. Consequently, each film may veer from one end of the spectrum to another in terms of its commitment to form. Therefore, rather than being static or binary, we may find more than one mode at work. Furthermore, the form continues to evolve. Take, for example, Roscoe and Hight's study of the rise of the 'mock-documenary' and its subversion of the art form.[22]

This group of texts have been labelled using a variety of terms; 'faux documentary (Francke, 1996), 'pseudo-documentary', 'mocumentary', 'cinéma vérité with a wink' (Harrington, 1994), 'cinéma un-vérité' (Ansen, 1997), black comedy presented as 'in-your-face documentary', 'spoof documentary' and 'quasi-documentary'. . . .[23]

This new form highlights the fact that documentary is a discursive practice in the sense that it shapes the way we think about the subject (like a lawyer representing a case). All of these modes have been present in varying degrees within the films in which I have participated, but what has been most important is having control of the narrative.

In the context of television documentary, narrative is essential for conjuring for at least two reasons. First, the development of a film narrative is one area where a documentary presenter can have the most influence and control. As I will describe in the following chapter, when making films I cannot completely control the person directing the camera or the editing, but I can structure the narrative. Second, in my work, narrative is not confined to one film alone but expresses a grand project: how a body of films combines to reveal a meta-narrative, an all-encompassing story that seeks to capture the 'grand scheme of things' in a cohesive fashion (emancipatory framework). Thus, documentary narrative as the space for the emancipatory framework requires analysis of more than one film to appreciate conjure. While postmodernity has nurtured an incredulity towards meta-narratives, for those of us seeking to challenge inequalities, meta-narratives help to create a thoughtful point of reference rather than immovable and fixed assertions bent on producing a totalizing theory.

## Poetic

Conjure takes place in the documentary narrative and to understand how it works it is necessary to appropriate the poetic mode of documentary. The poetic mode is deeply subjective as the filmmaker sets about creating a particular tone, mood, rhythm or overall scheme

Conjure in documentary

in the film. This approach breaks with the traditional argument structure of documentary because the defining motif is stylistic or a particular structure.[24] According to Paul Ward, a key component of the poetic is the 'aesthetic expression of aspects of the real that become the main focus, rather than the real per se'.[25] What this means in practice is quite varied because aesthetic expression can encompass a range of techniques and features. How it works for conjure is that is the emancipatory framework becomes the key aesthetic concern, but it is given expression in (1) the documentary narrative, the narration, and (2) at a subliminal level or double-voice.

On one level, narrative is ubiquitous; it is all around us and not confined to 'texts'. This universal view is based on the verb *narrate* which implies 'that we all have the capability to tell someone something about things that have happened to us and and their effects in our daily lives'. However, there is a more specific definition of narration that arises out of literary theory. In literary theory, there are at least three levels of narrative.[26] First there is *narration*, which is the act of a narrator. This first mode gives rise to auteur criticism. Next, there is the analysis that examines narrative and narrative structure, that is, *narratology*.[27] Finally, there is narrative as *history*; that is, the story that the narrator seeks to tell. These distinctions are by no means fixed and may be paired together to reveal tensions and binaries at work in a narrative. *Narration* defines the use of narrative in this study.

In my documentaries narration works at both a surface and subliminal level. On the surface, it is the author (me) narrating the story, the relating of events within a particular narrative style in a documentary. At the subliminal level, narration is conjure – it is how I encode religious meaning in the narrative. A useful way of thinking about this duality of authorial intent in the narrative is through the black Atlantic literary practice of double-*voice*. The double-voice is a literary practice that emerges from continental Africa and finds its way into African-Caribbean diaspora folk cultures. A groundbreaking study in this field is Henry Louis Gates' *The Signifying Monkey*.[28] Gates interprets the black vernacular of the African American literary tradition through the trickster figures of Esu-Elebara (from West Africa) and the signifying monkey (African American). He identifies a conscious articulation of language traditions of signifying as the 'double-voiced (epitomized by the Esu's depictions in sculpture as possessing two mouths)'.

Bakhtin's metaphor of the double-voice discourse, figured most literally in representational sculptures of Esu and implied in the Signifying Monkey's function as the rhetoric of a vernacular literature, comes to bear in black texts through the trope of the Talking Book. In the slave narratives . . . making the white written text speak with a black voice is the initial mode of inscription of the metaphor of the double-voiced.[29]

The double-voice has a diaspora counterpart in Caribbean literature, epitomized by the mythical 'Anancy' the spider. Anancy in the Caribbean manifestation is a liminal trickster figure using cunning and deception to ensure that things work in his favour. He speaks in the double-voice – in this case, saying one thing but meaning another. But the double-voice is more than verbal trickery; it is also 'a creative process of adjoining and constructing meaning(s)', so that signification provides new connections and possibilities:

Anancy's web is homespun out of the stuff of one's own being-in-the-world; it is also a fine-spun catch of sensibility that takes in every air-borne particle. Hence, the web is a place and space of hybridity that creates, by its very presence in the world (which is often invisible, unseen, a gossamer of the margins), new combinations and juxtapositions.[30]

In other words Anancy's signifying practice 'is a web or creative exercise designed to make connections. The web is therefore always a place of meeting and forging of new things'.[31]

Translating the double-voice into film theory is not new.[32] African diaspora film studies have been cognizant of the role of signifying practice in black film forms for at least 30 years. According to African American film theorist Marlon Yearwood the primary task of the double-voice is to 'reflect the cultural priorities and historical exigencies of the black experience'.[33] In the case of this study, the priority of the narration is to articulate the bewitchment exorcism nexus.

But there are limitations to the double-voice, as mentioned in Chapter Eight; communication within a sign system does not always fit. This is especially true in the aural-visual signs generated by television. In short, communication is articulated and meaning cannot reside in or be guaranteed.

Applied to documentary, the double-voice refers to the two levels of narration, the surface description and the subliminal encoding of the narrative or conjure. Conjure takes place at the subliminal level of the narrative. It is the use of the narrative to carry a deeper symbolism. For instance, as mentioned in the introduction to this chapter, the use of the 'n' word in the *Great African Scandal* is an example of double-voice. On one level, it describes the demeaning effects of corporate greed, and on another level, a subliminal level, it is the evocation of the ghost of slavery and its malevolent intent.

To summarize, as Nichols makes clear in the quote above, documentary as a form changes over time and is never a static genre. Thus, in this chapter, I have outlined the evolution of documentary film to show that rather than being a clear-cut genre and a homogeneous form it is in fact diverse and contradictory. There exist a variety of documentary modes and the central and defining mark of documentary is a tension between record and editing. In short, no documentary is free from interference and filmmakers must situate their work on a spectrum of ranging from empiricist realism and ideological schools. My approach veers towards the ideological school, where the documentary, while representing reality, is underscored by signifying practice, that is, a double-voice that facilitates on one level a conjuring or inscribing of the emancipatory framework in the film. Therefore, conjure is expressed in and through the poetic mode of documentary. In the following chapters, I will show how the narrative was mobilized in several films to encode the emancipatory framework. As we shall see, at a subliminal level, spanning a range of films, I conjure the bewitchment of black Pentecostalism and its exorcism.

# CHAPTER TEN

# Bewitchment in documentary

This chapter marks the beginning of disclosing conjure or religious encoding of the emancipatory paradigm in my documentary films. It engages in a description of narratives to reveal deeper levels of meaning that are aimed at the intended audience – black Pentecostals in Britain. Conjure, however, was not a uniform practice. It was not possible to conjure every film because not all films facilitated this critique. For instance, *Test of Time* (2001), a six-part series for BBC Religious Education, focused on the Religious Education component of the National Curriculum, and was therefore out of range for addressing black Pentecostalism directly or indirectly. Similarly, *Gospel Truth* (2005), *The Real Patron Saints* (2005), *The Passion: Film, Faith and Fury* (2006), *God Gave Rock and Roll to You* (2006), *Hidden Jerusalem* (2007) and *Christianity: A History, The Dark Ages* (2009) were religious-cultural explorations and outside of the narrative scope of bewitchment. Although a political film, the same narrative limitations restricted the conjuring of *Ghetto Britain* (2006). Another reason for my inability to conjure every film was the amount of influence I could exert over the narrative. Television documentary is not outside of the vicissitudes of representational politics, and these issues are often played out at a micro level while filming. Not surprisingly, I have worked with producers who ultimately seek to dominate the editorial process to suit their creative designs (their own conjure), rather than comply with my narrative trajectory. Indeed, every film has multiple 'authors' from the commissioning editor to the executive producer and studio editor. Thus, the task as presenter was to always ensure that my voice and authorial intent were dominant. This was generally easier to achieve when working with producers and production companies who trusted my voice and the experts I recommended. They simply desired to construct a commercial structure for the best possible reception of the film. The varying degrees of control influence the level of encoding, and it is necessary to think of encoding as having strong and weak forms. Strong forms describe films with a heavy emphasis on the emancipatory paradigm, and it is these films that best embody conjure. In contrast, weak forms describe films with little authorial or narrative concern with encoding. It is strong forms that are the focal point of the following chapters.

## The canon

| Film | Genre | Weak (W) Strong (S) | Conjure |
|------|-------|---------------------|---------|
| *Britain's Slave Trade* (1999) | Political | S | Bewitchment |
| *Black Messiah* (2001) | Political | S | Bewitchment |
| *Test of Time* (2001) | Religion and Culture | W | None |
| *Blood and Fire* (2002) | Political | W | Exorcism |
| *Ebony Towers* (2003) | Political | S | Bewitchment |
| *God is Black* (2004) | Political | S | Bewitchment |
| *Who Wrote the Bible?* (2004) | Bible | S | Exorcism |
| *Empire Pays Back* (2005) | Political | S | Exorcism |
| *Gospel Truth* (2005) | Religion and Culture | W | None |
| *The Real Patron Saints* (2005) | Religion and Culture | W | None |

| | | | |
|---|---|---|---|
| *Ghetto Britain* (2006) | Political | W | None |
| *God Gave Rock and Roll to You* (2006) | Religion and Culture | W | None |
| *The Passion: Film, Faith and Fury* (2006) | Religion and Culture | W | None |
| *The Secret Family of Jesus* (2006) | Bible | S | Exorcism |
| *The Great African Scandal* (2007) | Political | S | Exorcism |
| *Hidden Jerusalem* (2007) | Religion and Culture | W | None |
| *The Hidden Story of Jesus* (2007) | Bible | S | Exorcism |
| *The Nativity Decoded* (2008) | Bible | S | Exorcism |
| *The Secrets of the Twelve Disciples* (2008) | Bible | S | Exorcism |
| *Christianity: A History, The Dark Ages* (2009) | Religion and Culture | W | None |
| *God Bless You Barack Obama* (2010) | Political | S | Exorcism |
| *Revelation: The Final Judgment* (2010) | Bible | S | Exorcism |

My films as a canon can be structured in a variety of ways. However, for ease of analysis, I divide them into two stages of development: these are the early projects and the Channel 4 films.

The early projects consists of three films in which I was either invited to tell a particular story, such as *Britain's Slave Trade* (1999), or projects that I 'sold' to a broadcaster but acted as a main contributor ('talking head'). These were *Black Messiah* (2001) and *Ebony Towers: The New Black Intelligentsia* (2003). As we shall see below, these first three projects are crucial because they collectively identify bewitchment: how I (1) encoded the churches' collusion with empire and also (2) the bewitchment of black Pentecostalism. I went on to make two other films for the BBC. These were *Test of Time* (2001) and *Blood and Fire* (2002), which were weak narratives. As mentioned above, *Test of Time* was a film made for schools, not my target audience. *Blood and Fire* contained elements of exorcism, particularly a postcolonial political analysis. However, it was limited conjure because it relied on an incongruous production technique that involved a plethora of producers and executive producers, which weakened the extent of my voice in the narrative.

The second stage consists of films I made mostly for Channel 4 between 2003 and 2010. These films are separated into three subject areas. The first are *political* films. This group comprises: *Britain's Slave Trade* (1999), *Empire Pays Back* (2005), *Ghetto Britain* (2006), *The Great African Scandal* (2007) and *God Bless You Barack Obama* (BBC, 2010). As we shall see below, *Britain's Slave Trade* was an example of bewitchment and highlighted church collusion with empire. *Ghetto Britain* was a synchronic analysis of 'race' politics in Britain and focused on the contradictions and weaknesses of 'diversity' strategies. It was a challenge to non-prophetic ministry but not as strong a case as *Empire Pays Back* and *The Great African Scandal*. In contrast, as rich analyses of past and present economics, political relations and quests for power it was easier to encode exorcism in these narratives. *God Bless You Barack Obama*, was the epitome of an exorcism, that is, a critique of non-prophetic ministry and also academic-theology phobia. However, I want to make use of it in this study as an example of visual exorcism in the Conclusion.

Next are *Bible* films: *Who Wrote the Bible?* (2004), *The Secret Family of Jesus* (2006), *The Hidden Story of Jesus* (2007), *The Secrets of the Twelve Disciples* (2008), *The Nativity Decoded* (2008) and *Revelation: The Final Judgment* (2010). All of these films were a source of exorcism, identifying how black Pentecostals defeat academic-theology phobia. I have chosen two films, *Who Wrote the Bible?* and *Revelation: The Final Judgment* as examples of exorcism in the Bible film.

The final group is *religious-cultural*. These are *Test of Time* (2001), *God is Black* (2004), *Gospel Truth* (2005), *The Real Patron Saints* (2005), *Film, Faith and Fury* (2006), *God Gave Rock and Roll to You* (2006), *Hidden Jerusalem* (Discovery, 2007) and *Christianity: A History, The Dark Ages* (2009). These films are weak analyses. *Test of Time* was a film aimed at a school-age audience and therefore outside the scope of analysis. Likewise the preferred audience for *The Real Patron Saints, Film, Faith and Fury* and *God Gave Rock and Roll to You* was a mainstream audience rather than a black Pentecostal one. *Hidden Jerusalem* was made for Discovery USA and was directed towards engaging a diverse American audience. Finally, *Christianity: A History, The Dark Ages* explored ethnic diversity in the origins of Christianity in Britain and while having some potential for exorcism, I did not think that there was enough of the right kind of narrative material to exploit in a meaningful way.

The political and Bible films were the vehicles for inscribing exorcism. This chapter, however, is concerned with the first stage, that is, identifying bewitchment, and three early films exemplify the conjure of bewitchment.

## Bewitchment: *Britain's Slave Trade* (1999)

As mentioned above, one aspect of the emancipatory paradigm is 'bewitchment'. Bewitchment describes the presence of malevolence diagnosed through the language of the cannibal and zombie. I have suggested that the church's collusion with empire during slavery is bewitchment. I have argued that its influence is still felt in the contemporary world among black Pentecostals by highlighting the presence of a non-prophetic ministry and academic-theology phobia. The bewitching nature of colonial Christianity was registered in the narrative of *Britain's Slave Trade*, and its continued influence on black Pentecostalism in *Black Messiah* and *Ebony Towers*.

*Britain's Slave Trade* was a three-part series designed to tell the story of Britain's involvement in the slave trade through the great slave-owning families of the Caribbean, of which the white Beckford family are one. I had written a short news piece on the connection between the white slaveholding family and my family, and pitched it to Channel 4 as a documentary idea. Soon after, I was approached by the producer to consider telling my story as part of this particular series. What this meant in effect was being one of several contributors, and speaking off camera to the producer to express my thoughts at different points in the journey. I was not therefore the sole presenter but part of a group of contributors. My journey was one of discovery: to travel across Jamaica and Britain to trace the history of the white Beckford family, their acquisition of wealth through slavery and their legacy. *The Guardian*'s television reviewer described the series as:

> . . . an attempt to restore a missing chapter of British history. It places the history of slavery right at the heart of British life – and describes the present legacy of slavery, just as relevant to many white people as black.[1]

Given that the programme's subject was slavery, it was relatively easy to identify the role of the church within it. In fact, the narrative facilitated my understanding of the collusion of the Church of England with slavery in Jamaica. The only narrative consideration was that the channel wanted a programme that concentrated on the economic legacy of slavery. Thus, *I placed the church's complicity within the context of the economic history of the slaveholding Beckford family.* The style of the documentary was interactive and switched between individual stories and historical archives. So, in real terms, I had three or four opportunities to expose key themes.

In my first piece to the camera, I wanted to make sure that the audience understood that at the heart of slavery was an illicit exchange and that slavery was 'unfinished business'. Thus, when asked by the director at the beginning of the show about my initial feelings regarding my search of the white slave-owning family, I said:

> . . . now, how I feel . . . is that they represent the oppressors in my family history. We've got this family who were able to exploit my side of the family and do very well off it. And from the little I know about slavery we didn't get . . . much pay then and are still waiting for the 'back taxes' now.

This initial point aligned slavery with the overarching theme of bewitchment/exorcism but in the language of economic exploitation/recompense. This starting point not only set the stage for the rest of the film, but also challenged attempts to sanitize the white Beckford story.[2] After the initial comments, the film narrative went on to explore the Beckford slavery history.

I travelled across Jamaica, visited great houses, slave quarters and churches to tell the story of how the Beckford family made their fortune from slavery. At their height, they owned 22 plantations and some 1,600 African slaves. The first Beckford began slave trading and planting as early as the later part of the 1660s.[3] For almost 200 years, as a result of the huge profits from their plantations in Jamaica, a plethora of Beckford descendants lived lives of luxury and influence. I was able to ascertain that the Beckford annual income was between £30,000–150,000 per annum back in the nineteenth century. Even at the end of slavery in 1834, the white family received a lump sum for their losses – tens of thousands of pounds in compensation. In disbelief, I acknowledged how, in contrast, the enslaved black Beckford families received nothing. No compensation was or has ever been given.

Exploration of the white family's wealth continued in England. I investigated how the family converted economic wealth into political influence. For instance, Peter Beckford (d. 1711), one of the descendants of the early planting family, was a governor of Jamaica and his son, also named Peter, was speaker of the Jamaica Assembly (d. 1735). After the death of the father, his sons and relatives were able to reap the rewards of his slaving activities. The son of Peter Beckford was Alderman Beckford (1709–70), a very wealthy member of parliament and twice lord mayor of London.

Colonial Christianity, my central concern, was embedded in the narrative when I went to Spanish Town Cathedral to seek out the final resting place of some of the white Beckford family. At the altar of this austere Anglican church lie several graves of slaveholding families. Ironically, the Anglican Church, which refused to free, properly instruct or marry slaves, was naturally willing to bury the slaveholding plantocracy. I thought of what my ancestors would have thought of this man who enslaved and tortured them, and in some cases sanctioned their deaths. Thus, with 'set on' in mind, when asked how I felt after visiting the Cathedral, I said:

> I want to spit on their graves . . . [T]his is a clear example of how these people sanitized the history by being buried at the front of a church while overseeing the death of millions of Africans . . . It shows how the church was complicit with racial terror in slavery. . . .

This statement was doublespeak. On one level I was conveying my sense of disgust at discovering the Beckford graves; on another, subliminal level, I was offering a coded reference to the bewitchment of colonial Christianity, namely its participation in the devouring of black flesh through its collusion with slavery's racial terror.

## Non-prophetic ministry: *Black Messiah* (2001)

Intriguingly, *Britain's Slave Trade* was received with critical acclaim and I found myself in demand from television producers and companies. But I did not want to be anyone's stooge, and maintained a focus on developing films that would engage with black Pentecostal bewitchment.[4] As a result, I decided to foster my own ideas and find a willing partner to get them made for television. I was fortunate to meet a young producer at BBC Bristol, David Olusoga, while contributing to a radio programme on black history in 2000. David and I decided to collaborate on programme ideas for BBC4. I pitched two ideas to David, one on the church and politics, and the other on black education. These ideas were worked up into treatments by David and eventually commissioned as *Black Messiah* and *Ebony Towers*. Collaboration provided me less space for being as explicit about bewitchment as I was in *Britain's Slave Trade*. Furthermore, as was the case with *Britain's Slave Trade*, my role in the documentary was one of numerous contributors – with no more than two or three opportunities to get my point across. Nonetheless, I was determined to reveal the continued impact of bewitchment. I would do so by influencing the narrative structure of the films and ensuring that particular themes and contributors were included – both to secure the encoding of bewitchment. In terms of style, these films were also interactive, interview-based documentaries drawing on the experience and expertise of church leaders, laity and theologians from both sides of the Atlantic. Intercut with historical archive and church services, these interviews were edited to tell a 200-year-old history.

In *Black Messiah*, I sought to identify the continued influence of colonial Christianity in the form of *non-prophetic ministry* in black Pentecostalism. To achieve this aim, I decided to compare the black church in Britain to its African American counterpart. The purpose was to reveal how one tradition arose out of slavery with a political mandate and how the other remained disengaged from the political. I knew that African American churches were more engaged with the social world than their black British equivalents and therefore, as long as the narrative contrasted these competing traditions, I would achieve my aim of revealing the state of affairs in black Pentecostalism. The producer was very amenable and the contrast was the central theme of the film. The narrative had three major parts: the rise of the black church in Britain, political theological ideas and then a comparison with the black church in America.

The documentary commenced with the story of the formation of black churches in Britain. The film gave voice to early settlers who spoke of their high expectations regarding worshipping opportunities in post war Britain, and how their initial hopes were dashed when they experienced racism in mainstream churches. The result was that the Anglican and other indigenous churches forfeited a generation of followers, as many newcomers started setting up their own places of worship to 'practice a form of Christianity they had experienced back home'. For example, Melvin Powell of the Pentecostal denomination, the New Testament Assembly (NTA), spoke of how he began preaching in halls, community centres, homes and wherever people were willing to allow the congregation to meet. Eventually these fledging congregations were able to buy church buildings from mainstream denominations, grow in numbers and, in the case of the NTA, become one of the most successful black Pentecostal denominations.

Next, there was a discussion on the theology of black Pentecostal churches. It began with hymnody and ended with black theology. The focus of the film switched to the African American Christian experience. The bridge between these two traditions was gospel music. Dr Carol Tomlin, a preaching scholar, described the dynamics of black preaching styles in Britain and the importance of music ministry. Next, a discussion of the spirituals took in views from Dr Iain MacRobert and, again, Tomlin. The discussion continued with opinions from African American scholars and church people, for whom the spirituals were a product of African American Christianity. The spirituals in the United States grow out of the African American religious, social and cultural experience and often engender a political and revolutionary imagination or 'eschatological hope'. The discussion of the rise of a political faith allowed us to explore the emergence of Black Theology.

Black Theology was a response to the racism in the church and society in the 1960s. The architect of Black Theology in the United States, James Cone, spoke of its origins in a synthesis of Martin King and Malcolm X:

> We lived in a society that was defined by race and churches defined by race. So King was working against great odds. And Malcolm's critique forced us young black ministers who were deeply involved in the Civil Rights movement, struggling for justice but not emphasizing blackness. Malcolm persuaded us that we could not be Christian unless we re-interpreted the faith in such a way that embraced our blackness as well as justice.

The focus on Black Theology in the United States was the lens for re-evaluating the rise of the black church in Britain, and the result was stark. With respect to politics, the willingness to engage with party politics, political campaigns or the grassroots to agitate for political change, there was radical discontinuity between the United States and United Kingdom.

A defining moment occurred when we interviewed Bishop John Francis from Ruach, one of the largest black Pentecostal churches in Britain located in Brixton, London. When asked about the relationship between the church and politics he said:

> The important thing is to be a voice that all parties can turn to. Jesus said that we must be in the world but not of the world and he said 'the government will be upon his shoulder', and I really believe sincerely that we have the power to mould and make things happen and we need to be a voice reaching out there and getting out there in the community.

Francis positioned his church beyond party politics, but not completely separate from it. Indeed, the task of the church is to be a sort of neutral spiritual support that all political parties can turn to. Its role is to respond to rather than challenge government. After Francis's comment, the film cut to Ruach's outreach work among the homeless in Brixton to illustrate the church's community engagement or welfare work. When pushed on the specific question, 'Are you willing to engage in political matters on behalf of the black community?' Francis replied, 'We are not ready for that'. Even less interest in politics was shown at Kingsway International Christian

Centre, an east London church of some 12,000 black members. There the senior pastor Matthew Ashimolowo described political engagement as a 'stooping' or lower calling, compared to the role of minister of the Gospel. He did not see any meaningful way of combining faith and politics without appearing partisan.

In contrast, African American contributors expressed a greater clarity on the relationship between faith and politics through a willingness to advocate for equality and justice predicated on the Gospel's commitment to equality, justice and the empowerment of the poor. The history of the African American church's fight against segregation and for Civil Rights was the subject through which these themes were illustrated. Civil Rights campaigner Al Sharpton, paraphrasing Matthew 25, said that the church should not just 'have ceremonies but also feed the hungry, clothe the poor and tend to the sick'. Furthermore, he was befuddled by the British experience and described it as anti-faith or bewitchment:

> When I first came to Britain in the early 90s and we had rallies at the Friends House and other places, the churches were afraid to get involved. And you can't preach faith and then have fear of the political powers that be.

*Black Messiah* made clear the problem of political disengagement by black Pentecostal churches in Britain. Furthermore, while not directly mentioning colonial Christianity, the contrast with the African American experience revealed how one tradition had sought to rid itself of the shackles of the slave-master's religion by combining the theological with the political, and how the other (black British Pentecostalism) had not. Thus, from the vantage point of the emancipatory framework, this film encoded one aspect of 'set on' – the presence of a black, Pentecostal, non-prophetic ministry that failed to take seriously the political mandate of the Bible and the political needs of the black community.

## Academic-theology phobia: *Ebony Towers* (2003)

In *Ebony Towers*, I sought to highlight black Pentecostal zombism, that is, academic-theology phobia. This film was another black Atlantic study, but in this instance, the focus was on intellectual thought – critical thinking having a decisive role in identifying academic-theology phobia in black Pentecostalism. This time, however, it was necessary to find another way of encoding bewitchment. I decided to try a very different form of encoding based on a *politics of absence*. Thus, by foregrounding African American churches and academic theologians, I was simultaneously identifying the absence of similar academics and philosophies of education in the black Pentecostal context in Britain.

Building on the success of *Black Messiah*, this film followed a transatlantic journey. My goal was to encode the narrative so that it would reveal a problem: the struggle to build a black academy in the United Kingdom. My strategy was to reveal an African American Christian affirmation of critical thinking and academic theology and the absence of a black British comparison. This is not to say all African American Christian traditions readily embrace academic theology; rather, the film signalled the numerous traditions on the other side of the Atlantic that successfully nurture critical thinking. Paramount for me, was to have black intellectuals with roots in the church to speak about the role of education in the struggle for justice, in order to reveal the black church/intellectual thought axis. The producer had no knowledge of African American intellectuals such as Michael Eric Dyson and Cornel West, but was nonetheless willing to take my word of their appropriateness as contributors to the film. We were unable to secure Professor West, but Professor Dyson granted an interview. Dyson's presence was particularly important as a symbol of critical thought and academic theology because he trained as a philosopher of religion, served as a pastor and rose to prominence during the first decade of the twenty-first century as a leading African American public intellectual.

*Ebony Towers* told the story of the rise of black intellectual thought in late modernity in the United States, and what Britain can learn from this experience. The tease or introductory segment set out the status quo: the rise of African American intellectual thought and the relative inactivity in Britain:

> Black people dominate American popular culture. In sports, music, and entertainment the icons and fashions of black America have become a global phenomenon. In the last thirty years, a hugely successful black middle class has emerged and black Americans have finally reached the heart of the US

establishment. But there has been another success, one less well known here in Britain. New generations of black academics have stormed America's 'ivory towers' and black America has created a new class of superstar intellectuals who are almost as famous as its athletes and film stars. Today, these figures are leading and redirecting America's national debate on race . . . This is the story of how America has become the superpower of black thinking, and how new ideas about race and identity that are changing the world are now dominated by America's new black intelligentsia.

The narrative smoothly introduced the major point of contrast in the film. Over images of empty lecture theatres, the narrator continued with:

By contrast, we in Britain have not been able to emulate anything like this success. Black Britons are on the margins of intellectual life at our universities and the consequences of this historic failure are beginning to be felt in modern Britain . . . The result is a community without the intellectual role models to meet the educational crisis that threatens it.

The documentary had two parts: the rise of black intellectual thought in America and a comparison between the United States and United Kingdom. The first theme revealed how, in the post-slave world, education was a key for black advancement. Professor Manning Marable of Columbia University explained how slavery's racial terror included the denial of education, how 'laws were passed in Mississippi and other southern states in America that denied slaves the opportunity to learn to read, and threatened anyone who dared do so with the fear of receiving lashes'. This factor fostered a 'thirst for learning after the end of slavery, as 4 million illiterate African Americans began the quest for education'. The narrative then stated how historically black colleges such as Morehouse in Atlanta were established after slavery to educate the sons and daughters of slaves. Central to this task was the church. Commenting on this relationship, African American scholar and activist pastor Eugene Rivers stated:

The church was the one institution that the black community controlled. It was an institution that the slaves created, with its own discourse, rhetoric, language and imagery and its collectively celebrated and affirmed leadership class, so out of slavery, the black church evolves and creates the first bible colleges and black college network.

The second part of the film contrasted the experiences of black Americans and Britons. Of primary importance was the African American fight for academic desegregation in the United States, the struggle for inclusion in the mainstream of American academic life in the 1960s and the effort of agitated black students to secure black studies and black scholarship in the academy. The narrative then switched to Britain and told the hidden story of how, in the post-war years, the first generation of West Indian immigrants desired to advance themselves. This aim was not encouraged or supported by the British establishment, which viewed blacks as a reserve pool of cheap labour rather than future leaders. Contributors argued that as a result that blacks were not provided with significant conduits to higher education.

The documentary ended with two caveats. The first was the danger of a rising tide of anti-intellectualism in black expressive cultures. Dyson, who was featured throughout the film, explained how aspects of hip hop culture posed an anti-intellectual threat, especially '. . . in families and communities without the social and educational buffers to challenge the negative and sometimes nihilistic imagery presented in hip hop culture'. The second was the danger of ignoring 'race' in the development of the academy. Rivers concluded, at the end of the film, that even the colonial [sic] Americans realized that 'race' had to be a central component in addressing education and that the 'sophisticated Brits' court danger in ignoring this relationship:

> The United Kingdom ignores at her peril their failure to produce a black intelligentsia. How is it that blacks are underrepresented at your elite universities? That's a recipe for disaster. Learn from the United States. The primitives, even in the States, understood that the failure to politically incorporate at elite institutions, blacks, would result in a disaster, which they experienced, even the crude Americans. So I am baffled by the sophisticated Brits, who with all their smug refinement, could not figure out something as basic as, we must be an inclusive society.

In relation to bewitchment, *Ebony Towers* encoded bewitchment (non-prophetic ministry) through a politics of absence. The film revealed how in the post-slave world, the church in the United States played a seminal role in the intellectual advancement of blacks. What is more, educated theologians played a prominent role in discussions of 'race'. The blatant absence of black British examples in the film was a subliminal critique of the paucity of interest in intellectual life in black churches, including black Pentecostalism, in Britain. The focus on the African American church revealed how one Christian tradition had exorcized this aspect of the slave past and another remained captive to an academic-theology phobia.

Thus, before going on to make films at Channel 4 in 2003, I had conjured documentary – encoding bewitchment in documentary film in the form of colonial Christianity and its continued influence in the contemporary world of black Pentecostalism as non-prophetic ministry in *Black Messiah*, and academic-theology phobia in *Ebony Towers*. The next task was to find ways of exorcizing these remnants of colonial Christianity by conjuring political and Bible films.

# CHAPTER ELEVEN

# Exorcism in the political documentary

This chapter analyses exorcism, the 'cast out' or expulsion feature of the emancipatory framework that is embedded into the documentary. Once the documentary identifies detrimental beliefs, systems and structures that still plague communities or nations as the vestiges of colonialism, which I have characterized as bewitchment, the response to these forms of oppression is exorcism. To explain how exorcism functions in documentary film, I closely connect it with a set of beliefs and practices rooted in the wider church, and located in revolutionary Christianity, which I name as 'prophetic ministry'. Prophetic ministry is rooted in the biblical tradition of the eighth-century prophets who, at great cost, were called to foretell the will of God.

> The prophets gave a large measure of their address to proclaiming the emptiness and tragedy of Israel's present existence. The tragedy of Israel is due to her failure to remember the Exodus-Sinai tradition. . . . The people failed to recognize Yahweh's sovereignty in history, and thus began to trust their own power and the power of political alliances with other nations. (Isaiah 31.1)[1]

God's purposes for the community, while grounded in a religious covenant and nurtured through spiritual practices, had *concrete social and political consequences*. The prophet and community did not have the privilege of engaging solely in worship practices. Authentic worship required a committed lifestyle of pursuing justice and loving mercy. Therefore, failure to do so was represented as breakdown in the community's religious practice and the covenant with God:

> The disobedience of the first commandment always had consequences in the social life of the community. Israel, therefore, began to oppress the weak and the poor in their own community.[2]

The 'prophetic' is both an office and a type of practice and not surprisingly, it is prophetic ministry, a mode of thought and action, that is of interest here. In light of this understanding, when prophetic ministry is inscribed on political documentary, it is accompanied by exorcism as a practice of rooting out oppression and excluding evil from the community so that it might embrace justice. Thus, although prophetic ministry in documentary is directed towards the social world, it nonetheless exorcizes the non-prophetic ministry of black Pentecostalism by *silencing/exorcizing* the apoliticism of non-prophetic ministry.

Two films that best illustrate the exorcizing aspects of the political documentary are *Empire Pays Back* (2005) and *The Great African Scandal* (2007). The focus of the prophetic in these two films is socio-economic justice. The former demands recompense for slavery, and, the latter recompense for contemporary servitude brought about by globalization.

## *Empire Pays Back* (2005)

I had previously pitched the idea of a film on reparations for slavery several times to production companies before the project was eventually realized in early 2005. Reparations are a contentious subject due in part to a selective British historical amnesia that results in the marginalized study of Britain's slave past across all levels of historical inquiry. In this film, I did not want to rehearse the diverse arguments for and against reparations but instead present a polemic. The result was *Empire Pays Back*, a film that simply calculated the amount of reparations due and who should pay – a perspective expressed in the tease at the beginning of the film:

> A long time ago, a very bad empire captured millions of people in a far away land and ripped them away from their homes. They were forced onto ships and transported as cargo across the ocean to a foreign land and made to work as slaves. For hundreds of years, their blood and sweat helped to create a very rich empire. Slavery was finally done away with but the empire kept its riches and has never paid its debt to the slaves. The empire is Britain and the slaves, Africans taken to the Caribbean just like my own ancestors. The debt has been ignored for over two hundred years. But now I think its time, the empire pays back. My name is Robert Beckford, I am a lecturer in the school of historical studies at the University of Birmingham. I believe African slaves were ripped-off by the British Empire. I want to know who bankrolled it, who insured it and who made a mint from it. I've even hired a group of 'boffins' (intellectuals) to do some number crunching, so I know exactly how much is owed. I'm going to track down some heirs to Britain's slave past and ask them to pay reparations of the slave trade.

However, with exorcism in mind, I embedded a prophetic dynamic in the narrative, which is the quest for justice in the form of reparations. The programme had three main parts: identifying the workings of the slave trade, proffering examples of compensation and calculating how much is owed in reparations.

I began by telling the story of how Britain made money from slavery. To underscore the benefit to British cities, I went to Liverpool. Illustrating the Golden Triangle, the trade route from Africa to the colonies, and back to the mother country, we filmed the embarking and disembarking off the ferry across the Mersey, as a metaphor for the trade in slaves and goods from Africa and the West Indies back to England.

> I am on the famous, ferry across the Mersey. But in the eighteenth century this was the perfect port for slave trading and the gateway to Africa and the new world. Here is how it worked: goods were taken from here to Africa, where they were traded for slaves, the slaves were then taken to the Caribbean

to work on the plantation and finally the fruit of their labour, the tobacco, rum and sugar were loaded up and brought back to Britain. It was a brilliant money spinner and had a knock on effect for the rest of the city: from the people who built the ships to the people who made the shackles.

In Liverpool city centre, I teamed up with a local lay historian, Eric Lynch, who was determined to make sure the city owned up to its slave past. His tour took me to the site of Martins Bank, which was founded with the profits of slavery. There I came across a relic of the slave trade. Carved on the stone pillars of the august front door was a relief of Negro children at the feet of Neptune. Neptune's hands are placed on their heads and their feet are bound with irons. Mr Lynch described it as 'the arrogant symbol of power'.

I then travelled to Germany to explore a recent case of reparations for slave workers. In Berlin, I met up with American compensation expert Bert Neuborn. Neuborn was a leading lawyer in a compensation case for individuals who had been slave labourers during the Nazi reign. I asked him if he thought that African Caribbean people had a case against the British state for compensation for slavery. He said:

> There is no doubt that the case for African slavery is as strong as the case we had here . . . [A]s a matter of theory both groups should receive the same compensation. The problem is timing. If this had been done 50 years after the abolition of slavery, if it had been done within a time frame when individuals were still alive, I think they should and could have received compensation.

I reminded the audience that compensation did indeed occur at the end of slavery, but for the white owners. To illustrate this reality, I revisited the Beckford history in Britain and spoke to people involved in curating that history, specifically those in Beckford's Tower in the city of Bath. At the Tower, the curator at that time, Amy Frost, said that at the height of the slave trade, the Beckford family, one of the largest plantation families in Jamaica, owned about 1,200–1,600 slaves, some of whom might have been my ancestors.

Frost revealed how compensation was at the centre of the abolition of slavery in Jamaica, with the British government providing millions of pounds in compensation, the equivalent of two billion pounds in today's currency. In contrast, for their pain and suffering, the slaves received nothing.

## Prophetic ministry: The bill

The next step was to go in search of the bill to determine who was liable to pay reparations. To do so, I decided to calculate individual parts of the bill and identify who was liable. To work out this sum, I sat in a room for the best part of a day with three experts in particular fields related to compensation history and law. These were the economic historian Professor David Richardson, Peter Tomkins, an actuarian and leading expert on compensation claims and Mick Antonwin, a leading compensation lawyer. We worked through three calculations.

The first figure that the team addressed was compensation for loss of earnings – how much was owed to the slaves who were worked to death without pay. To compensate the descendants, it was necessary to determine the amount each slave would have made during his or her lifetime, and return it as compensation. The team decided that if a slave was being paid about £10 per year, the going rate for agricultural workers during that period (minus cost of living expenses), they could reckon on an average salary of £200 for a lifetime's work. The amount of £200 with compound interest paid, since the abolition of slavery, is calculated to be one million pounds in today's currency. The next task was to establish how many slaves could be accounted for. The team decided that there were at least, in the English-speaking Caribbean, 3 million slaves who survived the Middle Passage and were enslaved. At least another 1 million slaves were born into slavery. The total cost of compensation in the first category was arrived at by the calculation:

4 million slaves ×

1 million pounds in lost earnings =

4 trillion pounds.

I then set out to identify some of the clues hidden in national landmarks in London that would indicate who made money out of slavery. In an open-top, red London bus, I gave my 'alternative tour of London', the tour of shame. I revealed how the National Gallery was established by a slave trader, how Lloyds of London insurers got rich from insuring slaves and how the Bank of England, HSBC and Barclays banks have slavery at their roots:

> HSBC may stand for Hong Kong and Shanghai Banking Corporation, but this bank has slavery in its family tree. Back in Liverpool there is this guy, Thomas Leyland. He is a slave trader and sends over three and a half thousand pounds to Jamaica alone. He makes a fortune from the trade and establishes a bank with his nephew. Leyland and Bullings Bank is eventually taken over by North and South Wales Bank in 1901 that becomes a part of Midlands Bank. And as we know, in recent history, Midlands was taken over by HSBC.

Naturally, all the banks mentioned in the film spoke of how these events were long in the past and that the banks they took over had limited involvement in slavery. Lloyds refused me access to their archives, possibly because they were in the process of being sued for their involvement in the slave trade by blacks in the United States. I also drove past the Houses of Parliament and told of how, by 1766, 40 MPs were slave traders or plantation owners.

I ended by describing how the royal family and the church got in on the act. Historically, the royal family participated in the trade with Queen Elizabeth I funding one of the first slave voyages and providing a royal charter in 1563. Later, Charles I gave the Royal Africa Company a monopoly on slave trading, and many of the first investors were members of the royal family. I identified the role of the Church of England in the slave trade by pointing out the Codrington plantation in Barbados, in which the Church had a role.

The second round of calculations about compensation explored how much is owed for unjust enrichment. This category explained the profit Britain made from slavery and how reparation should be made to those who suffered from this exploitation. The team suggested that sugar added nearly 5 million pounds a year to the British economy during the height of the sugar industry, for 100 years from the middle of the seventeenth century. Taking this 100-year dominance and multiplying it by the 5 million pounds benefit, equalled 500 million pounds. Adding compound interest over a substantial time leaves us with a figure of 2.5 trillion pounds. We calculated that Africa owned nothing, as it was a net looser from slavery. The final category was pain and suffering.

The third and final calculation was for pain and suffering based on contemporary annual rates.

> **Robert**  I ask the team how we could arrive at a figure to compensate the slaves for pain and suffering?
>
> **Mick**  Perhaps looking at cases of miscarriages of justice, people who have been put into bondage in UK jails. And again it is quite difficult to assess but some cases have put a figure around about £12,500 a year. So, someone who is in slavery for twenty years that would work out at figure of around about a quarter of a million pounds or so.
>
> **Robert**  So being enslaved for twenty years or so at £12,500 or so compensation for wrongful imprisonment, works out at £250,000 for each slave's suffering.

These rates were then multiplied by the 4 million slaves, and also the duration of slavery, and amounted to one trillion pounds.

> So the team has come up with this: 4 trillion pounds in unpaid wages, 2.5 trillion in unjust enrichment of the British economy through the profits of the sugar industry and another 1 trillion pounds for pain and suffering. So, in total, we estimated that the debt due to the slaves was a whopping seven and a half trillion pounds.

The film ended with a conversation with a senior official in the then Labour government regarding how this amount should be paid. Fiona Mactaggart, a Home Office minster, however, argued against reparations. In her opinion, slavery took place too long ago to be considered under current British legislative frameworks, though *she did see the symbolic value of a public apology and offered one in the interview on behalf of Her Majesty's Government.* But I went further and ended the film by calling for money to be paid to establish institutions, bodies and events that would educate the nation of the horrors of the slave trade and the relationship between slavery and modern racism(s). I also suggested that the cancellation of debts of former slave colonies by the British government would be a means of facilitating reparations for slavery.

A cursory or surface reading of *Empire Pays Back* suggests that it was a film on reparations for slavery. At a deeper level, however, it was prophetic ministry, a quest for justice in the social world and therefore a nullification of non-prophetic ministry. As such, it was an exorcism of one of the spells of colonial Christianity.

## The Great African Scandal (2007)

*The Great African Scandal* also explored financial restitution. This time, the focus was corrupt economic practice or occult economies in the present; that is, a study of contemporary global economic inequality. The focus of enquiry and point of connection between the domestic audience and the subject at hand was consumerism and fair(er)[3] trade. At the outset of the film, I went out on the streets of London and asked people whether they would continue to buy particular high-street products (chocolate, gold and rice) if it could be demonstrated that there were dubious production ethics at work. Next walking across a supermarket aisle, I said in the first piece to camera:

> Be honest, rarely when you pick something up from the supermarket shelf do you consider the 'poor beggar' in Africa who had to produce it. 'Oh no', I hear you say, 'poor people being exploited in Africa, what can I do about it?' Well I believe consumers can influence the powers that be and I've come to Africa on the trail of our three high-street products, rice, chocolate and gold. I'm going to meet the people that produce them and see for myself the lives that they lead. Can I as a Westerner, do the work that they do? And I am also going to take on some powerful multi-national companies.

However, the film was also an exercise in prophetic ministry as it sought to challenge powerful corporations proposing change in practices in Africa. This time, however, there would be material change beyond a government apology. Indeed, one of the companies under scrutiny, *Cadbury*, later made significant changes to the way that it did business in Ghana. The filming took place in Ghana over a four-week period and explored how the practice and policies of corporations, the World Bank and the International Monetary Fund (IMF) impoverish Ghana. The film received logistical support from the development charity Christian Aid, without which it would have been impossible for the project to be realized. I went in search of the story behind three high-street goods – rice, gold and cocoa – to disclose the basic economic practices that keep most Africans poor. In this case, prophetic ministry as the agency of exorcism was expressed in a call for trade justice.

# Rice

Rice farming in Ghana demonstrates how Western economic policies can devastate local economies in developing countries. In Gbirima, I assumed the role of a rice worker, and I struggled to keep up with the physical demands of rice farming and the general day-to-day living experience of rural poverty. My wage was 50 pence per day, the average for agricultural farmers. To identify the wrongdoing, I explored the history of rice farming to reveal how the profitability of the industry had been decimated by liberalization of the Ghanaian economy in the 1980s:

> In the 1980s, as part of their strategy to open up the Ghanaian market, the American government provided (American) rice as food aid. It was like sending snow to Eskimos. Along with the sweetener of food aid, the IMF, the World Bank, and the American government told the Ghanaian government to cut farm aid to farmers and open up its markets to foreign imports. The food aid tailed off but cheap foreign rice flooded in and Ghana's rice production stagnated.

There was a hidden cost to the destruction of rice farming, including rural migration to the cities, particularly among young, vulnerable girls who went to work as domestic or commercial servants in homes and marketplaces. I went in search of three girls from the village I was living in, who had run away to Ghana's second largest city, Kumasi. After a day of searching, I eventually found them living in squalid conditions in shacks in a slum, working as occasional domestic servants or carrying other people's goods like human forklifts in the food markets. It appeared to me that these young women, 14- and 15-year-olds, were incredibly vulnerable to criminal activity in the area. In light of their experience, I believe that those who design policies which condemn young girls to near destitution are nothing more than gangsters dressed up as global economists:

> The worse thing, the worse, absolute, degrading, nasty thing about all of this is that it's not adults, it's not people who are trained and skilled and can look after themselves; it's teenage girls. IMF, World Bank policies leading to teenage girls to have to hustle money. These policies are not policies, it's international gangsterism.

## Cocoa

Next I travelled to central Ghana to learn about the cocoa industry and to investigate the hidden cost of Europe's sweet tooth. Having lived in Birmingham, England, I had first-hand knowledge of the success of the *Cadbury* chocolate business, and its progressive model housing estate built by the business for its English workers. In contrast, in Ghana, huts, shacks and underdeveloped regions were the status quo where cocoa was sourced. I spoke to family cocoa businesses to find out how and why they were unable to add value to their business. I was told of the lack of investment in the secondary stages of processing cocoa and how any development in this area would not necessarily lead to greater exports because tariffs from the European Union and various countries discouraged secondary development in this sector of agriculture. I also spent a day working with child labourers, trafficked from poorer areas to work on cocoa farms. This labour is often hidden from official statistics because it takes place within families. The wrongdoing here was personally overwhelming. Was this not a modern dynamic equivalent of the slave story of my people? Working as 'slave labour' for Western industries? One ray of hope was the Kopacocoa fair trade farm I visited, where a higher price was paid for cocoa in order to enable farmers to invest in equipment and the education of their children. Nonetheless, it was shocking to learn that, at that time, less than five per cent of all fair trade beans were bought at the higher price. Due to lack of demand, the rest were thrown back into the cheaper pool. At the fair trade warehouse a fair trade farmer gave me the startling facts that challenged the notion of fair trade being 'fair':

Robert     At the port what percentage of your beans actually sells at the fair trade price?

Farmer     We have about 3 per cent.

Robert     Hold on a minute, let me get that clear, you are saying of all the beans you get in from the collective, fair traded, only 3 per cent of them are actually at the fair trade price?

Farmer     Yes, just 3 per cent.

Robert     I am really shocked. Nearly all the beans produced by the fair trade cooperative isn't bought at the fair trade price and ends up mixed in with cocoa that may have been picked by children.

## Gold

The production of gold, the last commodity, was an example of corporate malfeasance. In the final leg of the film, I came 'face-to-face' with the predicament of illegal gold miners. I travelled to the gold mining capital, Obuasi, to hear both sides of the gold mining divide. On one side, there were mining officials working for Anglo-Gold Ashanti who told of the wealth, job creation and environmental management that gold mining had brought to Ghana. These Anglo-Gold Ashanti executives lived on the wealthy side of the gold divide. On the other side were communities living in mining areas who spoke of impoverishment, stolen land and pollution from mining production.

I travelled to one deprived village bordering Obuasi to see for myself the impact of mining. What was clear from the outset was that despite the mineral wealth below ground, above ground there was very little evidence of economic development or wealth creation:

> Gold is one of Ghana's most lucrative exports. Here in Obuasi, the biggest player is part British owned Anglo-Gold Ashanti. . . . Last year Anglo-Gold Ashanti registered profits of around half a billion pounds from its global operations, but it does not look as if the people here are sharing in the bonanza.

I travelled to a village called Dotcuwa which borders Obuasi. I walked with a group of young men around the village and confronted a wasteland with a water supply that I would be cautious about drinking from or bathing in – but I had a choice, they did not.

> Robert    What did this village use to look like
>
> Farmer    This area here was full of cocoa, yam, cassava, but ever since the takeover these things are no more.

Local people showed what they perceived to be the environmental damage caused by gold mining. A University of Ghana survey had revealed high levels of toxic materials in the water and fruit in Obuasi. In one surrounding village, arsenic levels were nearly 2,000 times higher than the level deemed safe by the World Health Organization. I was also introduced to the illegal mining popular among unemployed young men, and the risks involved in this underground trade. It is a terrible activity, highlighted by international publicity in recent years as a result of the influx of Chinese workers joining the illicit trade.[4] What was clear to me was that, despite the incredible gold wealth that Anglo-Gold Ashanti was reaping (registering half a billion pounds from its global operation that year), there was little physical evidence of material benefit for the people in areas where the precious metal was mined.

## Prophetic ministry: Fair(er) trade

The solutions proposed at the end of the film are, in the short term, increased support for fair trade products in the West, a solution that requires education, consciousness-raising and the ongoing support of British consumers. A long term solution, however, is a radical approach to trade injustice, which takes seriously the urgency of biblical exorcism, for one cannot be complacent about the nefarious presence of evil. I think of this second approach as a new 'war' of independence based on trade justice for Africa:

> The reality is that Ghana is a poor country when it should be rich. In the 21st century, foreign masters are still pulling the economic strings. But as consumers we can make a difference with our buying power. We can hold big corporations to account. We can demand that Europe and the United States end unfair trade practices and we can insist that the IMF and World Bank act in the interests of poor countries. Ghana may have its independence politically, but its economic independence is yet to be realized. I believe that there needs to be a new war of independence for Africa, and in this new war the soldiers are the consumers – like you and me. This new war isn't about a military struggle but it has to be militant. And in this new war, there has to be a slogan that drives us all forward. And its not one settler one bullet, but trade justice for Africa.

As mentioned above, one of the companies under scrutiny, *Cadbury*, later decided to change policy and participate in fair trade. This change in practice underscores the power of prophetic ministry, and that 'exorcism' has material consequences. Although this quote is rather long, it highlights the power of prophetic ministry to transform the lives of persons, communities and nations:

> The Fairtrade movement hailed a major breakthrough yesterday with the announcement that Britain's biggest-selling chocolate brand was switching to the ethical standard. Cadbury's Dairy Milk, which sells 300 million bars a year in the UK and Ireland, will source its cocoa from Fairtrade farmers in Ghana, the biggest brand of its kind to make the move. 'This is groundbreaking news for thousands of small farmers in Ghana, enabling all those who buy it to make a real difference', said Cadbury's chief executive, Todd Stitzer. The Fairtrade mark was set up as a way of guaranteeing developing world farmers a bigger share of the money generated from products using their raw materials.

Some 7.5 million people, including farmers, workers and their families, benefit from products displaying the Fairtrade symbol. 'Farmers are saying that it's impossible to make ends meet', said Fairtrade's head, Harriet Lamb. 'People don't see cocoa as a future. They don't get enough cash from cocoa so there's not enough investment'. The new project is designed to create a 'virtuous circle' by putting a floor on the price and offering a premium for higher quality beans. 'With more income, farmers invest to improve quality and productivity', she added. 'Then they start to spread the benefits and you see banks popping up in villages and thriving markets appearing'. Forty thousand of Ghana's 700,000 cocoa farmers will benefit from the first phase of the Cadbury venture, tripling the country's Fairtrade cocoa production. 'Young people are giving up and moving to the cities where there are often no jobs', Ms Lamb said. 'We hope this can be a turning point for the industry.'[5]

As a result of the policy change, tens of thousands of farmers will receive a better price for the produce, which will positively impact their families and communities. Moreover, this exercise in prophetic ministry was an encoding of exorcism of black Pentecostal non-prophetic ministry. Again, by proclaiming the prophetic we silence the non-prophetic.

While both films, *Empire Pays Back* and *The Great African Scandal*, engage in sociopolitical action and take aim at vestiges of colonialism and current systems of globalization, the intended audience was black Pentecostals. Indeed, considering that the legacy of slavery and failed economic systems in Ghana and other parts of Africa disproportionately impact black Britons, many of whom are believers, it is my hope that black Pentecostals narrate their own stories through the stories that I share, and that they see their own faces through the many persons that I interview. Consequently, it is my hope that they would also view the struggle for justice as their own. Prophetic ministry demonstrates that engagement with politics is one means of remedying the world's brokenness.

# CHAPTER TWELVE

# Exorcism in the Bible documentary

In this chapter, I want to highlight the necessity of academic theological education in black Pentecostalism in order that the church might engage in social transformation in an informed way. Specifically, I prescribe ongoing engagement with academic scholarship, particularly theological and biblical scholarship, in the hope that black Pentecostals might interpret Scripture, and the social contexts through which they 'make sense' of Scripture, in more rigorous and compelling ways. A deliberate Pentecostal partnership with academic study is the desired outcome of exorcism. In this instance, exorcism targets what is generally referred to as anti-intellectualism. With respect to black Pentecostalism, I refer to the perspective that disregards or disparages the need for higher education for those aspiring to ministry, and the need for theological scholarship to inform the life of the church, as *academic-theology phobia*. Therefore, if Pentecostals are going to engage in social exorcism by actively opposing oppression and driving out injustice in the wider society, they first must have their own excessive fears and enslaving beliefs exorcized. As I demonstrate in other chapters, this anti-intellectual stance has its roots and formation in colonial Christianity and its practices. I encode the practice of exorcism in my Bible documentaries by interacting with the Bible, which is beloved by Pentecostals, on the one hand, and by dialoguing with biblical scholarship, which is suspect and even feared by some Pentecostals, on the other. The aim of my Bible films is to demonstrate how biblical scholarship can inform how Pentecostals read and embody the biblical text transformationally, in a manner that is both spiritual and social.

## Bible films and exorcism

Indeed, my understanding of the role of exorcism within Pentecostalism is informed by biblical narratives and readers of the Bible. Within my hermeneutic, the readers of Scripture are, at times, also specialized readers of postcolonial studies. As I noted in Chapter Four, my understanding of exorcism in the story of the Gerasene demoniac, informed by postcolonial interpretation, is that exorcism enabled the return to sanity of a man who was mentally deranged by his encounter with the occupying Roman army. The return to sanity is not only the restoration of normality but also a new way of perceiving one's life and the wider world. Applied to black Pentecostalism, the continued influence of colonial Christianity's anti-intellectualism and the denial of theological education, to the degree that advanced theological learning is something to be feared or thoroughly repudiated because of its perceived detrimental impact on personal faith and spirituality, functions as an occult force that enslaves far too many Pentecostals. The remedy for this ailment is *academic theological practice* – a restoration of a right mind (that entails clear and critical thinking), coupled by a new perception of scripture that leads to critical and innovative ways of reading the text as a resource for social change. Central to this task are the Bible documentaries.

The Bible documentaries are documentary films exploring an aspect of biblical history, a particular book of the Bible or biblical interpretation. These films were all personal journeys that involved an evolution of thought and practice, and, as such, permitted me to engage directly with a black Pentecostal audience. My personal journey stemmed from how I was taught to read the Bible in my home church. From there, the narrative progressed to show how I went on to challenge this view through deeper reflection. My hope was that my story would resonate with Pentecostals and become an example of how they might develop their approach to the Bible. But the narrative was also conjured, that is, inscribed with 'individual exorcism' (Chapter Four), and, consequently, my primary goal was to identify and expel academic-theology phobia. As an outcome, conjure was signalled in the Bible documentary narrative by 1) reference to *the way I was taught* to read the Bible as a child and 2) by seeking out a *new interpretation* to displace my earlier reading strategy. In other words, the Bible documentaries not only seek to repudiate the remnants of colonial Christianity but also contour a *new perception* of the text itself.

The Bible film category consists of several films (*Who Wrote the Bible? The Secret Family of Jesus, The Hidden Story of Jesus, The Secrets of the Twelve Disciples, The Nativity Decoded* and *The Book of Revelation: The Final Judgment*). Two films best embody this form of exorcism. These are *Who Wrote the Bible?* and *The Book of Revelation: The Final Judgment*.

## *Who Wrote the Bible?* (2004)

On the surface, this film was a limited exploration of biblical authorship to tell the story of how the Christian scriptures were formed and how some of the traditional ideas about authorship of particular texts deserve to be challenged. This film entailed a journey across the Middle East and Europe in search of biblical authorship and canon formation focusing on paradigmatic texts from the Old and New Testament. It was historical criticism in a simple and uncomplicated style for a Christmas Day audience. Stylistically, the film was shot as a journey with me speaking 'off' and 'on' camera to convey a sense of informality and formality, respectively. Exorcism was encoded at the start of the film in the departure from black Pentecostalism, or how I was taught to understand as a child, and then in the new interpretation of the Bible.

## How I was taught

The first part of the film was a critique of black Pentecostalism's limited engagement with academic scholarship. To illustrate this reality, I began with a visit to my mother's church in Handsworth, Birmingham. I explained how I was taught a concordist or surface reading of the Bible.[1] This method accepted the biblical narrative as a whole and simply searched for references and issues that corresponded with our everyday concerns. In the sequence, my mother could be seen in the background explaining the story of Jonah to a group of Sunday school children. As she taught the children, I remarked that despite its limitations, the reading strategy was nonetheless capable of producing a powerful and transforming Christian experience. But it was also lacking – it did not probe the biblical text to understand its history, including authorship and context of its books. I wanted to find out more about the Bible to enhance the reading strategy that I had been taught at Sunday school.

> I am in the Wesleyan Holiness Church in Handsworth (Birmingham) and my mother is teaching Sunday School the story of Jonah. This (place) is so important to me because this is where I learned about the Bible, and learned to read it as the Word of God. The Bible shaped what we said what we thought and what we did, and I am grateful for that because if I did not have that (upbringing) I would not have a doctorate in Theology. . . . So although it was pretty rigid, it kept me in check. As I grew older, I tried to hold onto that simple faith, but my studies taught me that it was not going to be that simple: the stories about Creation and the Garden of Eden were more symbolic than literal and if the bible is more literal (than factual), what is there to hold onto? Is it really the word of God? So I have lived a kind of schizophrenic existence and I now think it's time to plant myself in one camp or the other, or find a way of bringing the two together. I need to know who wrote the Bible.

## New interpretation

I then went in search of this more critical approach. This narrative change also signalled a critique of Pentecostalism, a rebuke that also underlined a move towards exorcizing this tradition. To this end, I set out across the Middle East and Europe to explore the evolution of Scripture by taking in numerous locations and speaking to experts and everyday people caught up in the sociopolitical ramifications of biblical interpretation. It was not possible to address the authorship of every book of the Bible in the limited time we had for the film, so the film focused on the Pentateuch (the first five books of the Bible) the synoptic Gospels and some of St. Paul's letters. The first part of the programme examined the Old Testament. In this section, I examined editing, collation and revision practices within the texts and also how the meaning of the Old Testament (Exodus) is still being fought over today in contemporary Palestine.

Regarding the Old Testament, we focused on the evolution of the Pentateuch. I began by travelling to the Sinai desert to retell the traditional view of Mosaic authorship, but then returned to Britain to show how Mosaic authorship was contested by biblical scholars. Dr Jill Middlemas explained it this way when I asked her about Moses:

**Robert**   Tradition says that Moses wrote the first five books of the Bible.

How likely is that?

Jill    Not very likely, partly because Moses would be speaking about his own death. At least from the medieval period, we have rabbis already arguing about parts of the Torah. It wasn't really until the 19th century that we find a German scholar by the name of Wellhausen that we come up with the theory that there were four different literary sources that underlie the Pentateuch.

Using the Exodus stories as an example, Dr Middlemas went on to explain the basis of an alternative view of the authorship of the Pentateuch, including 'documentary hypothesis', the argument that several authors or communities of authors wrote and edited versions of the Pentateuch over a given period. Armed with this new critical approach to interpretation, I set out to Israel to discover how these texts were collated.

In order to discover how these versions were collated, I then went in search of the editing practices. In Tel Aviv, I spoke to leading Hebrew Bible scholar Yari Zakovitch from the Hebrew University, who argued that editing began in the seventh-century BCE by a thin layer of intellectuals who wrote and rewrote traditions in competition with each other. He identified the combination of traditions in the Psalms, which were often revised to fit the ideological and political views of the day as well as the cult of Yahweh.

> I do believe that most of the Torah, the five book of Moses, the scroll that we are holding right now was written in the seventh century (BC). Major parts of it had been written earlier, but it reached some semi-final form in the seventh century. . . . When I read Psalms 78, which still believes that Judah will last forever, I can see that the author of this Psalms is actually making a great mosaic. He is using different traditions from the Torah to form a different document, J E D and P and all of them I can trace, the footprints of all of them, in this Psalms for instance. . . . These are the verses of the manna coming down from heaven and here again he combines the tradition from Exodus and the tradition from the book of Numbers.

Returning to Jerusalem, I then examined later revisions of the traditions with the expert guidance of Israel Knohl of the Shalom Hartman Institute. Knohl showed how further revisions occurred in the seventh-century BCE after the death of King Josiah, and how the death of Josiah and the exile of the Jews were the beginning of messianism. Using the book of Isaiah as an example, Knohl revealed how Isaiah develops a new idea; the appearance of a new Eden with all nations seeking the Word of God. Isaiah develops this idea (Isaiah 40–66) to introduce a rationale for the exile – the suffering of the Jewish people-and their mission to bring light to the nations. The Old Testament part of the documentary, concluded with contrasting views on what the Torah meant in Israel today for both Jews and Palestinians. I wanted to show how the meaning of the text was still being fought over today and to this end, took in views from Jewish settlers in Hebron and Palestinian Christians in Bethlehem. In Hebron, Rabbi Simcha Hochbaum says:

> We believe every word of the Bible to be divinely ordained, God giving it to Moses and being written down for future generations. The Torah describes in great detail, in chapter 23 in the book of

Genesis the purchase of the cave and the fields surrounding it, Abraham negotiating. . . . the purchase of this place.

As far as Rabbi Hochbaum was concerned, the Bible, read literally, justifies the presence of Jews in Hebron. In contrast, in Bethlehem, Palestinian Christians, who also accept the Bible as the word of God, read the Exodus and conquest stories in a different way. Not as legitimating the ownership of land for one group over another for posterity but instead as divine commitment to all people struggling for justice. One of the Palestinians, Nuha Khoury, puts it this way:

> What does it mean as a Christian today living in Palestine under occupation – by somebody who is using that particular book to say, I am not supposed to be? Turn it on the other side, and I say no, because that book says. . . . even that book for the Jews . . . it gave the right for the people of God to seek liberation and we are the people of God too, not people of a lesser God.

The New Testament part of the film followed the same pattern as the Old Testament: a review of selected texts followed by contemporary examples. We began in Ephesus in modern-day Turkey. I spoke to Kings College London New Testament scholar Dr Eddie Adams, who explained the context of Paul's letters. Dr Adams explained how Paul, after his conversion, ends up in this city as a fanatic for the Gospel to convert others:

> I like to think of Paul as something like a boxer – keeps getting knocked down continually, but keeps getting back up, takes more punishment but keeps on fighting. He is zealous and ardent for the faith. He is a fanatic, and he's a fanatic for the Gospel.

Dr Adams continued by explaining how Paul wrote letters to address problems in the early church communities, but feels that he is writing with the Spirit's insight:

> Paul has a mentality that is similar to the Old Testament Prophets. He feels he is writing with the Spirit's insight, writing the Word of the Lord. It's the Word of the Lord for a particular

situation; but nevertheless, he feels he is writing with God's or the Spirit's insights.

However, Dr Adams also explained that Paul's scribes also played a role in writing his letters, and that the scribes could have had an influence on what was written down and attributed to Paul. Therefore, it was not always easy to distinguish between Paul's voice and those writing in his name.

The idea of multiple layers of editing was further developed in a discussion on the synoptic Gospels in which I examined the writings of the life of Jesus. To tell the story of the writing of the Gospels, in Rome I met up with my then Birmingham University colleague and New Testament expert Mark Goodacre to identify the context of each Gospel, the audience, author(s) and sociopolitical contexts. We began with the Gospel of Mark and Dr Goodacre painted the picture of the author(s) and their general motivations:

> We don't know precisely who Mark is. He does not sign his book at the end and say this is where I have come from and this is who I am. But you can pick up clues from the Gospel about who he is. It's quite possible, that Mark like many of the other Christians in this period actually has personally experienced persecution. It's very realistic and gripping, you know you can smell the dirt and the blood in Mark's Gospel. Some of it is because of the persecution, that Mark wants to write the first gospel, because you have got to try and make sense of it and what better way of making sense of it than telling the story of the first real martyr of this new faith, Jesus himself. . . . The thing is, when you are looking at the Gospels we don't know that its true there are no independent archeological records where you can check things up, no one was out there with a camcorder recording these things, there was not even anyone taking notes as far as we know. So a lot of it we are being asked to take on trust. I don't think Mark himself is an eyewitness, for a start, he never says, 'I did this or I did that' so there is not any claiming to be an eyewitness. But what I do think you find in Mark is some quite interesting reminiscences from some of the earliest people that were involved with Jesus.

Goodacre then explained the difficulties surrounding authorship, how schools of authors developed Gospels, and how the Gospels, rather than being eyewitness accounts, represent the theologizing of the early church. However, the question of historicity is not something to be feared, as Goodacre proposed:

> Just because something (a Gospel) is trying to tell a particular story to a particular group of people does not mean it's not got any history in it.

I wanted to know how issues of authorship intersected with gender politics, that is, if gender was prevalent in questions of Biblical authorship. In Rome, Fr Stephen Pisano of the Pontifical Biblical Institute told me that the Holy Spirit inspired the canon and that the exclusion of women was part of the Lord 'working in mysterious ways'. I did not agree with him and set out to investigate gender bias in canon formation. I travelled to Boston in the United States to speak to Professor Karen King about one account of the Gospel from a female author, the deutero-canonical Gospel of Mary. Professor King explained how the Gospel was written in the name of a woman, and offers an alternative view of the relationship of Jesus to His disciples. That is to say a more dynamic image of Jesus as one who embraced male and female followers as equals. It became clear to me that while the Spirit may indeed have been present in the development, and that canon formation was a complex and lengthy process with numerous checks and balances throughout church history, the Spirit is also present today encouraging us to see through the biases that were present back then. In a piece to camera I said:

> At this point, it seems to me that canon formation is all about a group of rich and powerful people putting a text together and deciding whom they want to include in orthodoxy and whom they want to exclude. Now where is the Spirit in this? You know what I think: the Spirit is at work today. It gives you the ability to see the ignorance, the bias and the prejudice that was involved and raise questions about the legitimacy and accuracy of what took place. That's the power of the Spirit for me – to see through what was really going on.

# New perception: A hermeneutic of suspicion

In closing the film, I wanted to encourage my intended audience to think about reading the Bible as a complex text, consisting of numerous genres and authors spanning hundreds of years. By identifying the contested authorship and question of gender exclusion, I hoped that the audience would be primed for a more radical challenge. To this end, the close of the film included the encoding of a new perception of the Bible – a hermeneutic of suspicion[2] or a critical assessment of the motives behind every text and interpretation. A hermeneutic of suspicion is aimed at strengthening interpretation by encouraging a discussion of the motivation and layers of editing behind any interpretation. As such it encourages all readers never to accept any interpretation without considering issues of power lurking in the background. I ended by warning of the dangers of ignoring this kind of critical thinking:

> Who wrote the Bible? Well, it's a complex question and it takes some thinking through. And that tells me that to have faith in the world today is to ask questions and never have the wool pulled over your eyes.

Yet, a hermeneutic of suspicion in and of itself can lead to an unbridled scepticism of the Bible or even the rejection of Scripture. When this approach to interpretation is employed as a stand-alone methodology that merely interrogates Scripture, it can undermine thoughtful approaches to questioning Scripture in a holistic fashion that includes both pastoral and theological aims. Therefore, a hermeneutic of suspicion is only one facet of a more comprehensive approach to biblical exorcism. In all of my film work that encodes exorcism, a hermeneutic of suspicion is necessarily followed by an approach that enables a new perception and new interpretation of the biblical text. Indeed, it is the use of a questioning approach to Scripture that provides the space for a new outlook and reading of the Bible. This second step will become more apparent through my sketch below of a more recent biblical documentary. Thus, on the surface, *Who Wrote the Bible?* is a critique of fundamentalism in interpretation and an affirmation of critical approaches to the text as part of a search for a liberating exegesis. It was also an example of an encoded exorcism of black Pentecostalism, specifically, a rebuke of academic-theology phobia.

## *The Book of Revelation: The Last Judgment* (2010)

The second example of exorcizing the effects of colonial Christianity is *The Book of Revelation: The Last Judgment*. This film was an examination of the Book of Revelation as part of a series on the Bible in which each programme consisted of a personal reflection on a Book of the Bible. The commissioning editor asked me to explore the Book of Revelation from my own theological perspective. This commission provided a license to make explicit a range of black theological readings of the Book. As was the case with *Who Wrote the Bible?* I began by identifying my context, then engaged in a critique to arrive at a new perception.

## How I was taught

Referring to my upbringing in the Pilgrim Holiness Church, I reflected on how I was taught to read Revelation as a guidebook to the end of the world or through the correspondence approach.[3] In this frame, Revelation was used to find similarities between themes in the Book and events in the contemporary social world. As a result, my family spent an inordinate amount of time seeking out 'signs of the times' – that is trying to locate contemporary events in the Book of Revelation in order to work out how close we were to the return of Jesus. But this literal approach to the text was also a point of departure from the old ways:

> I was taught that the Book of Revelation was literal truth. But I believe there is more to it than the death and destruction most people know. I want to discover if this strange and confusing Book deserves its bad reputation, or whether centuries of misuse and abuse have obscured its true meaning.

This point of departure, however, also gestured towards a 'rebuke' of the lack of sustained critical thinking in light of biblical scholarship in black Pentecostalism and the need for a new approach to Scriptures.

## New interpretation

In search of a new interpretation, I began exploring various approaches to the Book but centred on a historical critical perspective. This approach argues that to make sense of Revelation we must understand the context of the author, and the social and political world in which he lived and addressed. To clarify this view, I spoke again to New Testament scholar, Dr Goodacre, who was by then based at Duke University in North America. He explained that the Book was apocalyptic literature, an unveiling of something otherwise hidden. Further, Goodacre argued that the Book worked best when understood as a testimony to those who had suffered under Roman rule. It uses 'picture language' (not unlike filmmakers) to paint the world in which they were living. But this did not mean that the Book had no relevance for today. On the contrary, when recontextualized, it has a recurring theme for each age and generation: it asserts that one should resist empire and tyranny wherever it is found.

But what did this text mean today? In order to contour a 'neo-apocalyptic' perspective or add contemporary relevance to this view of Revelation, I sought out examples of how diaspora blacks and political groups have reinterpreted the Book to support their struggles for justice.[4] The first example was from the Civil Rights Movement and the second from contemporary urban Boston, an American city that struggles against gang warfare.

I travelled to New York and retold the story of how certain black theologians in the middle of the twentieth century decided to side with the Black Power struggle, and in doing so gave birth to a Black Liberation Theology. I interviewed Professor James Cone, the noted father of Black Liberation Theology. Cone relayed how the Book of Revelation inspired theologians and activists, including Dr King, because of its resonance with their struggle:

> The key thing about the Book of Revelation and the oppressed is that John himself and the Christian churches he is writing to in the Book of Revelation are living under a similar situation

to which blacks perceived themselves to be living under. Black people did not have to go to seminary to know that the Bible spoke to them; they did not have to go to university to know that their situation was analogous to that of the poor, the weak, and the helpless within the Bible . . . Who was the *beast* in the black community? White supremacy, white power, and the US government which refused to acknowledge their right of citizenship. We were fighting for the right to vote in the 1960s.

Next I spoke to Rev. Eugene Rivers. Rivers came to national and international prominence for his work with at-risk young people in Boston in the 1990s. In voiceover, I introduced Rivers by setting the scene of the rise of the Ten Point Coalition, a coalition of clergy, law enforcement personnel, social workers and community activists that focused on reaching vulnerable urban youth:

In the early 1990s, stories of gang warfare and drug-related violence dominated the headlines of Boston's newspapers. Within the relatively poor Latino and African-American neighbourhoods of the city [of Boston], youth crime was spiralling out of control. In 1992, after a gang shooting at a funeral, a group of church ministers banded together to tackle the problem. What the police could not solve, the church would. The Reverend Eugene Rivers, a Pentecostal minister, was a founding member of the Ten Point Coalition.

In the late 1980s, the 'beast' of Revelation was no longer defined as white supremacy but as the capitalist system. For Rivers, the devouring forces he confronted on a daily basis – drug-fuelled violence within poor neighbourhoods – was a direct result of consumer capitalism. He thinks a consumerist society devours scare resources and sets communities against each other. Therefore, to collude with the mythologies of capitalism, such as unrestricted growth and conspicuous consumption, was to do the work of the 'beast':

One of the ways that we have taken some of the theological themes of Revelation and some of the images and symbols is to talk about the nature of the beast. The image of a source of evil that exists in the cosmos, in the world, whose bidding I may unwittingly do by acts of evil. When I go to prisons, dudes get it . . . 'Don't disrespect yourself by doing the work of the beast.' So the image of the beast now must be re-interpreted for a generation of young people who do not understand the nature of the evil and the system that's against them.

For Rivers, the 'beast' had to be tackled by radical intervention by church communities that encouraged working collaboratively and meaningfully with the local police to restrict criminal activity and support positive initiatives to reform young offenders. He alleged that the church often ignores the revolutionary imagery of the Book, particularly its egalitarian impulse at the end.

## New perception: Fighting injustice

In concluding the film, I sided with the vision of the Book as a book of hope – a resource for the quest for justice in the present:

I am now convinced that the last Book of the Bible is the most misunderstood Book in history. Today I cannot accept that terrifying literal interpretation that I was taught as a boy in the Pentecostal church. Everything I've discovered and learned has proven that the Book of Revelation is best not, and probably *should not* be read, as a guidebook to the end of the earth. Instead, I am with those revolutionaries from the early Christians onward who were inspired by its message to the oppressed and persecuted. Today, 2000 years on from John having his vision, I believe his message still speaks to all of us committed to building the new heaven and the new earth.

In short, the film called for a new perception of the Book as a resource for social justice. The fight against collusion and tyranny identified by John provided resources for present struggles from racial equality to the fight against environmental degradation. On a deeper level, the film encoded exorcism, how black Pentecostals might move beyond the confines of surface readings of the text[5] and embrace a more critical approaches to the text.

*Revelation*, like *Who Wrote the Bible?* was fundamentally a silencing of colonial Christianity's academic-theology phobia and a restoration of a 'right mind', which in this case was a more critical approach to scripture. The approach facilitated an understanding of the text as a complex document that nonetheless functions as a powerful redemptive resource for Pentecostals seeking to remedy social ills. By embracing this exorcism, I believe, black Pentecostalism in Britain can realize its full potential as a prophetic institution that seeks to liberate believers from all forms of oppression and can do so on the basis of being a witness to what it means to be 'free' in Christ – individually and communally.

# Conclusion: Towards an exorcism aesthetic

The publicity photo shoot was better than I thought. This was due in part to the preparation beforehand as well as the expertise of the photographer that day. Prior to the event, I had discussed with the producer of the documentary how we might best represent the core idea of the film in the publicity material. All documentaries have to have a publicity photo to promote the film in the media. In this case, the documentary in question was, *God is Black*, a two-part series on the rise of fundamentalist Christianity in Africa. The film chronicled the changing geopolitics of Christianity, and the rise of the global south as the new numerical powerhouse of Christianity at the turn of the twenty-first century.

We decided to reproduce an image of a black Jesus. The reason was to signify the title of the documentary, 'God is Black'. But we also wanted to communicate in the image the idea that all concepts about God are, in part, human efforts to express the infinite. Therefore, location and even imagination play an important role in doing theology. To convey this second meaning, we decided that the shoot would take place in an artist's studio and that the setting would include all the artist's paraphernalia such as brushes, paints and other materials.

So in the publicity photo (front cover), I stand in the foreground looking directly into the camera to invite the viewer into the scene. Wearing my customary black suit, I stand in the foreground, arms crossed with my chin perched on my hand to represent seriousness, intensity and engagement. The viewer might assume that having reflected on the construction behind me, I am about to comment on it or solicit the views of the spectator. In the background, a black dreadlocked Jesus adopts a classic (even romanticized) pose of the crucifixion event, but in this case, he is unaccompanied and stationed on top of an artist's trestle table. The exhibiting of Jesus, as an artistic practice implies not only a sense of reconstruction of the original crucifixion event but also that reconstruction is also a deeply subjective and creative enterprise.

The creation of the photograph is a metaphor for documentary filmmaking. This is because, as I have demonstrated in this book, documentary filmmaking is a constructed and also multi-vocal task. It is a construction in the sense that documentary filmmaking is always part record and part signifying practice. As such, filmmaking is subject to layers of editing and reworking so that the final product is a representation of what took place. The photograph was also a multi-vocal project. It was the result of the input of many individuals, but ultimately my role and positioning were central because I was the presenter of the film. Being in the foreground signified the centrality of my voice. Documentary production is also multi-vocal. There are many specialist involved in the process who make a film possible. However, central to every film is the role of the author or narrator. In this book, I have demonstrated how I went about the business of ensuring that my voice, narrative and perspective informed my documentary practice and also shaped my documentary canon. This book has disclosed how I encoded documentary films, so that while covering a range of subjects and disciplines across numerous films, my primary concern was to address my intended audience of black Pentecostals in Britain. I have contended that black Pentecostalism is bewitched by colonial Christianity and that my films are exorcisms.

# Summary

In this book, I have argued that colonial Christianity was complicit with slavery and imperialism and produced a corrupt version of the Christian faith for West Indian slaves and their descendants in the Caribbean. I have interpreted this corrupt missionary activity and gospel through the idioms of witchcraft, so that 'bewitchment' is diagnosed through the rapacious and avaricious tropes of the cannibal and zombie. Applied to colonial Christianity, I have argued that both these utterly compromised forms of Christianity (Catholics, Protestants) 'ate' African substance, that is, it participated in slavery's economic devouring of Africans during the slave trade. To add insult to injury, colonial Christianity also sought to create Christian zombies – compliant Christian blacks who would not think too much about their faith. I have suggested that rather than ending with the abolition of slavery, the influence of colonial Christianity is still experienced among the Caribbean diaspora in Britain, especially among African Caribbean black Pentecostals. Black Pentecostal bewitchment, therefore, represents a reconfiguration of colonial Christianity's bewitchment but in the very real and present forms of apoliticism and anti-intellectualism: two undesirable features of this tradition that I have described as non-prophetic ministry and academic-theology phobia, respectively.

I have argued that my documentary films are acts of exorcism of the bewitchment of colonial Christianity. Making a centrepiece of Jesus' exorcisms in Mark's Gospel, I have demonstrated that exorcism is both theological and political. To exorcize is not only a sign of divine power but also a driving out of evil in both the physical body and the social world. This interpretation of exorcism is given a decisive anti-colonial leitmotif when interpreted through the lens of postcolonial biblical studies. The result of this combination, exorcism and postcolonial hermeneutics, is that we may think of Jesus' exorcisms as political activity designed to reveal the evil of the colonialism and how it was to be removed by healing acts that restored sanity to individuals and gestured towards the expulsion of the occupying force from the land.

Biblical exorcism is translated into a visual practice for use in documentary film. In order to do so, I have appropriated the encoding/decoding traditions of black Pentecostalism. Black Pentecostalism in Britain has a convention of inscribing theological ideas on cultural products in places of worship. This transfer of meaning is never arbitrary but represents deliberate attempts to fix meaning for the sake of creating theological-cultural products that point beyond themselves to another reality. Based on this practice, I have encoded religious meaning onto documentary film. The religious meanings in this case arise from the emancipatory framework. The emancipatory framework is a contextual way of speaking about oppression and liberation as Christian modes of though and action. In the emancipatory framework, oppression is bewitchment – the continued evil of colonial Christianity in black Pentecostalism, and liberation is exorcism – a theological-political reality focused on the removal of occupying forces in individual and social spheres. I have contended that encoding the emancipatory framework in documentary film, inadvertently, creates a new mode of documentary.

This book also revealed a new mode of filmmaking that I term documentary conjure. Conjure describes a dynamic process in black Atlantic cultures, where religious meaning is attributed to cultural products. When actualized or conjured these products have spiritual dynamism. Applied to documentary, conjure describes the inscribing of the emancipatory framework on documentary film for the sake of religious-political healing – the exorcism of black Pentecostalism.

The exorcism of black Pentecostals takes place in the narrative of my documentary films. Through the auspices of the double-voice, the narrative at a subliminal level reveals the encoding of bewitchment and exorcism. In the political films, I seek to challenge the presence of non-prophetic ministry with the exorcizing presence of *prophetic ministry*. Prophetic ministry features in all but one of the political films and, by way of illustration, I reveal the prophetic in *Empire Pays Back* and *The Great African Scandal*. Similarly, the Bible documentaries are the site for challenging academic-theology phobia by embracing *academic theological practice*. Academic theological practice takes the form of developing not only an appreciation of critical thought, but also the aligning of the Biblical text with social justice. The Bible films, *Who Wrote the Bible?* and *The Book of Revelation: The Final Judgment* were mobilized to exemplify exorcism of academic-theology phobia. In concluding this study, I want to make three recommendations. The first two, a call for political engagement and theological education, are obvious outcomes of the exorcism trope. However, the third, the call for an exorcism aesthetic in black Pentecostal churches, is a less obvious move. This is because it goes against the grain of black churches' use of images in places of worship. Even so, I believe it represents a legitimate theological practice that, despite its radicalism, is in line with the signifying traditions of black Pentecostalism outlined above. Naturally, to outline this innovation, I spend more time reflecting on this third point than the first two recommendations.

# For political engagement

Implicit in this study is a desire for black Pentecostal political engagement based on a commitment to social and economic justice at home and abroad. This is not a new demand or concern and it would be disingenuous to suggest that all black Pentecostals have been completely silent on political matters. On the contrary, there have been a few *individuals* who have taken seriously the prophetic role of the church and become leaders in particular fields. For example, black Pentecostals are playing a prominent role in the London Citizens, a leading community-organizing charity in Britain.[1] Equally important is the political role of Bishop Derek Webley in Birmingham. Bishop Webley is a bishop in the New Testament Church of God. For a period of time, he was the chair of the West Midlands Police Authority, and in 2012 the runner-up for the post of Police Commissioner of the West Midlands Police Force. Moreover, the victorious candidate appointed a black Pentecostal, Yvonne Mosquito, as one of his deputies. Rev. George Hargreaves has worked consistently with mainstream Christian political organizations including the Christian Party and also with the centre right, UK Independence Party (UKIP). Finally, Dr Joe Aldred, who is also a bishop in the Church of God of Prophesy, has engaged in raising awareness of the need for political engagement in his role at Churches Together in Britain and Ireland. But these individual efforts do not compensate for the historic structural indolence of major denominations and their leadership. As mentioned above, the need for meaningful black Pentecostal political activity has existed in the black community for some time. What is new here is the framing of this predicament. In this book, I have suggested that we view non-prophetic ministry as bewitchment or the consequence of captivity to a malevolent spirituality.

# For theological education

I also recommend that black Pentecostal churches take seriously theological education as a fundamental necessity of ministerial formation. The basic theological courses that currently exist must be replaced by contextual theological education. A contextual approach takes seriously the particular needs of black Pentecostal ministerial training, including the necessary academic tools for urban ministry. But the issue is more than just raising the standard of education among clergy; it is also a matter of what kind of theological education is foregrounded. A contextual approach also means that we have to ensure that the courses and modules are structured to relate to the needs and issues of the urban landscape. A good model of a contextual and staged approach is the Centre for Black Ministries and Leadership headed by Lynette Mullings at the Queen's Ecumenical Foundation in Birmingham.[2] The Queen's model, while offering education and training for black clergy from all denominations, is in fact a mission of an ecumenical college that began in the 1987 as a result of the work of Anglican priest and scholar Rev. John Wilkinson, and was further developed by myself in the late 1990s and by Dr Anthony Reddie, a black Methodist scholar, in the Noughties. Thus, the Queen's centre is an example of exorcism at work from the context of both black and white Christians.

I also want to propose a new requirement for ministry – that each major denomination make a Bachelor's degree equivalent the minimum academic requirement for ordination, and that mandatory educational development is introduced for new and existing clergy. Additionally, priority should be given to academically qualified or theologically trained people to run educational departments on behalf of denominations. Finally, churches should make clear to congregations the distinction between earned and honorary degrees to ensure that these communities of faith are not misled into believing that honorary qualifications reflect academic theological competence. As part of this clarification of existing qualifications, the current trend of black British Pentecostal clergy 'buying' doctorates from unrecognized and dubious institutions in North America must be shunned. These recommendations if adopted would, I believe, begin to align black Pentecostalism with the radical potential of its Azusa Street origins.[3]

## For an exorcism aesthetic

My third recommendation concerns aesthetics. I want to prescribe an exorcism aesthetic. An exorcism aesthetic is one way that my documentary as exorcism can be adopted by church communities seeking to rid themselves of the colonial past. I want to therefore show how conjure can be translated into a visual artistic practice within the church. Specifically, I want to cultivate an exorcism aesthetic expressed in church art. This idea is not as far-fetched as it may seem. After all, Pentecostal aesthetic practices, which, as I have demonstrated in Chapter Eight, willingly combine theological ideas with a range of artistic practices that are more implicit than explicit. I simply desire for these practice to become less opaque and channelled into the use of visual art in places of worship. To help make this leap of faith, I draw on theoretical tools and practical examples. In terms of theory, first, I will show how visual art functions as a Christian picture language or religious symbolism. Thought of this way, we can begin to imagine how an exorcism aesthetic may take form as 'picture language about God'. However, this picture language must connect with political realities that engulf the world of scripture and the social world in which faith is lived out. To undertake this political concern, my second theoretical tool is the notion of 'committed-art', the black political tradition of producing art with political meanings. Combined, religious symbols and committed-art provide the theoretical underpinnings for a theological-political artistic practice capable of conveying the types of social and individual exorcisms described in Chapter Four and elaborated upon in Chapters Eleven and Twelve. To move from theory to practice, I want to provide two existing examples of an exorcism aesthetic. The first is the example of an exorcism aesthetic in a specific piece of black British art, 'The Ghosts of Christendom' by Keith Piper. The second is an example of the visual art practice at Trinity United Church of Christ in Chicago, as revealed in my documentary *God Bless You Barack Obama* (2010).

Christian visual art, such as images (paintings, sculptures) of Jesus, biblical scenes or concepts about God in history have a particular theological role. Art is 'picture language' and as such has the ability to convey ideas about God, inspire devotion and enthuse action.

But like all theological language, art is also limited in its ability to reveal the divine. This is because human language is inept at completely capturing the qualities of God. Consequently, the biblical writers draw on human experience to describe the nature and being of God, for example, the idea of God as 'father'. Thus, images of God tell us as much about ourselves as they do who we perceive God to be. Religious art is therefore always 'two-sided'.[4] Even so, religious art has the capacity to inspire devotion and foremost action, and these outcomes interest me. To this end, I want to review the characteristics of religious symbols to help us think about religious art as a form of exorcism.

According to Paul Tillich, religious symbols have at least six characteristics, which I will briefly outline.[5] First, as picture language Christian art is symbolic. As symbols, works of art are inscribed with theological ideas that anticipate a faith reaction from the viewer. This is not a new idea for black Pentecostals because, as I have shown above, theological ideas are routinely inscribed on cultural products (music/broadcast equipment, décor, attire) so that the artefact communicates meaning and represents something else – it is a symbol. Second, religious symbols point to a reality beyond themselves. For example, reflecting on our discussion of black church aesthetics in Chapter Eight, we can say that the dress codes in black Pentecostalism are also religious symbols because they are signifiers of holiness (another reality). Religious symbols, however, differ from signs because they participate in the world to which they point. In this sense, they are not arbitrary or haphazard but bear some comparison to what they signify. In other words, religious symbols are iconic (Greek word for 'image') or have some resemblance to that which is signified. As we shall see below, the religious imagery of Keith Piper is iconic because it seeks to imitate perceived attributes of God.

Third, symbols reveal what might have otherwise been hidden. There are layers of reality that cannot be comprehended without religious symbols. This perspective has generally been ignored in black Pentecostal places of worship, particularly with respect to the display of large iconic religious portraits of Jesus or the paintings of scenes from the Bible. But the revelatory use of art is not completely shunned. This is because church music as an art form enables black Pentecostals to experience God in ways that are not possible through other media. For instance, as was illustrated in Chapter Five, worship at New Church was a vehicle for channelling knowledge about God; that is, it was revelatory. Fourth, because they are revelatory, religious symbols also unlock aspects of our own being. They disclose otherwise hidden aspects of our soul. Returning to the example of black Pentecostal décor, we can surmise that the lack of imagery and plain simplicity of style in black Pentecostal churches is also a revelation about the human condition – humanity as an empty vessel to be filled by the Holy Spirit. But as we shall see below, religious symbols can also reveal problematic predicaments such as the paradoxical role of Christianity in the lives of blacks in the diaspora. The penultimate characteristic is that religious symbols cannot be manufactured. The symbol's meaning is stored up over time and entrusted to the symbol. We might think of the cross of Jesus as such a symbol because of the meanings that have been associated with it and the powerful resonance it has for Christians and non-Christians alike.

Finally, religious symbols have a life span. That is to say they emerge, develop and eventually fade away. For instance, the image of Jesus has changed over time, just as the geographical centre of Christianity has moved from east to west and now to the southern hemisphere, as have the growing number of adherents and Christian intellectuals. Similarly, the images of Jesus have accompanied the development of Christianity and as a result some images have emerged and then disappeared.

Religious art is therefore a profoundly important medium for communicating religious truths. However, the use of art in Christianity has not been uniform or without controversy. Theological traditions have come to interpret images, icons and representations in history from numerous perspectives and social locations, and have revealed a fractious history that is as equally appreciative as it is dismissive.[6]

Religious art is not created in a political vacuum, for all art is in some way bound up with the social and political world. Take, for example, one of the most popular images of Jesus in the twentieth century, the Werner Salman portrait of the mid-twentieth century. In this painting, Jesus is given the physical characteristics of a Northern European man with flowing blond hair and gentle blue eyes. However, by recasting Jesus the Palestinian Jew as a twentieth-century Aryan, the image cannot escape resonance, even unwittingly, with discourses of white supremacy in eighteenth- and nineteenth-century European missionary endeavours in Africa and the Caribbean, and mid-twentieth-century European anti-Semitism. However, despite the inevitability of political interpretation of art, not all artists seek to produce art that is political, and this issue leads to our second theoretical tool, committed-art.

There are artists who claim to avoid the political, while others suggest that avoidance is impossible. In black Atlantic cultures, this debate has given rise to two competing schools of thought. On the one hand, there exists a group, the committed-art school, who believe that art *must* reflect the political aspirations of black people. In contrast, the detached-art school argues for the primacy of art over politics. It stresses the universal and human dimensions of art.[7] This debate is also played out in the United Kingdom. As cultural theorist Gen Doy shows in *Black Visual Culture: Modernity and Postmodernity*, the discussion is distilled into a tension between those who prefer to describe their work as 'black' or as an open signifier designating the non-white 'other', and those who want to move beyond blackness by describing their work as diasporan, ethnic and hybrid.[8] However, while the motives of this second camp may be apolitical, their commitment does not inhibit a political interpretation of their work, or evade the question of how their work relates to other discourses such as 'race', gender, sexuality and class. In this sense, political *interpretation* is inescapable. Not surprisingly, I am interested in the committed-art school and how this tradition lends itself to the creation of an exorcism aesthetic.

I want to combine the notion of religious symbols and the committed-art school to sketch a threefold guide for an exorcism aesthetic, which I will now outline. First, it is self-evident that an exorcism aesthetic must be grounded in black political reality and the quest for justice. The political reality must prioritize the struggle against colonial Christianity in the present. Second, exorcism as a religious symbol points towards a reality beyond itself. In this case, reflect divine engagement with the struggle. Third, exorcism as a religious symbol also opens us up to a new reality of the black Pentecostal condition, that is, the practice for an on-going exorcism of the colonial past.

# Keith Piper

The first example of an exorcism aesthetic in visual art is found in Keith Piper's 'The Ghosts of Christendom' (1990–1; Figure 1). In this case the artwork in question seeks to explore the two sides of black faith – namely that Christianity was an oppressive force ('put on') as well as the raw material for positive transformation ('cast out').

Piper explores the theological-political intersections at work in slave trade and Christianity. In describing the piece, the Birmingham art gallery states that it is 'a . . . variety of photographic images including the figure of a slave ship occupied by slaves, a crucifix,

**FIGURE 1** *'The Ghosts of Christendon Past'* 1991.
Courtesy of the Artist

and the feet of the artist'. Furthermore, 'within the artist's feet are crucifixes akin to the nails hammered into Jesus' feet'.

What is important here is that the image points to a reality beyond itself and expresses a paradox of faith. Christianity is portrayed as an oppressive, corrupting force complicit with the terror of the Middle Passage and slavery. In the language of this book, it identifies the occult of Christianity and its 'ghosts that are very much with us today'. But the image can also be read incarnationally or in ways that image how Jesus is present in the lives of black people in the past and present. This incarnational interpretation arises from viewing the presence of black bodies inside the cross as a statement that makes contemporaneous the treatment of slaves with the passion of Christ. Moreover, Jesus is cast in the form of the oppressed, the 'least of these' (Matthew 25.40). Thus we may surmise that in this artistic interpretation, Jesus is not only sufferer but also ultimately the redeemer, a God of the oppressed. The image opens up a new world of meaning for black Pentecostals including the deep suffering of the past and Christianity's complicity and also the fact that we cannot ignore the underside of Christianity, its collusion with the empire's occult, because 'naming the demon' is essential to exorcizing it.

## Trinity United Church of Christ

The second example provides us with another example of exorcism at work, but this time in the context of church art. This example of a working exorcism aesthetic appears in my documentary on the faith of Barack Obama (*God Bless You Barack Obama*). Central to the narrative of the documentary was the role of Chicago's Trinity United Church of Christ in the president's faith formation. The motivation for making the film came straight from the head of the history department at BBC2. In our first meeting, she said, 'We want to know why Americans are so fascinated with the faith of their leaders, what Barack Obama believes, and, if at all possible, what relationships exist between his faith and politics'. My exploration, however, was placed within the recent history of faith and politics in America, and specifically the relationship between Barack Obama and Trinity. Trinity was the church that Barack Obama attended for over 20 years, which also became the focus of attention during the 2008 election due to a controversy that arose between Barack Obama and Rev. Jeremiah Wright, its pastor at that time.[9]

One immediately becomes aware that aesthetics are grounded in a political reality in this church. When approaching the building from the highway, one observes the African liberation flags adorning the building, which reflect a deeper theo-politics realized inside of the building. Inside I was able to capture on film a sophisticated use of religious symbols at Trinity.

At the descriptive level, there were heroic scenes from black history and black Christian experience painted on stained glass windows, flanking both sides of the building. These images were inclusive in terms of faith perspectives in that they included depictions of the black nationalism of Marcus Garvey and the Islamic faith of Malcolm X. Likewise, in the foyer outside of the sanctuary on the upper level stood a large image depicting a reworking of Da Vinci's *The Last Supper*. In this picture, the 13 characters sit around a table with their faces covered in traditional masks associated with traditional African cultures and religions.

At the symbolic level, the art at Trinity United Church of Christ points to a black liberation theology aesthetic. At the time of filming in 2010, the theological orientation of Trinity was Black Liberation Theology. Black Liberation Theology is a complex tradition of thought and action and can be described generally as a contextual theology that makes its starting point the experience(s) of God in the history, culture and the experience of black people. Liberation describes the work of God in the world to free humanity from the bondage of sin. Sin is not only individual but also structural, and black theology foregrounds the sins of racism, sexism, classism and homophobia. At Trinity, liberation is the central and defining motif, which informs what is considered worthy of depiction or considered good taste for the artwork in the building. In this specific case, the images in the stained glass that portray the story of African American social and political history disclose God's abiding presence in the multifarious political struggles of African Americans.

The art at Trinity embodies the exorcism aesthetic. But in this case, the new reality is that the site of healing is memory. This is because the focus on African heritage, and also the historic journey from slavery to full citizenship, hints at an all-too-familiar struggle over memory. As discussed in Chapter Six, struggles over memory, particularly the memory of slavery, represent a new battlefield for a very old struggle. Trinity's emphasis on remembering black history in visual art is therefore, on one level, an exorcism of an evil I have termed 'memory cannibalism'.

One of the things that these examples reveal is that it is possible to construct and actualize an exorcism aesthetic. However, for black Pentecostals, for this to happen, it is necessary for them to undergo an internal exorcism, in order to 'destroy the yoke' of colonial Christianity.

## For those who are *not* black Pentecostals

My final recommendation is for progressive whites to embrace exorcism as a modality for confronting colonial history and its continued impact on Christian theology and church life in Britain. While a handful of white theologians have begun to recognize the existence of Black Liberation Theology the vast majority have failed to take seriously the ways that British theological ideas in Britain were crafted inside of the British Empire and are therefore infected with the empire's occult logic. For instance, at the time of writing, there was no British equivalent to James W. Perkinson's *White Theology: Outing Supremacy in Modernity* (2004). Such is the enduring power of colonial Christianity in white British theology that even six decades of black Caribbean, Asian and more recently African Christian rejection by British churches have failed to alert it to the fundamental reality that the theological categories in British Christian theology are faulty – they have failed to produce a Christian tradition that seriously reflects on 'race' colonial history and the post-war failure to embrace the black and brown strangers. In fact the opposite is true, white theology in Britain has not decolonized itself and is therefore still very much anti-black. Hence, I am calling on progressive white theologians to end the selective historical and theological amnesia, and exorcize their colonial past and produce exorcized white theologies that have the categories of thought and action to embrace their black and brown brothers and sisters and strive towards a new inclusive British Christian theology and church life.

As I have suggested throughout this book, the aesthetic has the potential to remake the world[10] and it is in this spirit of renewal and re-creation that I am exhorting not just black Pentecostals in Britain, but all Christians to develop a new picture language to overcome not only colonial Christianity, but all forms of tyranny that seek to 'steal, kill and destroy' (John 10.10) all of God's children.

# NOTES

## Introduction

1  F. Fanon (1990), *The Wretched of the Earth*. London: Penguin, p. 206.

2  S. Hall (1980), 'Encoding/decoding', in Centre for Contemporary Cultural Studies, *Culture, Media, Language*. London: Routledge, pp. 128–38; G. Rose (2011), *Visual Methodologies: An Introduction to Researching with Visual Materials* (3rd edn). London: Sage, pp. 20–7.

3  A. Rosenthal and J. Corner (eds) (2005), *New Challenges for Documentary* (2nd edn). Manchester: Manchester University Press, introduction; M. Renov (ed.) (1993), *Theorizing Documentary*. London: Routledge, introduction.

4  J. Corner (2005), 'Television, Documentary and the Category of the Aesthetic', in A. Rosenthal and J. Corner (eds), *New Challenges for Documentary* (2nd edn). Manchester: Manchester University Press, pp. 48–59.

5  G. Lynch (2005), *Understanding Theology and Popular Culture*. Oxford: Blackwell; K. Cobb (2005), *The Blackwell Guide to Theology and Popular Culture*, Blackwell Publishing: Oxford; D. B. Forbes and J. H. Mahan (2000), *Religion and Popular Culture in America*. Berkeley: University of California Press.

6  See reviews of this perspective in A. Reddie (2012), *Black Theology*. London: SCM; C. Shanahan (2010), *Voices from the Borderland: Re-imagining Cross-cultural Urban Theology in the Twenty-first Century*. London: Equinox.

7  M. Karenga (2002), *Introduction to Black Studies* (2nd edn). Los Angeles, CA: University of Sankore Press, p. 398; R. Beckford (2006), *Jesus Dub: Theology, Music and Social Change*. Abingdon: Routledge, p. 149ff; Lynch, *Understanding Theology*, p. 40.

8  I am appropriating Frantz Fanon's idea with regard to 'race' but substituting it for 'white theology'. F. Fanon (1991), *Black Skins White Masks* (2nd edn). London: Pluto, p. 116.

9  A good example of this theological orientation is found in J. W. Perkinson (2004), *White Theology: Outing Supremacy in Modernity*. London: Palgrave Macmillan.

10  Reddie, *Black Theology*, pp. 64–71.

11  R. Beckford (2001), *God of the Rhatid: Redeeming Rage*. London: DLT.

12  M. Wilkinson and S. M. Studebaker (2010), *A Liberating Spirit: Pentecostals and Social Action in North America*. Eugene, OR: Pickwick.

13  A. Anderson (2004), *An Introduction to Global Pentecostalism*. Cambridge: Cambridge University Press.

14  J. H. Stanfield (2011), *Black Reflective Sociology: Epistemology, Theory and Methodology*. Walnut Creek, CA: Left Coast; P. H. Collins (1990), *Black Feminist Thought: Knowledge, Consciousness and the Politics of Empowerment*. London: Routledge.

15  G. Rose (2012), *Visual Methodologies: An Introduction to Researching with Visual Materials*. London: Sage, p. 26; S. Hall (1997), 'The Work of Representation', in S. Hall (ed.), *Representation: Cultural Representations and Signifying Practices*. London: Sage, p. 35.

16  S. Burke (2010), *The Death and Return of the Author: Criticism and Subjectivity in Barthes, Foucault, and Derrida* (3rd edn). Edinburgh: Edinburgh University Press.

17  For example, the excellent book on religion and media, G. Lynch and J. Mitchell (eds) (2012), *Religion, Media and Culture: A Reader*. London: Routledge, is exclusively a reflection on media from theorists and analysts with no discernable substantial input from cultural practitioners or media professionals.

18  S. Ortner (1984), 'Theory in Anthropology since the Sixties', *Comparative Studies in Society and History*, 26 (1), 126–66; P. Bourdieu (1977), *Outline of a Theory of Practice*. Cambridge: Cambridge University Press.

# Chapter 1

1  H. Rosen (1998), *Speaking from Memory: The Study of Autobiographical Discourse*. Stoke on Trent: Trentham Books, p. 30.

2  M. Foucault (1990), *The History of Sexuality, Vol. 1: An Introduction*. Robert Hurley (trans.). New York: Vintage Books, pp. 95–6; J. Curran and J. Seaton (2009), *Power Without Responsibility: Press, Broadcasting and the Internet in Britain*. London: Routledge.

3  A. Kobayashi (2003), 'GPC Ten Years On: Is Self-reflexivity Enough?' *Gender, Place and Culture*, 10 (4), 345–9.

4  R. Miles (1993), *Racism after Race Relations*. London: Routledge, p. 135.

5  S. Malik (2002), *Representing Black Britain: Black and Asian Images on Television*. London: Sage, pp. 70–1.

6  S. Lambert (1982), *Channel 4: Television with a Difference?* London: British Film Institute, pp. 144–6; D. Hobson (2008), *Channel 4: The Early Years and the Jeremy Isaacs Legacy*. London: I.B.Tauris, pp. 68–70.

7  For an example of the subtle shift see, R. Ferguson (1998), *Representing Race: Ideology, Identity and the Media*. London: Bloomsbury Academic, pp. 181–90.

8  M. E. L. Bush (2011), *Everyday Forms of Whiteness: Understanding Race in a 'Post-Racial World'* (2nd edn). Plymouth: Rowman and Littlefield; W. C. Rich (2013), *The Post-Racial Society is Here: Recognition, Critics and the Nation-State*. London: Routledge.

9  S. Ali (2003), *Mixed-Race, Post-Race: Gender, New Ethnicities and Cultural Practices*. Oxford: Berg.

10  T. Wise (2010), *Colorblind: The Rise of Post-Racial Politics and the Retreat from Racial Equity*. San Francisco, CA: City Lights Books.

11  Even within this genre, a critique was possible. See S. Dunn (2008), *Baad Bitches and Sassy Supermamas: Black Power Action Films*. Chicago: University of Illinois Press, pp. 1–55; M. J. Koven (2010), *Blaxsploitation Films*. Harpenden, Herts: Kamera Books, pp. 10–13.

12  E. Chambers (2012), *Things Done Change: The Cultural Politics of Recent Black Artists in Britain*. New York and Amsterdam: Rodopi, p. 97ff; J. Nesbitt (2010), *Chris Ofili*. London: Tate.

13  S. Hall (ed.) (1997), *Representation: Cultural Representations and Signifying Practices*. London: Sage, pp. 1–13; M. Sturken and L. Cartwright (eds) (2001), *Practices of Looking: An Introduction to Visual Culture*. Oxford: Oxford University Press, pp. 21–5.

14  See S. Hall and T. Jefferson (2006), *Resistance through Rituals: Youth Subcultures in Post-War Britain* (2nd edn). London:

Routledge; P. Gilroy (1993), *The Black Atlantic: Modernity and Double Consciousness*. London: Verso.

15 P. H. Collins (1998), *Fighting Words: Black Women and the Search for Justice*. Minneapolis: University of Minnesota Press, p. 14.

16 Ibid., p. 14.

17 See bell hooks discussion of 'the gaze' as black kinesis in b. hooks (1992), *Black Looks: Race and Representation*. Cambridge, MA: South End; K. R. Johnson (1971), *Black Kinesics – Some Non-verbal Patterns in Black Culture. Florida F/L Reporter*, 9 (1 and 2) (Spring/Fall), 17–20.

18 Quoted in, J. Webb, T. Schirato and G. Danaher (2002), *Understanding Bourdieu*. London: Sage, p. 25.

19 P. Bourdieu (1992), 'Thinking about Limits', *Theory, Culture and Society*, 9, 37–49.

20 Ibid.

21 S. A. Smith (2009), *British Black Gospel: The Foundations of this Vibrant UK Sound*. Oxford: Monarch Books.

22 According to D. Dixon (2005), 'Black Theology Forum', Research paper, Queens College.

23 G. Martin and J. Greennough (2011), *A Boy, A Journey, A Dream: The Story of Basil Meade and the London Community Gospel Choir*. 1st edn). Oxford, UK and Grand Rapids, MI: Monarch Books. pp. 117–33.

24 C. A. Kirk-Duggan (1997), *Exorcizing Evil: A Womanist Perspective on the Spirituals*. Maryknoll, NY: Orbis Books; J. H. Cone (1992), *The Spiritual and the Blues: An Interpretation*. Maryknoll, NY: Orbis Books.

25 E. Lott (1995), *Love and Theft: Blackface Minstrely and the American Working Class*. New York: Oxford University Press, pp. 15–18.

26 M. Pickering (2001), *Stereotyping: The Politics of Representation*. London: Palgrave Macmillan; C. Stangor and C. Crandall (eds) (2013), *Stereotyping and Prejudice*. Florence, KY: Psychology.

27 The most recent study on religions broadcasting by Ruth Deller does not 'whiten' religious broadcasting or the representation of mainstream Christianity. See R. A. Deller (2012), *Faith in View: Religion and Spirituality in Factual British Television 2000–2009*. Doctoral thesis, Sheffield Hallam University. See also as examples of text that fail to acknowledge whiteness in representation of Christians on television in Britain, A. Quicke and J. Quicke (1993),

*Hidden Agendas: The Politics of Religious Broadcasting in Britain, 1987–1991*. Doncaster, UK: Dominion King Grant. The Archbishop of Canterbury (1986), *Religious Broadcasting Today*. London, UK: Centre for the Study of Religion and Society.

28 I am referring to the intersection of ethnicity and sexuality in the Curse of Ham narrative in the book of Genesis. For a detailed analysis of the interplay between blackness, sexuality and slavery see, D. M. Goldenberg (2005), *The Curse of Ham: Race and Slavery in Early Judaism, Christianity and Islam*. Princeton, NJ: Princeton University Press; S. R. Haynes (2002), *Noah's Curse: Biblical Justification of American Slavery*. Oxford: Oxford University Press.

29 See www.christian.org.uk/news/bbc-accused-of-anti-christian-bias-by-viewers/; also see http://metro.co.uk/2010/07/12/bbc-defends-eastenders-lucas-plot-after-anti-christian-complaints-rise-445106/

30 D. J. Austin-Broos (1997), *Jamaica Genesis: Religion and the Politics of Moral Orders*. Chicago: University of Chicago Press.

31 Austin-Broos terms this the 'trickster' motif to describe this dynamic; *Jamaica Genesis*, p. 12.

32 C. Jackson (2010), *Violence, Visual Culture, and the Black Male Body*. London: Routledge, introduction.

33 Ibid., p. 6.

34 Ethicist, Victor Anderson, uses the term postmodern blackness to describe a commitment to black diversity and multiplicity. See V. Anderson (1997), *Beyond Ontological Blackness: Essays in African American Religious and Cultural Criticism*. New York/London: Continuum. Spivak coins the term 'strategic essentialism' to describe a black essentialism for political engagement. See M. Sanders (2006), *Gayatri Chakravorty Spivak: Live Theory*. London/New York: Continuum.

35 D. Hopkins (1999), *Introducing Black Theology of Liberation*. Maryknoll, NY: Orbis Books.

36 S. Y. Mitchem (2002), *Introducing Womanist Theology*. Maryknoll, NY: Orbis Books.

37 S. Hall (1997), 'The Spectacle of the "Other"', in S. Hall (ed.), *Representation: Cultural Representations and Signifying Practices*. London: Sage, pp. 223–90.

38 Ibid.

39 Chambers, *Things Done Change*, p. 72.

40 Hall 'The Spectacle of the "Other"', pp. 223–90.

41 Ibid.
42 Ibid., p. 274.

# Chapter 2

1  C. H. Long (1986), *Significations*. Minneapolis: Fortress, p. 7.
2  J. W. Perkinson (2005), *Shamanism, Racism and Hip Hop Culture*. New York: Palgrave Macmillan; Perkinson, *White Theology*.
3  T. Muncey (2010), *Creating Autoethnographies*. London: Sage, pp. 3–8, 30–4.
4  Ibid., p. 2; H. V. Chang (2008), *Autoethnography as Method*. California: Left Coast, p. 2; R.-D. Danahay (1997), *Auto/ethnography: Rewriting the Self and the Social*. Oxford: Berg.
5  G. Maréchal (2010), 'Autoethnography', in A. J. Mills, G. Durepos and E. Wiebe (eds), *Encyclopedia of Case Study Research* (vol. 2). Thousand Oaks, CA: Sage, pp. 43–5.
6  Muncey, *Creating Autoethnographies*, p. 33.
7  C. Ellis and A. P. Bochner (2006), 'Analyzing Analytic Autoethnography – An Autopsy', *Journal of Contemporary Ethnography*, 35 (4), 404–29.
8  L. Anderson (2006), 'Analytic Autoethnography', *Journal of Contemporary Ethnography*, 35 (4), 373–95.
9  See, for example, a combined approach in D. Matsumoto and L. Juang (2008), *Culture and Psychology* (4th edn). Belmont, CA: Thompson Wadsworth.
10  For discussion of the syncretism of religion and its oppositional role see R. D. E. Burton (1997), *Afro-Creole: Power, Opposition, and Play in the Caribbean*. New York: Cornel University Press. For examination of the African soul in Caribbean religion, particularly Christianity, see K. Davis (1990), *Emancipation Still Commin': Explorations in Caribbean Emancipatory Theology*. New York: Orbis.
11  Ibid.
12  C. Long (1986), *Significations Signs, Symbols, and Images in the Interpretation of Religion*. Philadelphia: Fortress, p. 7.
13  A. Anderson (1999), 'Global Pentecostalism in the New Millennium', in A. Anderson and W. J. Hollenweger (eds),

*Pentecostals after a Century.* Sheffield, UK: Sheffield Academic Press, pp. 209–24.

14  R. Beckford (2000), *Dread and Pentecostal: A Political Theology for the Black Church in Britain.* London: SPCK.

15  I. Morrish (1982), *Obeah, Christ and Rastaman: Jamaica and its Religion.* Cambridge: James Clarke and Co., p. 43; B. Chevannes (ed.) (1995), *Rastafari and other African-Caribbean Worldviews.* Basingstoke, UK: Macmillan Press.

16  Morrish, *Obeah, Christ and Rastaman*, p. 43.

17  O. M. Fernández and L. Parvisini-Gebert (eds) (2011), *Creole Religions of the Caribbean, An Introduction from Vodou and Santeria to Obeah and Espiritismo.* New York: New York University Press, p. 127.

18  C. Grant (2011), *I & I: The Natural Mystics: Marley, Tosh and Wailer.* London: Jonathan Cape.

19  J. Mbiti (1991), *Introduction to African Religion* (2nd edn). Heinemann: England.

20  B. Chevannes (ed.) (1998), *Rastafari and Other African-Caribbean Worldviews.* London: Macmillan, p. 23.

21  See M. Sheller (2003), *Consuming the Caribbean: From Arawaks to Zombies.* London: Routledge.

22  S. A. Ellington (1996), 'Pentecostalism and the Authority of Scripture', *Journal of Pentecostal Theology*, 9 (17), 16–38.

23  www.wesleyan.org/beliefs

24  D. M. Stewart (2005), *Three Eyes for the Journey: African Dimensions of the Jamaican Religious Experience.* Oxford: Oxford University Press, p. 102; Austin-Broos, *Jamaica Genesis*, pp. 51–74.

25  J. M. Collins (2009), *Exorcism and Deliverance Ministry in the Twentieth Century: An Analysis of the Practice and Theology of Exorcism in Modern Western Christianity.* Eugene, OR: Wipf & Stock, p. 4.

26  M. W. Cuneo (2001), *American Exorcism: Expelling Demons in the Land of Plenty.* New York: Doubleday, p. 81.

27  Ibid.

28  G. Wilmore (1998), *Black Religion and Black Radicalism: An Interpretation of the Religious History of African Americans.* New York: Orbis, chapter 10.

29  See Anderson, *Beyond Ontological Blackness*; C. Alexander (1996), *The Art of Being Black.* Oxford: Oxford University Press.

30  J. Adred (2005), *Respect: Understanding Caribbean British Christianity.* Peterborough, UK: Epworth.

# Chapter 3

1  Steel Pulse, 'Soldiers' *Handsworth Revolution*, composed by Selwyn Brown, Basil Gabbidon, David Hinds, Alphonso Martin, Ronnie McQueen and Steve Nesbitt, Island Records, UK. 1978.

2  M. N. Olmos and L. Paravisini-Gebert (eds) (2003), *Creole Religions of the Caribbean: An Introduction from Vodou and Santeria to Obeah and Espiritismo.* New York: New York University Press, p. 15; M. Warner-Lewis (2003), *Central Africa in the Caribbean: Transcending Time, Transforming Culture.* Barbados: University of West Indies Press, p. 139.

3  M. Gaskill (2010), *Witchcraft: A Very Short Introduction.* Oxford: Oxford University Press, p. 1.

4  Ibid., p. 2.

5  Ibid., p. 47.

6  Ibid., chapter 2.

7  See John Hall, 'Torso of African Boy Detectives Believe was Killed in a Ritual Sacrifice before being Tossed into the Thames is 'Identified' by Key Witness', *Independent*, Thursday, 7 February 2013.

8  House of Commons Health Committee (2003), *The Victoria Climbié Inquiry Report, Sixth Report of Session 2002–3.* London: Stationary Office Books; Great Britain, Department for Education (2003), *Keeping Children Safe: Government Responses to the Victoria Climbié Inquiry.* London: Stationary Office Books.

9  The relationship between the media, policing and moral panics are discussed in S. Hall, Chas Critcher, Tony Jefferson, John N. Clarke and Brian Roberts. (1978), *Policing the Crisis: Muggings, the State and Law and Order.* London: Palgrave Macmillan.

10  Steven Morris and Rosie Cowan, *Guardian*, Saturday, 14 May 2005.

11  A. Sanders (1995), *A Deed without a Name: The Witch in Society and History.* Oxford: Berg, pp. 151–7.

12  K. Thomas (1973), *Religion and the Decline of Magic: Studies in Popular Beliefs in Sixteenth and Seventeenth Century England.* London: Penguin.

13  H. P. Broedel (2003), *The Malleus Maleficarum and the Construction of Witchcraft.* Manchester: Manchester University Press, p. 3.

14  Sanders, *A Deed without a Name*, p. 15.

15  Ibid., p. 151.

16  P. G. Maxwell-Stuart (2001), *Witchcraft in Europe and the New World, 1400–1800*. Basingstoke: Palgrave Macmillan, p. 10.

17  Ibid., p. 151.

18  Gaskill, *Witchcraft*.

19  O. Onyinah (2011), *Pentecostal Exorcism: Witchcraft and Demonology in Ghana*. Bryanston: Deo; W. K. Kay and R. A. Parry (eds) (2009), *Exorcism and Deliverance: Multi-Disciplinary Perspectives*. Milton Keynes: Paternoster; Collins, *Exorcism and Deliverance Ministry*.

20  Gaskill, *Witchcraft: A Very Short Introduction*. Oxford: Oxford University Press, p. 46.

21  N. Miguez, J. Rieger and J. Mo Sung (2009), *Beyond the Spirit of Empire*. London: SCM.

22  S. Jones and P. Lakeland (eds) (2005), *Constructive Theology: A Contemporary Approach to Classical Themes* Minneapolis: Fortress, p. 120.

23  Ibid.

24  Ibid., p. 118.

25  Ibid.

26  Ibid., p. 134.

27  C. D. Moe-Lobeda (2013), *Resisting Structural Evil: Love as Ecological-Economic Vocation*. Minneapolis: Spark House, p. 3.

28  Ibid., p. 134.

29  Ibid.

30  Ibid.

31  W. Wink (1992), *Engaging the Powers: Discernment and Resistance in a World of Domination*. Minneapolis: Fortress, p. 7.

32  J. Comaroff and J. L. Comaroff (1993), 'Introduction', in J. Comaroff and J. L. Comaroff (eds) *Modernity and its Malcontents: Ritual and Power in Postcolonial Africa*. Chicago: University of Chicago Press, 98–110.

33  B. Meyer (1999), *Translating the Devil: Religion and Modernity amongst the Ewe in Ghana*. London: Edinburgh University Press; J. Parish (2000), 'From the Body to the Wallet: Conceptualizing Akan Witchcraft at Home and Abroad', *Journal of the Royal Anthropological Institute*, 6 (3), 487–500.

34  Ibid.

35  E. E. Evans-Prichard (1976), *Witchcraft, Oracles and Magic among the Azande*. Oxford: Clarendon.

36  M. G. Marwick (1965), *Sorcery in its Social Setting: A Study of the Northern Rhodesia Ceŵa*. Manchester: Manchester University Press.

37  V. Turner (1996), *Schism and Continuity in an African Society: A Study of Ndembu Village*. Manchester: Manchester University Press.

38  M. Gluckman (1959), *Custom and Conflict in Africa*. Oxford: Basil Blackwell.

39  P. Geschiere (1997), *The Modernity of Witchcraft: Politics and the Occult in Postcolonial Africa*. Charlottesville: University of Virginia Press; R. Pool (1994), *Dialogue and the Interpretation of Illness. Conversations in a Cameroon Village*. Oxford, UK and Providence, RI: Berg; R. Shaw (1997), 'The Production of Witchcraft/Witchcraft as Production: Memory, Modernity and the Slave Trade in Sierra Leone', *American Ethnologist*, 24 (4), 856–67.

40  J. Comaroff and J. L. Comaroff (eds) (1993), *Modernity and its Malcontents: Ritual and Power in Postcolonial Africa*. Chicago: University of Chicago Press, p. xxvi.

41  Ibid.

42  H. L. Moore and T. Sanders (2001), *Magical Interpretations, Material Realities*, p. 15.

43  Ibid.

44  Ibid., p. 14.

45  R. Austen (1993), 'The Moral Economy of Witchcraft: An Essay in Comparative History', in J. Comaroff and J. L. Comaroff (eds), *Modernity and its Malcontents: Ritual and Power in Postcolonial Africa*. Chicago: University of Chicago Press, pp. 89–110, 92.

46  L. White (2000), *Speaking with Vampires: Rumor and History in Colonial Africa*. Berkeley: University of California Press.

47  This term is derived from the concept of the numinous in the work of theologian Rudolf Otto. In *The Idea of the Holy*. Otto uses the concept of the numinous to describe the presence of a supernatural force. How one responds to this force is varied; one might be drawn to it or conversely experience 'awfulness' and 'overpoweringness', that is, 'mystrium tremendum'. R. Otto (1958), *The Idea of the Holy*. Oxford: Oxford University Press, pp. 12–23.

48  Long, *Significations*, p. 7.

49  V. Turner (1996), *Schism and Continuity in an African Society: A Study of Ndembu Village*. Manchester: Manchester University Press. p. 23.

50  P. J. Stewart and A. Strathern (eds) (2004), *Witchcraft, Sorcery, Rumors, and Gossip*. Cambridge: Cambridge University Press, pp. 50–1.

51  Geschiere, *The Modernity of Witchcraft*.

52  W. Davis (1988), *Passage of Darkness: The Ethnobiology of the Hatian Zombie*. Chapel Hill: University of North Carolina Press, p. 186.

# Chapter 4

1  C. S. Pero (2013), *Liberation from Empire: Demonic Possession and Exorcism in the Gospel of Mark*. New York: Peter Laing, preface.

2  Ibid., p. 4.

3  Collins, *Exorcism and Deliverance Ministry*, pp. 15–17.

4  A. Witmer (2012), *Jesus, the Galilean Exorcist: His Exorcisms in Social and Political Context*. London: T&T Clark, p. 3.

5  E. Bourguignon (1976), *Possession*. San Francisco: Chandler and Sharp, p. 24.

6  E. Sorensen (2002), *Possession and Exorcism in the New Testament and Early Christianity*. Tubingen: J.C. Mohr, p. 47.

7  Ibid., pp. 51–2.

8  Ibid., p. 53.

9  Ibid.

10  Ibid., pp. 118–23.

11  W. Burkert (1985), *Greek Religion*. Cambridge, MA: Harvard University Press, pp. 181–7.

12  Bourguignon, *Possession*, pp. 7, 45.

13  Sorensen, *Possession and Exorcism*, p. 118.

14  See E. Eshel (2003), 'Genres of Magical Texts in the Dead Sea Scrolls', in A. Lange, H. Lichtenberger and K. H. Römheld (eds), *Demons*. Tubingen: J.C. Mohr, pp. 395–415.

15  Sorensen, *Possession and Exorcism*, pp. 118–24.

16  G. Parrinder (2005), 'Exorcism', in L. Jones (ed.), *Encyclopedia of Religion, vol. 3, 15 vols*. Detroit: Thompson/Gale, pp. 225–33.

17 P. Hollenbach (1981), 'Jesus, Demoniacs, and Public Authorities: A Socio-Historical Study', *JAAR*, 49 (4), 565–88.

18 H. C. Kee (1988), *Medicine, Miracle and Magic in New Testament Times*. Cambridge: Cambridge University Press, pp. 75–6.

19 Witmer, *Jesus, the Galilean Exorcist*, p. 203.

20 R. J. S. Barrett-Lennard (1994), *Christian Healing after the New Testament: Some Approaches to Illness in the Second, Third, and Fourth Centuries*. Lanham, MD: University Press of America, p. 42.

21 Sorensen, *Possession and Exorcism*, pp. 132–6.

22 Ibid., pp. 148 ff.

23 W. Wink (1987), *The Powers that Be: Theology for a New Millennium*. New York: Doubleday Dell.

24 R. Bultmann (1960), *Jesus Christ and Mythology*. London: SCM.

25 Ibid.

26 See S. V. McCasland (1951), *The Finger of God: Demon Possession and Exorcism in the Light of Modern Views of Mental Illness*. New York: MacMillan.

27 H. Naegeli-Osjord (1988), *Possession and Exorcism: Understanding the Human Psyche in turmoil*. Oregon, WI: New Frontiers Centre, pp. 3–10.

28 K. Warrington (2008), *Pentecostal Theology: A Theology of Encounter*. London: T&T Clark, p. 265ff; S. J. Land (2010), *Pentecostal Spirituality: A Passion for the Kingdom*. Sheffield: Sheffield Academic, pp. 1–10.

29 R. S. Sugirtharajah (2002), *Postcolonial Criticism and Biblical Interpretation*. Oxford: Oxford University Press, pp. 11–70; C. Keller, N. Michael and R. Mayra (eds) (2004), *Postcolonial Theologies: Divinity and Empire*. St Louis, MO: Chalice, introduction.

30 B. Ashcroft, G. Griffith and H. Tiffin (2000), *Post-colonial Studies: The Key Concepts*. London: Routledge, pp. 186–7.

31 R. S. Sugirtharajah (ed.) (1998), *The Postcolonial Bible*. Sheffield: Sheffield Academic.

32 R. S. Sugirtharajah (2003), *Postcolonial Reconfigurations: An Alternative Way to Read the Bible and Doing Theology*, St Louis, MO: Chalice, p. 4.

33 R. S. Sugirtharajah (ed.) (1988), *The Postcolonial Bible*. Sheffield: Sheffield Academic; R. C. Bailey (2003), *Yet with a Steady Beat:*

*Contemporary U.S. Afrocentric Biblical Interpretation.* Semeia Studies 42. Atlanta: Society of Biblical Literature.

34 Bible and Culture Collective (1997), *The Postmodern Bible.* New Haven and London: Yale University Press, p. 275.

35 C. Keller et al., *Postcolonial Theologies,* pp. 13–15.

36 S. D. Moore (2006), 'Mark and Empire: "Zealot" and "Postcolonial" Readings', in R. S. Sugirtharajah, *The Postcolonial Biblical Reader.* Oxford: Blackwell, pp. 193–206.

37 See, Pero, *Liberation from Empire.*

38 See the discussion in G. H. Twelftree (2007), *In the Name of Jesus: Exorcism among Early Christians.* Grand Rapids, MI: Baker Academic, 105–11.

39 P. Hollenbach (1993), *Help for Interpreting Jesus' Exorcisms.* SBL Seminar Papers. Atlanta: Scholars, p. 125.

40 R. Horsley (2004), *Jesus and the Spiral of Violence: Popular Jewish Resistance in Roman Palestine.* Minneapolis, MN: Fortress, pp. 187–8.

41 Witmer, *Jesus, the Galilean Exorcist.*

42 S. L. Davies (1995), *Jesus the Healer.* London: SCM, p. 79.

43 A. Meier (1994), *A Marginal Jew: Rethinking the Historical Jesus, Vol. 2: Mentor, Message, and Miracles* (1st edn). New Haven and London: Yale University Press. p. 251.

44 Ibid., p. 653.

45 G. Theissen (2004), *The Gospels in Context.* London: Continuum, p. 110.

46 R. Grundy (1993), *Mark: A Commentary on His Apology for the Cross.* Grand Rapids, MI: William B. Eerdmans, p. 260.

47 C. Myers (2008), *Binding the Strong Man: A Political Reading of Mark's Story of Jesus.* New York: Orbis, pp. 190–4; J. D. Crossan (2009), *Jesus: A Revolutionary Biography.* New York: Harper Collins, pp. 88–91.

48 Sugirtharajah, *The Postcolonial Biblical Reader,* pp. 92–3.

49 Ibid., p. 92.

50 Ibid., p. 93.

51 Witmer, *Jesus, the Galilean Exorcist,* pp. 172–3.

52 Ibid.

53 F. Fanon (2005), *The Wretched of the Earth.* London: Grove.

54  Wink, *Engaging the Powers*.

55  F. Fanon (1963), *The Wretched of the Earth*. London: Pluto.

56  R. A. Horsley (2001), *Hearing the Whole Story: The Politics of Plot in Mark's Gospel*. Louisville, KY: Westminster John Knox, p. 143.

57  Ibid.

58  Ibid., p. 148.

59  Moore, 'Mark and Empire', pp. 193–205.

60  Witmer, *Jesus, the Galilean Exorcist*, p. 172.

61  Ibid.

# Chapter 5

1   I. Dookhan (1971), *A Pre-emancipation History of the West Indies*. Kingston, Jamaica: Longman Jamaica Limited, p. 125.

2   D. Lin, 'Structural Evil', *Third Way*, 17 (10) (December 2004), 20–21.

3   C. Card (2010), *Confronting Evils: Terrorism, Torture, Genocide*. New York: Cambridge University Press, p. 84.

4   Ibid.

5   Ibid.

6   W. J. Jennings (2010), *The Christian Imagination: Theology and the Origins of Race*. New Haven: Yale University Press, p. 22.

7   N. S. Murrell (2000), 'Dangerous Memories: Underdevelopment, and the Bible in Colonial Caribbean Experience', in H. Gossai and N. S. Murrell *Religion, Culture and Tradition in the Caribbean*. Basingstoke: Palgrave Macmillan, p. 11.

8   J. H. Elliot (1992), *The Old World and the New 1492–1650*. Cambridge: Cambridge University Press, p. 7.

9   L. A. Clayton (2011), *Bartolomé de las Casaas and the Conquest of the Americas*. Chichester, Sussex: Wiley-Blackwell, p. 7.

10  D. Castro (2007), *Another Face of Empire: Bartolomé de Las Casas, Indigenous Rights, and Ecclesiastical Imperialism*. Durham, NC: Duke University Press Books, p. 19.

11  Ibid., p. 23.

12  D. Greenblatt (1992), *Marvelous Possessions: The Wonder of the New World*. Chicago: University of Chicago Press, p. 9.

13  T. Todorov (1987), *The Conquest of America: The Question of the Other*. Richard Howard (trans.). London: Harper & Row, p. 43.

14  L. A. Clayton, *Bartolomé de las Casas and the Conquest of the Americas*. Chichester, Sussex: Wiley-Blackwell, p. 43.

15  J. Meier (2001), 'The Beginnings of the Catholic Church in the Caribbean', in A. Lampe (ed.), *Christianity in the Caribbean: Essays on Church History*. Barbados: University of West Indies Press, pp. 1–23.

16  Todorov, *The Conquest of America*, p. 170.

17  B. D. L. Casas (1992), *A Short Account of the Destruction of the Indies*. Harlow: Penguin Books, p. 15.

18  Ibid.

19  A. Aimé Césaire (2000), *Discourse on Colonialism*. New York: Monthly Review, p. 13.

20  Meier, 'The Beginnings of the Catholic Church in the Caribbean', p. 5.

21  Castro, *Another Face of Empire*, p. 14.

22  Ibid.

23  Quoted in Todorov, *The Conquest of America*, p. 171.

24  G. E. Tinker (1993), *Missionary Conquest: The Gospel and Native American Cultural Genocide*. Minneapolis: Fortress.

25  Ibid.

26  F. A. MacNutt (2008), *Bartholomew de las Casas: His Life, His Apostolate, and His Writings*. New York: G.P. Putnam's Sons, p. 108.

27  Ibid.

28  Ibid., p. 15.

29  Todorov, *The Conquest of America*, p. 170.

30  M. Rediker (2007), *The Slave Ship: A Human History*. Harlow: Penguin Books.

31  J. B. Ellis (1913), *The Diocese of Jamaica: A Short Account of its History, Growth and Organisation*. London: Society for Promoting Christian Knowledge, p. 41.

32  A. C. Dayfoot (1998), *The Shaping of the West Indian Church: 1492–1962*. Barbados: University of West Indies Press.

33  Ibid.

34  C. Hall (2002), *Civilizing Subjects: Metropole and Colony in the English Imagination 1830–1867*. London: Polity, p. 77.

35  B. Bush (1990), *Slave Women in Caribbean Society, 1650–1838*. Kingston, Jamaica: Heinemann. See also the Dutch colonial study by E. Donoghue (2006), *Black Women/ White Men: The Sexual Eploitation of Female Slaves in the Danish West Indies*. Trenton, NJ: Africa World.

36  Ibid.

37  G. E. Simpson (1978), *Black Religions in the New World*. New York: Columbia University Press, p. 26.

38  K. Hunte (2001), 'Protestantism and Slavery in the British Caribbean', in Lampe (ed.), *Christianity in the Caribbean: Essays on Church History*. Barbados: University of West Indies Press, p. 91.

39  Simpson, *Black Religions in the New World*, pp. 22 ff.

40  Ibid.

41  Ibid.

42  Ibid.

43  Ibid.

44  Hall, *Civilizing Subjects*, p. 77.

45  Ibid.

46  Simpson, *Black Religions in the New World*, pp. 21 ff.

47  See G. W. Bridges (1828), *The Annals of Jamaica*. London: John Murray.

48  www.ncte.org/library/NCTEFiles/Resources/Journals/CCC/0611-sep09/CCC0611Good.pdf

49  A. Hochschld (2005), *Bury the Chains: The British Struggle to Abolish Slavery*. London: Macmillan, pp. 60 ff.

50  T. Glasson (2012), *Mastering Christianity: Missionary Anglicanism and Slavery in the Atlantic World*. Oxford: Oxford University Press, chapter 2.

51  N. M. Beasley (2006), 'Christian Liturgy and the Creation of British Slave Societies, 1650–1780'. PhD Dissertation, Vanderbilt University, pp. 3–5.

52  Glasson, *Mastering Christianity*, chapter 2.

53  Ibid.

54  H. Beckles (1990), *A History of Barbados: From Amerindian Settlement to Nation-state*. Cambridge, UK: Cambridge University Press, p. 88.

55 Dookhan, *A Pre-emancipation History of the West Indies*, p. 130.

56 J. Cox (2008), *The British Missionary Enterprise since 1700*. Christianity and Society in the Modern World. London: Routledge, p. 38.

57 O. Patterson (1982), *Slavery and Social Death: A Comparative Study*. Cambridge, MA: Harvard University Press, p. 39.

58 Ibid.

59 Glasson, *Mastering Christianity*, pp. 159 ff.

60 This term is derived from the concept of the numinous in the work of theologian Rudolf Otto.

# Chapter 6

1 P. L. Walton (2004), *Our Cannibals, Ourselves*. Chicago: University of Illinois Press, p. 4.

2 M. Foucault (2002), *Archeology of Knowledge*. London: Routledge; M. Foucault (1984), 'Nietzsche, Genealogy, History', in P. Rabinow (ed.) *The Foucault Reader*. New York: Pantheon, pp. 76–100.

3 C. C. Ragin (1992), *The Comparative Method: Moving Beyond Qualitative and Quantitative Strategies*. Berkley and Los Angeles: University of California Press.

4 D. Root (1996), *Cannibal Culture: Art, Appropriation, and the Commodification of Difference*. Boulder, CO: Westview, pp. 8–16.

5 Sheller, *Consuming the Caribbean*, p. 145.

6 Open University (2004), *Religion, Exploration and Slavery*. Milton Keynes: Open University, pp. 139–75.

7 O. Equiano (1995), *The Interesting Narrative and Other Writings*. Vincent Carretta (ed.). London: Penguin, p. 41.

8 Ibid., p. 55.

9 Ibid.

10 M. Prince (2000), *The History of Mary Prince: A West Indian Slave*. London: Penguin, p. 8.

11 *Morning Times*, Monday, 7 November 1831, p. 4.

12 Prince, *The History of Mary Prince*, p. 10.

13 Ibid., p. 11.

14 Patterson, *Slavery and Social Death*, pp. 334 ff.

15  Sheller, *Consuming the Caribbean*, p. 88.

16  Ibid., p. 89.

17  P. P. Sherlock and H. Bennett (1998), *The Story of the Jamaican People*. Kingston, Jamaica: Ian Randle.

18  Ibid.

19  K. Marx (1992), *Capital: Volume 1: A Critique of Political Economy*. London: Penguin Classics, chapter 10.

20  The term eschatology comes from the Greek term *ta eschata*, 'the last things', and refers to Christian belief in the resurrection, judgment or the closing of the present age. For Christians the foundations of eschatology are the New Testament teachings of Jesus and Paul, where the term has both present and future associations. For Jesus, it is a present reality in the sense that the Kingdom is near but also belongs to the future, in that the Kingdom is still to arrive in its fullness. J. L. Walls (ed.) (2008), *The Oxford Handbook of Eschatology*. Oxford: Oxford University Press, pp. 4–6.

21  A. E. McGrath (2001), *Christian Theology: An Introduction* (3rd edn). Chichester: John Wiley & Sons, p. 546.

22  Ibid.

23  See F. D. Macchia (2008), 'Pentecostal and Charismatic Theology', in J. L. Walls (ed.) *The Oxford Handbook of Eschatology*. Oxford: Oxford University Press, pp. 280 ff.

24  See N. Ferguson (2004), *Empire: How Britain Made the Modern World*. London: Penguin. Also, S. Cobb (2011), *Britain's Empire: Resistance, Repression and Revolt*. London: Verso.

25  G. C. Spivak (1994), 'Can the Subaltern Speak?' in P. Williams and L. Chrisman (eds), *Colonial Discourse and Post-Colonial Theory, A Reader*. New York: Columbia University Press, pp. 66–111.

26  T. R. Williams (2006), 'Proclaiming the Lord's Death until He Comes: Toward a Theology of the Lord's Supper', PhD dissertation, Fuller Theological Seminary, p. 165.

27  J. B. Metz (1986), *The Emergent Church*. New York: Crossroad, p. 29.

28  Ibid.

29  Ibid.

30  J. B. Metz (1980), *Faith in History and Society: Towards a Practical Fundamental Theology*. David Smith (trans.). New York: Seabury, pp. 170, 172.

**31** Ibid. p. 105.

**32** Ibid.

**33** David Smith, *The Guardian*, Tuesday, 27 March 2007.

**34** Ibid.

**35** See R. Hart (1985), *Slaves Who Abolished Slavery Vol. 2: Blacks in Rebellion*. Kingston, Jamaica: University of the West Indies Press.

**36** The opposite of prophetic thought as identified in the work of Cornel West. See, C. West, (1993), *Beyond Eurocentrism and Multiculturalism vol 1: Prophetic Thought in Postmodern Times*. Monroe, ME: Common Courage.

**37** See, for example, Wilkinson and Studebaker, *A Liberating Spirit*.

# Chapter 7

**1** J. Russell (2005), *Book of the Dead: The Complete History of Zombie Movies: The Complete History of Zombie Cinema*. England: Godalming: FAB, pp. 19 ff.

**2** C. L. R. James (2001), *The Black Jacobins: Toussaint L'ouverture and the San Domingo Revolution*. London: Penguin, pp. 5–22.

**3** M. W. Ghachem (2012), *The Old Regime and the Haitian Revolution*. Cambridge: Cambridge University Press, p. 457.

**4** E. B. Edmonds and M. A. Gonzalez (2010), *Caribbean Religious History: An Introduction*. New York: New York University Press, p. 58; L. G. Desmangles (1992), *The Faces of the Gods: Vodou and Roman Catholicism in Haiti*. Chapel Hill: University of North Carolina Press, pp. 21–32.

**5** S. Turlington (1999), *Do You Do Voodoo?: The Real Religion behind Zombies and Voodoo Dolls*. Reading: South Street, pp. 2–6.

**6** Desmangles, *The Faces of the Gods*, p. 15.

**7** Ibid., pp. 33–57.

**8** L. Hurbon (1995), *Voodoo: Truth and Fantasy*. London: Thames and Hudson, p. 14.

**9** Ibid.

**10** R. F. Thompson (1984), *Flash of Spirit: African and Afro-American Art and Philosophy*. New York: Random House, pp. 165–6.

11 G. E. Simpson (1980), *Religious Cults of the Caribbean: Trinidad, Jamaica and Haiti.* Rio Piedras, San Juan, Puerto Rico: Institute of Caribbean Studies, University of Puerto Rico, p. 238.

12 Ibid.

13 Ibid.

14 M. Rigaud (1985), *Secrets of Voodoo.* Robert Cross (trans). San Francisco: City Light Books, p. 132.

15 Ibid.

16 James, *The Black Jacobins*, pp. 86–7.

17 M. Laguerre (1980), *Voodoo Heritage.* Beverly Hills: Sage, pp. 107–10.

18 Ibid.

19 M. Deren (1991), *Divine Horsemen: Living Gods of Haiti.* Kingston, NY: McPherson and Co., pp. 15–16, 27–30.

20 Ibid.

21 Ibid.

22 Hurbon, *Voodoo*, p. 44.

23 Ibid.

24 Ibid.

25 Ibid.

26 Despite becoming the first black republic in 1804, Haiti became a pariah nation and was never fully able to access the financial and commercial resources necessary for sustained development. A low point in the history of this first black republic was the early twentieth century when, under the pretext of restoring stability after social and economic breakdown, the American military took control of the island. 'The Seizure of Haiti by the United States; A Report on the Military Occupation of the Republic of Haiti and the History of the Treaty Forced Upon Her'. http://archive.org/details/seizureofhaitiby00newy

27 Sheller, *Consuming the Caribbean*, p. 145.

28 The research method was participant-observation but as a complete participant. As a complete participant, I sought out to discover the 'structuring properties' of the worship. What this means in practice is noting the layers of thought and action in the worship and relating them to the wider social, political and cultural forces at work in the congregation and beyond. Thought and action ranges from the personal-emotional (feelings) to the structural-organizational (shaping of the congregation). I recognize both of these poles in

my investigation – indeed at times they overlap since worship provides a space for agency and self-development as well as shaping organizations and behaviour. In other words, worship is always embedded in practice.

29  J. L. Walton (2009), *Watch This!: The Ethics and Aesthetics of Black Televangelism*. New York: New York University Press, chapter 3. K. William (2011), *Pentecostalism: A Very Short Introduction*. Oxford: Oxford University Press, pp. 126 ff.

30  See C. Bell (2009), *Ritual Theory, Ritual Practice*. New York: Oxford University Press.

31  A. Young and E. Y. Alexander (2011), *Afro-Pentecostalism: Black Pentecostal and Charismatic Christianity in History and Culture*. New York: New York University Press, pp. 172–8.

32  Austin-Broos, *Jamaica Genesis*, p. 19.

33  Worship at New Church is a 'Spirit encounter' in which the Spirit leads believers into the presence of God. It also reflects the Pentecostal worldview, particularly a radical openness to God. Consequently, in terms of hymnody the focus is to lead the congregation into an experience of worship. 'Come let us worship', 'We are here to worship You' and 'Holy Spirit come' are regular themes in choruses and exhortations from worship leaders. Worship is conducted through a 'megachurch aesthetic' including the use of audio-visual equipment (projectors and screens), and a theatrical environment (stage, evocative lighting). Also evident was the black Pentecostal emphasis on kinetic (expressive movement) and tactile (physical touch) modes of expression where people may hug, hold hands or embrace each other in greeting or during special moments expressive of congregational unity. See Roswith Gerloff's 1992 study of the apostolic tradition in Birmingham in *A Plea for British Black Theologies: The Black Church Movement in its Transatlantic Cultural and Theological Interaction* (vol. 1). Frankfurt, Bern and New York: Peter Lang; P. Ward (2005), *Selling Worship: How what We Sing has Changed the Church*. Milton Keynes: Paternoster.

34  The question of ethics and ethical worship were never far from the surface. 'Ethical worship' describes the biblical tradition of worship as truth and justice (Romans 12.1). It is understood as both vertical and horizontal inasmuch as believers are expected to enter into a state of spiritual harmony with God (vertical) and with each other (horizontal). Consequently, it is vitally important to be 'right' with the God to ensure that one's worship is 'true'. However, despite its importance, the demand for ethical worship is not consistent and at New Church I identified weak and strong examples. In the

case of weak ethical worship, the form (aesthetic) is placed over content (ethics). As a result, 'sounding good, looking good' is given priority over meaningful theological reflection. This emphasis was played-out in the volume of the music in worship. At the 10.30 am service, the music was loud, even by Pentecostal standards, and at times overwhelmed the singing of the congregation. When I asked the technician why the music was so loud he responded by saying 'people need it loud to feel the music'. In contrast, strong demands emphasize ethics over aesthetics and values content over form. In short, in the second mode it does not matter how it looks or sounds, as long as 'God is glorified' and the congregation 'feel' the presence of the Spirit, generally evidenced in super-rational experiences, rather than through the acoustic dynamic of the hi-fidelity amplification. For this reason, on several occasions the pastors exhorted congregations to stop and then start worshiping again and again, until there was a sense that the worship was genuine. Weak and strong demands are rarely outside of church politics because, at New Church, those with the most power create a discourse on ethical worship. See B. Wannenwetsch (2004), *Political Worship: Ethics for Christian Citizens*. Margaret Kohl (trans.). Oxford: Oxford University Press, pp. 58 ff.

35  Worship cannot be separated from power. Within the specificity of diaspora, particularly the historic threat of living with varied forms of racial terror, worship has taken on added importance as a place of black empowerment. As one of the few spaces where a people weighted down by the existential absurdity of habitual anti-blackness, worship is regularly metamorphosed by an implicit biblical black love. This is expressed at New Church in expressive physicality that affirms an embodied blackness.

36  K. A. Smith (2010), *Thinking in Tongues: Pentecostal Contributions to Christian Philosophy*. Grand Rapids, MI: William B. Eerdmans, pp. 64, 71.

37  R. Gerloff (1992), *A Plea for British Black Theologies: The Black Church Movement in Britain in its Transatlantic Cultural and Theological Interaction, with Special References to the Pentecostal Oneness (Apostolic) and Sabbatarian Movements, Part 1.* Frankfurt and New York: Peter Lang.

38  W. Hollenweger (1973), 'Pentecostalism and Black Power', *Theology Today*, 30, 234.

39  C. B. Johns (2010), *Pentecostal Formation: A Pedagogy among the Oppressed*. Sheffield: Sheffield Academic, pp. 22 ff.

40  I explore the socio-economic context in R. Beckford (2004), *God and the Gangs*, London: DLT.

41  R. Gerloff (1992), *A Plea for British Black Theologies: The Black Church Movement in Britain in its Transatlantic Cultural and Theological Interaction* (vol. 1). Frankfurt and New York: Peter Lang, p. 64.

42  Ibid.

43  Walton, *Watch This*, pp. 80–1.

44  V. Turner (1982), *From Ritual to Theater: The Human Seriousness of Play*. New York: PAJ, pp. 25–7.

45  C. Scandrett-Leatherman (2011), 'Rites of Lynching and Rights of Dance: Historic, Anthropological, and Afro-Pentecostal Perspectives on Black Manhood after 1865', in A. Young and E. Y. Alexander (eds), *Afro-Pentecostalism: Black Pentecostal and Charismatic Christianity in History and Culture*. New York: New York University Press, pp. 95–117.

46  P. Heelas and L. Woodhead (2005), *The Spiritual Revolution: Why Religion in Giving Way to Spirituality*. Oxford: Blackwell, p. 2.

47  Ibid., p. 3.

# Chapter 8

1  S. Hall (1980), 'Encoding/Decoding', in S. Hall, L. Hobson, A. Love and P. Willis (eds), *Culture, Media, Language: Working Papers in Cultural Studies, 1972–79*. London: Routledge, pp. 134.

2  S. Hall (1973), 'Encoding and Decoding in the Television Discourse', in Stencilled Paper 7. pp. 1–20; S. Hall, L. Hobson, A. Love and P. Willis (eds) (1980), *Culture, Media, Language*. London: Routledge, pp. 128–38.

3  Hall et al., *Culture, Media, Language*, pp. 128–9.

4  W. A. Elwell (1984), *Evangelical Dictionary of Theology*. Grand Rapids, MI: Baker Book House, pp. 969–70.

5  Ibid.

6  D. Peterson (1995), *Possessed by God: New Testament Theology of Sanctification and Holiness*. Nottingham: IVP.

7  R. Mark (2004), *A Century of Holiness: The Doctrine of Entire Sanctification in the Church of the Nazarene: 1905 to 2004*. Kansas: Beacon Hill.

8  Land, *Pentecostal Spirituality*, pp. 20–47.

9  *Birmingham Mail*, 29 May 2012. See www.birminghammail.net/news/birmingham-news/2012/05/29/row-over-handsworth-church-extension-plan-97319–31064421/

10  Music is a cipher for the 'popular'. The 'popular' is a commitment to making the Gospel contemporary by appropriating aspects of popular culture. (It is an evangelistic method.) Applied to music ministry the major outcome has been the appropriation of popular music forms to embellish church music. The 'popular' in music ministry is attractive to young people because it conveys a sense that faith in God is not outside of the social world, but a vital renewing resource within it.

11  The music culture of black Pentecostalism is also shaped by what I want to call the 'sonic faith'. This is the filling of worship space with sonic faith – church music, voices in praise or communal prayer. This cacophony of sound is by no means disorganized. Rather, it is the manifestation of the polyrhythmic cultural practice of diaspora culture: the simultaneous existence of several themes and rhythmic patterns. Theologically, sonic faith is integral to meaningful worship, in the sense that it is a recognition that God is present in the praises of His people (Psalm 22.3). Further, for black Pentecostals, volume often mediates divine presence (Psalm 100.1). As a result, saturating worship with sound denotes a state of sanctification because in such moments the church hall, sanctuary or meeting place *becomes* sanctified or 'holy ground'.

12  W. E. MacNair (2009), *Unraveling the Mega-Church: True Faith or Fast Promise?* New York: Praeger.

13  Walton, *Watch This!*, pp. 80–1.

14  Ibid., pp. 66–7.

15  A. Butler (2007), *Women in the Church of God in Christ: Making a Sanctified World*. Chapel Hill, NC: University of North Carolina Press, pp. 79–80.

16  Ibid.

17  M. McMillan (2007), 'Aesthetics of the West Indian Front Room,' in R. V. Arana (ed.), *'Black' British Aesthetics Today*. Newcastle: Cambridge Scholars, pp. 297–312.

18  Ibid.

19  Ibid.

20  W. A. Dyrness (2001), *Visual Faith: Art Theology and Worship in Dialogue (Engaging Culture)*. Grand Rapids, MI: Baker Publishing Group.

21  J. Inge (2003), *A Christian Theology of Place*. Farnham: Ashgate, p. 1.

22  Ibid., pp. 33–58.

23  Ibid., p. 53.

24  R. Barthes (1967), *Elements of Semiology*. London: Cape; R. Barthes (1972), *Mythologies*. London: Cape.

25  Hall et al., *Culture, Media, Language*, p. 133.

26  Ibid.

27  Ibid.

28  Ibid., vol. 2, p. 229.

29  C. S. Peirce (1931–58), *Collected Writings* (8 vols). C. Hartshorne, P. Weiss and A. W. Burks (eds). Cambridge, MA: Harvard University Press.

30  Smith, *Thinking in Tongues*, p. 40.

31  Ibid., p. 41.

32  Ibid.

33  T. Smith (1996), *Conjuring Culture: Biblical Foundations for Black America*. Oxford: Oxford University Press, p. 5.

34  Y. Chireau (2006), *Black Magic: Religion and the African American Conjuring Tradition*. Berkeley, CA: University of California Press.

35  Ibid.

36  W. Rucker (2001), 'Conjure, Magic, and Power: The Influence of Afro-Atlantic Religious Practices on Slave Resistance and Rebellion', *Journal of Black Studies*, 32 (1), 84–103.

# Chapter 9

1  B. Nichols (2001), *Introduction to Documentary*. Bloomington and Indianapolis: Indiana University Press, p. xi.

2  Ibid., pp. 1–2.

3  B. Nichols (2001), *Representing Reality*. Bloomington and Indianapolis: Indiana University Press.

4  M. Chanon (2007), *The Politics of Documentary*. London: British Film Institute, p. vi.

5  E. Barnouw (1993), *Documentary: A History of the Non-fiction Film*. Oxford: Oxford University Press, pp. 31–83.

6   J. Grierson (1933), 'The Documentary Producer', *Cinema Quarterly*, 2 (1), 8.

7   P. Ward (2005), *Documentary: The Margins of Reality*. London and New York: Wallflower, p. 1.

8   S. Bruzzi (2000), *New Documentary: A Critical Introduction*. Abingdon: Routledge, p. 4.

9   Ibid., p. 11.

10  R. Kilborn and J. Izod (1997), *Confronting Reality: An Introduction to Documentary*. Manchester: Manchester University Press, p. 35.

11  See the preface to E. Souriau (1953), *L'Universe Filmique*. Paris: Flammarion.

12  French scholar, Etienne Souriau, divides filmmaking between the 'profilmic,' 'afilmic' and 'filmic'. 'Profilmic' refers to what is viewed from the lenses of the camera. The world upon which the camera is trained is the 'afilmic' – what would have occurred if the camera was not there. The layers of editing, subjective judgements and aesthetic choices or the 'filmic' conventions are what make a documentary film. See preface to Souraiu, *L'Univers Filmique*.

13  See a discussion of the political and legal ramifications in B. Wilson (2000), *Lies, Damn Lies and Documentaries*. London: BFI.

14  Nichols, *Introduction to Documentary*, p. 4.

15  R. Kilborn and J. Izod (1997), *An Introduction to Documentary: Confronting Reality*. Manchester: Manchester University Press, p. 37.

16  Corner, 'Television, Documentary and the Category of the Aesthetic', pp. 49–58.

17  Kilborn and Izod, *An Introduction to Documentary*, p. 44.

18  Ibid.

19  D. Vaughan (1983), *Portrait of an Invisible Man: The Working Life of Stewart McAllister, Film Editor*. London: BFI.

20  Nichols, *Representing Reality*, pp. 32–3.

21  See B. Nichols (1994), *Blurred Boundaries: Questions of Meaning in Contemporary Culture*. New York: John Wiley & Sons, pp. 93–4.

22  J. Roscoe and C. Hight (2001), *Faking it: Mock-documentary and the Subversion of Factuality*. Manchester: Manchester University Press.

23  Ibid., p. 1.

24  Nichols, *Introduction to Documentary*, p. 102.

25  Ward, *Documentary*, p. 14.

26  G. Gérarad (1980), *Narrative Discourse: An Essay in Method*. Oxford: Basil Blackwell. Gérarad distinguishes between three meanings of the French word *récit*.

27  Gérarad, *Narrative Discourse*.

28  H. L. Gates Jr. (1988), *The Signifying Monkey: A Theory of African-American Literary Criticism*. Oxford: Oxford University Press, p. xxv.

29  Ibid., p. 13.

30  H. Baker in J. Jonas (1990), *Anancy In The Great House: Ways of Reading West Indian Fiction*. New York: Greenwood, forward.

31  Ibid.

32  M. M. Yearwood (1999), *Black Film as a Signifying Practice, Cinema, Narration and the African American Aesthetic Tradition*. Trenton, NJ: African World Press.

33  Ibid., p. 17.

# Chapter 10

1  *Guardian*, 20 September 1999.

2  J. Lees-Milne (1976), *William Beckford*. London: Century, p. 1.

3  Ibid.

4  I did, however, accept to present two films in the interim, these were *Test of Time* and *Blood and Fire*.

# Chapter 11

1  J. Cone (1975), *God of the Oppressed*. New York: Harper Collins, pp. 66–7.

2  Ibid., p. 67.

3  Because fair trade is not always completely fair.

4  Jonathan Kaiman, *Guardian*, 6 June 2013. See www.guardian.co.uk/world/2013/jun/06/ghana-arrest-chinese-illegal-gold-mining

5  Daniel Howden, *Independent*, 4 March 2009.

# Chapter 12

1  J. S. Croatto (1987), *Biblical Hermeneutics: Towards a Theory of Reading as the Production of Meaning* New York: Orbis Books.

2  J. L. Segundo (1976), *The Liberation of the Bible.* New York: Orbis Books.

3  E. S. Fiorenza (1991), *Revelation: Vision of a Just World.* Edinburgh: T&T Clark, pp. 7–10.

4  C. Keller (1996), *Apocalypse Now and Then: A Feminist Guide to the End of the World.* Minneapolis: Fortress.

5  Croatto, *Biblical Hermeneutics.*

# Conclusion

1  www.citizensuk.org/about/staff/

2  www.queens.ac.uk/index.php/about/centre/centre-for-black-ministries-and-leadership

3  Wilkinson and Studebaker, *A Liberating Spirit.*

4  P. Tillich (1973), *Systematic Theology* (vol. I). Chicago: University of Chicago Press, p. 40.

5  P. Tillich (1957), *Dynamics of Faith.* New York: Harper & Row, pp. 41–54; Tillich, *Systematic Theology* (vol. I), pp. 239–41; P. Tillich (ed.) (1959), *Theology of Culture.* New York: Oxford University Press, pp. 53–67.

6  Dyrness, *Visual Faith*; R. M. Jensen and K. J. Vrudny (2009), *Visual Theology: Forming and Transforming the Community through the Arts.* Collegeville, MN: Liturgical.

7  M. Karenga (1993), *Introduction to Black Studies* (2nd edn). Los Angeles, CA: University of Sankore Press, pp. 394–7.

8  Anderson, *Beyond Ontological Blackness.*

9  Ibid.

10  M. Stephens (1998), *The Rise of the Image and Fall of the Word.* Oxford: Oxford University Press.

# BIBLIOGRAPHY

Adred, J. (2005), *Respect: Understanding Caribbean British Christianity*. Peterborough, UK: Epworth Press.

Aimé Césaire, A. (2000), *Discourse on Colonialism*. New York: Monthly Review Press.

Alexander, C. (1996), *The Art of being Black*. Oxford: Oxford University Press.

Ali, S. (2003), *Mixed-Race, Post-Race: Gender, New Ethnicities and Cultural Practices*. Oxford: Berg.

Anderson, A. (1999), 'Global Pentecostalism in the New Millennium', in A. Anderson and W. J. Hollenweger (eds), *Pentecostals after a Century*. Sheffield: Sheffield Academic Press, pp. 209–24.

—. (2004), *An Introduction to Global Pentecostalism*. Cambridge: Cambridge University Press.

Anderson, L. (2006), 'Analytic Autoethnography', *Journal of Contemporary Ethnography*, 35 (4), 373–95.

Anderson, V. (1995), *Beyond Ontological Blackness: An Essay on African American Religious and Cultural Criticism*. New York: Continuum.

Ashcroft, B., Griffith, G. and Tiffin, H. (2000), *Post-Colonial Studies: The Key Concepts*. London: Routledge.

Austen, R. (1993), 'The Moral Economy of Witchcraft: An Essay in Comparative History', in J. Comaroff and J. Comaroff (eds), *Modernity and Its Malcontents*. Chicago: University of Chicago Press, pp. 89–110.

Austin-Broos, D. J. (1997), *Jamaica Genesis: Religion and the Politics of Moral Orders*. Chicago: University Of Chicago Press.

Bailey, R. C. (ed.) (2003), *Yet with a Steady Beat: Contemporary U.S. Afrocentric Biblical Interpretation*. Semeia Studies 42. Atlanta: Society of Biblical Literature.

Baker, H. (1990), 'Foreword', in J. Jonas, *Anancy in the Great House: Ways of Reading West Indian Fiction*. New York: Greenwood Press, pp. vii–xi.

Barnouw, E. (1993), *Documentary: A History of the Non-Fiction Film*. Oxford: Oxford University Press.

Barrett-Lennard, R. J. S. (1994), *Christian Healing After the New Testament: Some Approaches to Illness in the Second, Third, and Fourth Centuries*. Lanham, MD: University Press of America.

Barthes, R. (1961), *Elements of Semiology*. London: Cape.

—. (1972), *Mythologies*. London: Cape.

Beckford, R. (2000), *Dread and Pentecostal: A Political Theology for the Black Church in Britain*. London: SPCK.

—. (2001), *God of the Rhatid: Redeeming Rage*. London: DLT.

—. (2004), *God and the Gangs*. London: DLT.

—. (2006), *Jesus Dub: Theology, Music and Social Change*. Abingdon: Routledge.

Beckles, H. (1990), *A History of Barbados: From Amerindian Settlement to Nation-State*. Cambridge UK: Cambridge University Press.

Bell, C. (2009), *Ritual Theory, Ritual Practice*. New York: Oxford University Press.

Bible and Culture Collective (1995), *The Postmodern Bible*. New Haven and London: Yale University Press.

Bourdieu, P. (1977), *Outline of a Theory of Practice*. Cambridge: Cambridge University Press.

—. (1992), 'Thinking about limits', *Theory, Culture and Society*, 9, 37–49.

Bourguignon, E. (1976), *Possession*. Novato, CA: Chandler and Sharp.

Bridges, G. W. (1828), *The Annals of Jamaica*. London: John Murray.

Broedel, H. P. (2003), *The Malleus Maleficarum and the Construction of Witchcraft*. Manchester: Manchester University Press.

Bruzzi, S. (2000), *New Documentary: A Critical Introduction*. Abingdon: Routledge.

Bultmann, R. (1960), *Jesus Christ and Mythology*. London: SCM.

Burke, S. (2010), *The Death and Return of the Author: Criticism and Subjectivity in Barthes, Foucault, and Derrida*. Edinburgh: Edinburgh University Press.

Burkert, W. (1987), *Greek Religion: Archaic and Classical*. J. Raffan (trans.). Oxford: Blackwell.

Burton, R. D. E. (1997), *Afro-Creole: Power, Opposition, and Play in the Caribbean*. New York: Cornel University Press.

Bush, B. (1990), *Slave Women in Caribbean Society, 1650–1838*. Kingston, Jamaica: Heinemann.

Bush, M. E. L. (2011), *Everyday Forms of Whiteness: Understanding Race in a 'Post-Racial World'* (2nd edn). Plymouth: Rowman and Littlefield.

Butler, A. (2007), *Women in the Church of God in Christ: Making a Sanctified World*. Chapel Hill, NC: University of North Carolina Press.

Card, C. (2010), *Confronting Evils: Terrorism, Torture, Genocide*. New York: Cambridge University Press.

Casas, B. D. L. (1992), *A Short Account of the Destruction of the Indies*. Harlow: Penguin Books.

Castro, D. (2007), *Another Face of Empire: Bartolomé de Las Casas, Indigenous Rights, and Ecclesiastical. Imperialism*. Durham, NC: Duke University Press Books.

Chambers, E. (2012), *Things Done Change: The Cultural Politics of Recent Black Artists in Britain*. Amersterdam: Editions Rodopi B.V.

Chang, H. V. (2008), *Autoethnography as Method*. Walnut Creek, CA: Left Coast.

Chanon, M. (2007), *The Politics of Documentary*. London: British Film Institute.

Chevannes, B. (ed.) (1995), *Rastafari and other African-Caribbean Worldviews*. Basingstoke, UK: Macmillan Press.

Chireau, Y. (2006), *Black Magic: Religion and the African American Conjuring Tradition*. Berkeley, CA: University of California Press.

Clayton, L. A. (2011), *Bartolomé de las Casaas and the Conquest of the Americas*. Chichester, Sussex: Wiley-Blackwell.

Clough, P. and Nutbrown, C. (2002), *A Student's Guide to Methodology: Justifying Enquiry*. London: Sage.

Cobb, K. (2005), *The Blackwell Guide to Theology and Popular Culture*. Blackwell Publishing: Oxford.

Cobb, S. (2011), *Britain's Empire: Resistance, Repression and Revolt*. London: Verso.

Collins, J. M. (2009), *Exorcism and Deliverance Ministry in the Twentieth Century: An Analysis of the Practice and Theology of Exorcism in Modern Western Christianity*. Eugene, OR: Wipf & Stock.

Collins, P. H. (1998), *Fighting Words: Black Women and the Search for Justice*. Minneapolis: University of Minnesota Press.

—. (1990), *Black Feminist Thought: Knowledge, Consciousness and the Politics of Empowerment*. London: Routledge.

Comaroff, J. and Comaroff, J. L. (1993), 'Introduction', in J. Comaroff and J. L. Comaroff (eds), *Modernity and Its Malcontents: Ritual and Power in Postcolonial Africa*. Chicago: University of Chicago Press, pp. xi–xxxi.

Cone, J. (1975), *God of the Oppressed*. New York: Harper Collins.

—. (1992), *The Spirituals and the Blues: An Interpretation*. Maryknoll, NY: Orbis Books.

Corner, J. (2003), 'Television, Documentary and the Category of the Aesthetic'. *Screen*, 44 (1), 55.

—. (2005), 'Television, Documentary and the Category of the Aesthetic', in A. Rosenthal and J. Corner (eds), *New Challenges for Documentary* (2nd edn). Manchester: Manchester University Press, p. 48–59.

Cox, J. (2008), *The British Missionary Enterprise since 1700: (Christianity and Society in the Modern World)*. London: Routledge.

Croatto, J. S. (1987), *Biblical Hermeneutics: Towards a Theory of Reading as the Production of Meaning*. New York: Orbis Books.

Crossan, J. D. (2009), *Jesus: A Revolutionary Biography*. New York: Harper Collins.

Cuneo, M. W. (2001), *American Exorcism: Expelling Demons in the Land of Plenty*. New York: Doubleday.

Curran, J. and Seaton, J. (2009), *Power without Responsibility: Press, Broadcasting and the Internet in Britain*. London: Routledge.

Davies, S. L. (1995), *Jesus the Healer*. London: SCM.

Davis, K. (1990), *Emancipation Still Comin'*. Explorations in Caribbean Emancipatory Theology. New York: Orbis.

Davis, W. (1988), *Passage of Darkness: The Ethnobiology of The Hatian Zombie*. Chapel Hill: University of North Carolina Press.

Dayfoot, A. C. (1998), *The Shaping of the West Indian Church: 1492–1962*. Barbados: University of West Indies Press.

Deller, R. (2012), *Faith in View: Religion and Spirituality in Factual British Television 2000–2009*. Doctoral thesis, Sheffield Hallam University.Department for Education and Skills Department of Health, Home Office (2003), 'Keeping children safe: the Government's response to the Victoria Climbie Inquiry Report and Joint Chief Inspector's report Safeguarding Children'. London: Stationery Office.

Deren, M. (1991), *Divine Horsemen: Living Gods of Haiti*. Kingston, NY: McPherson, pp. 15–16 and 27–30.

Desmangles, L. G. (1992), *The Faces of the Gods: Vodou and Roman Catholicism in Haiti*. Chapel Hill: University of North Carolina Press.

Donoghue, E. (2006), *Black Women/White Men: The Sexual Exploitation of Female Slaves in the Danish West Indies*. Trenton, NJ: Africa World Press.

Dookhan, I. (1971), *A Pre-emancipation History of the West Indies*. Kingston, Jamaica: Longman Jamaica Limited, p. 125.

Dulcie Dixon (2005), 'Black Theology Forum', Queens College. Research paper.

Dunn, S. (2008), *Baad Bitches and Sassy Supermamas: Black Power Action Films*. Chicago: University of Illinois Press.

Dyrness, W. A. (2001), *Visual Faith: Art Theology and Worship in Dialogue (Engaging Culture)*. Grand Rapids: Baker Publishing Group.

Edmonds, E. B. and Gonzalez, M. A. (2010), *Caribbean Religious History: An Introduction*. New York: New York University Press, p. 58.

Elkes, N. (2012), 'Row over Handsworth Church Extension Plan', *Birmingham Mail*, 29 May, viewed 14 August 2013, www. birminghammail.net/news/birmingham-news/2012/05/29/row-over-handsworth-church-extension-plan-97319-31064421/

Ellington, S. A. (1996), 'Pentecostalism and the Authority of Scripture', *Journal of Pentecostal Theology*, 9, 16–38.

Elliot, J. H. (1992), *The Old World and the New 1492–1650*. Cambridge: Cambridge University Press, p. 7.

Ellis, C. and Bochner, A. P. (2006), 'Analyzing Analytic Autoethnography – An Autopsy', *Journal of Contemporary Ethnography*, 35 (4), 404–29.

Ellis, J. B. (1913), *The Diocese of Jamaica: A Short Account of Its History, Growth and Organisation*. London: Society for Promoting Christian Knowledge.

Elwell, W. A. (1984), *Evangelical Dictionary of Theology*. Grand Rapids, MI: Baker Book House.

Equiano, O. (1995), *The Interesting Narrative and Other Writings*. Vincent Carretta (ed.). London: Penguin.

Eshel, E. (2003), 'Genres of Magical Texts in the Dead Sea Scrolls', in A. Lange, H. Lichtenberger and K. H. Römheld (eds), *Demons*. Tubingen: J.C. Mohr, pp. 395–415.

Evans-Prichard, E. E. (1976), *Witchcraft, Oracles and Magic among the Azande*. Oxford: Clarendon.

Fanon, F. (1963), *The Wretched of the Earth*. London: Pluto.

—. (1991), *Black Skins White Masks* (2nd edn). London: Pluto.

—. (2005), *The Wretched of the Earth*. London: Grove.

Ferguson, N. (2004), *Empire: How Britain Made the Modern World*. London: Penguin.

Ferguson, R. (1998), *Representing Race: Ideology, Identity and the Media*. London: Bloomsbury Academic.

Fernández, Olmos. M. and Parvisini-Gebert, L. (eds) (2003), *Creole Religions of the Caribbean, An Introduction from Voodoo and Santeria to Obeah and Espiritismo*. New York: New York University Press.

Fiorenza, E. S. (1991), *Revelation: Vision of a Just World*. Edinburgh: T&T Clark.

Forbes, D. B. and Mahan, J. H. (eds) (2000), *Religion and Popular Culture in America*. Berkeley: University of California Press.

Foucault, M. (1984), 'Nietzsche, Genealogy, History', in P. Rabinow (ed.), *The Foucault Reader*, New York: Pantheon, pp. 76–100.

—. (1990), *The History of Sexuality, Vol. 1: An Introduction*. R. Hurley (trans.). New York: Vintage Books.

—. (2002), *Archeology of Knowledge*. London: Routledge.

Gaskill, M. (2010), *Witchcraft: A Very Short Introduction*. Oxford: Oxford University Press.

Gates Jr., H. L. (1988), *The Signifying Monkey: A Theory of African-American Literary Criticism*. Oxford: Oxford University Press.

Gérarad, G. (1980) *Narrative Discourse: An Essay in Method*. Oxford: Basil Blackwell.

Gerloff, R. (1992), *A Plea for British Black Theologies: The Black Church Movement in its Transatlantic Cultural and Theological Interaction with Special References to the Pentecostal Oneness (Apostolic) and Sabbatarian Movements, Part 1*. Frankfurt, Bern and New York: Peter Lang.

Geschiere, P. (1997), *The Modernity of Witchcraft: Politics and the Occult in Postcolonial Africa*. Charlottesville: University of Virginia Press.

Ghachem, M. W. (2012), *The Old Regime and the Haitian Revolution*. Cambridge: Cambridge University Press.

Gilroy, P. (1993), *The Black Atlantic: Modernity and Double Consciousness*. London: Verso.

Glasson, T. (2011), *Mastering Christianity: Missionary Anglicanism and Slavery in the Atlantic World*. Oxford: Oxford University Press.

Gluckman, M. (1959), *Custom and Conflict in Africa*. Oxford: Basil Blackwell.

Goldenberg, D. M. (2005), *The Curse of Ham: Race and Slavery in Early Judaism, Christianity and Islam*. Princeton, NJ: Princeton University Press.

Grant, C. (2011), *I & I: The Natural Mystics: Marley, Tosh and Wailer*. London: Jonathan Cape.

Greenblatt, S. (1992), *Marvelous Possessions: The Wonder of the New World*. Chicago: University of Chicago Press.

Grierson, J. (1933), 'The Documentary Producer', *Cinema Quarterly*, 2 (1), 8.

Grundy, R. (1993), *Mark: A Commentary on His Apology for the Cross*. Grand Rapids: Eerdmans.

Hall, C. (2002), *Civilizing Subjects: Metropole and Colony in the English Imagination 1830–1867*. London: Polity, p. 77.

Hall, S. (1973), 'Encoding and Decoding in the Television Discourse', CCCS stencilled Paper no. 7. Birmingham: pp. 1–20.

—. (1980), 'Encoding/Decoding', in S. Hall, L. Hobson, A. Love and P. Willis (eds), *Culture, Media, Language: Working Papers in Cultural Studies, 1972–79*. London: Routledge, pp. 128–38.

—. (1997a), 'The Spectacle of the "Other"', in S. Hall (ed.), *Representation: Cultural Representations and Signifying Practices*. London: Sage, pp. 223–90.

—. (1997b), 'The Work of Representation', in S. Hall (ed.), *Representation: Cultural Representations and Signifying Practices*. London: Sage, pp. 13–74.

Hall, S., Critcher, C., Jefferson, T., Clarke, J. N. and Roberts, B. (1978), *Policing the Crisis: Muggings, the State and Law and Order*. London: Palgrave Macmillan.

Hall, S. and Jefferson, T. (2006), *Resistance through Rituals: Youth Subcultures in Post-War Britain* (2nd edn). London: Routledge.

Hart, R. (1985), *Slaves Who Abolished Slavery Vol. 2: Blacks in Rebellion*. Kingston, Jamaica: University of the West Indies.

Haynes, S. R. (2002), *Noah's Curse: Biblical Justification of American Slavery*. Oxford: Oxford University Press.

Heelas, P. and Woodhead, L. (2005), *The Spiritual Revolution: Why Religion in Giving Way to Spirituality*. Oxford: Blackwell.

Hobson, D. (2008), *Channel 4: The Early Years and the Jeremy Isaacs Legacy*. London: I.B.Tauris.

Hochschld, A. (2005), *Bury the Chains: The British Struggle to Abolish Slavery*. London: Macmillan.

Hollenbach, P. (1981), 'Jesus, Demoniacs, and Public Authorities: A Socio-historical Study', *JAAR*, 49 (4), 565–88.

—. (1993), 'Help for Interpreting Jesus' Exorcisms,' SBL Seminar Paper. Atlanta: Scholars Press.

Hollenweger, W. (1973), 'Pentecostalism and Black Power', *Theology Today*, 30, 234.

hooks, b. (1992), *Black Looks: Race and Representation*. Cambridge, MA: South End.

Hopkins, D. (1999), *Introducing Black Theology of Liberation*. Maryknoll, NY: Orbis Books.

Horsley, R. A. (2001), *Hearing the Whole Story: The Politics of Plot in Mark's Gospel*. Louisville, KY: Westminster John Knox.

—. (2004), *Jesus and the Spiral of Violence: Popular Jewish Resistance in Roman Palestine*. Minneapolis, MN: Fortress Press.

House of Commons Health Committee (2003), *The Victoria Climbié Inquiry Report, Sixth Report of Session 2002–3*. London: Stationary Office.

Hunte, K. (2001), 'Protestantism and Slavery in the British Caribbean', in A. Lampe (ed.), *Christianity in the Caribbean: Essays on Church History*. Kingston, Jamaica: University of the West Indies Press. pp. 86–125.

Hurbon, L. (1995), *Voodoo: Truth and Fantasy*. London: Thames and Hudson.

Inge, J. (2003), *A Christian Theology of Place*. Farnham: Ashgate.

Jackson, C. (2010), *Violence, Visual Culture, and the Black Male Body*. London: Routledge.

James, C. L. R. (1963), *The Black Jacobins: Toussaint L'Ouverture and the San Domingo Revolution* (2nd edn). New York: Vintage Books.

—. (2001), *The Black Jacobins: Toussaint L'ouverture and the San Domingo Revolution*. London: Penguin.

Jennings, W. J. (2010), *The Christian Imagination: Theology and the Origins of Race*. New Haven: Yale University Press.

Johns, C. B. (2010), *Pentecostal Formation: A Pedagogy among the Oppressed*. Sheffield: Sheffield Academic.

Johnson, L. (2010), 'BBC defends EastEnders' Lucas Plot after Anti-Christian Complaints Rise', *Metro*, 12 July, www.christian.org.uk/news/bbc-accused-of-anti-christian-bias-by-viewers/; also http://metro.co.uk/2010/07/12/bbc-defends-eastenders-lucas-plot-after-anti-christian-complaints-rise-445106/

Johnson, K. R. (1971), 'Black Kinesics – Some Non-verbal Patterns in Black Culture'. *Florida: F/L Reporter* 9 (1 and 2) (Spring/Fall): 17–20.

Jones, S. and Lakeland, P. (eds) (2005), *Constructive Theology: A Contemporary Approach to Classical Themes*. Minneapolis: Fortress.

Kaiman, J. (2013), 'Ghana arrests 124 Chinese Citizens for Illegal Gold Mining', *The Guardian*, 6 June, viewed 14 August 2013, www.guardian.co.uk/world/2013/jun/06/ghana-arrest-chinese-illegal-gold-mining

Karenga, M. (2002), *Introduction to Black Studies* (3rd edn). Los Angeles: University of Sankore Press.

Kay, W. K. and Parry, R. A. (eds) (2009), *Exorcism and Deliverance: Multi-Disciplinary Perspectives*. Milton Keynes, Buckinghamshire: Paternoster.

Kee, H. C. (1988), *Medicine, Miracle and Magic in New Testament Times*. Cambridge: Cambridge University Press.

Keller, C. (1997), *Apocalypse Now and Then: A Feminist Guide to the End of the World*. Minneapolis: Fortress.

Keller, C., Nausner, M. and Rivera, M. (eds) (2004), *Postcolonial Theologies: Divinity and Empire*. St Louis, MO: Chalice.

Kilborn, R. and Izod, J. (1997), *Confronting Reality: An Introduction to Documentary.* Manchester: Manchester University Press, p. 35.

Kirk-Duggan, C. A. (1997), *Exorcizing Evil: A Womanist Perspective on the Spirituals.* Maryknoll, NY: Orbis Books.

Kobayashi, A. (2003), 'GPC Ten Years On: Is Self-Reflexivity Enough?' *Gender, Place and Culture,* 10 (4), 345–9.

Koven, M. J. (2010), *Blaxsploitation Films.* Harpenden, Herts: Kamera Books.

Laguerre, M. (1980), *Voodoo Heritage.* Beverly Hills: Sage.

Lambert, S. (1982), *Channel 4: Television with a Difference?* London: British Film Institute, pp. 144–6.

Lampe, A. (2001), *Christianity in the Caribbean: Essays on Church History.* Barbados: University of the West Indies Press.

Land, S. J. (2010), *Pentecostal Spirituality: A Passion for the Kingdom.* Cleveland, TN: CPT.

Lees-Milne, J. (1976), *William Beckford.* London: Century.

Lin, D. (2004), 'Third Way', December. 27 (10): 20–1.

Long, C. H. (1986), *Significations: Signs, Symbols, and Images in the Interpretation of Religion.* Philadelphia: Fortress.

Lott, E. (1995), *Love and Theft: Blackface Minstrelsy and the American Working Class.* New York: Oxford University Press, pp. 15–18.

Lynch, G. (2005), *Understanding Theology and Popular Culture.* Oxford: Blackwell.

Lynch, G. and Mitchell, J. (eds) (2012), *Religion, Media and Culture: A Reader.* London: Routledge.

Macchia, F. D. (2008), 'Pentecostal and Charismatic theology', in J. L. Walls (ed.) *The Oxford Handbook of Eschatology.* Oxford: Oxford University Press, pp. 280–94.

MacNair, W. E. (2009), *Unravelling the Mega-Church: True Faith or Fast Promise?* New York: Praeger.

MacNutt, F. A (2008), *Bartholomew de las Casas: His Life, His Apostolate, and His Writings.* New York: G.P. Putnam's Sons.

Madison, D. S. (2011), *Critical Ethnography: Methods, Ethics and Performance* (2nd edn). London: Sage. (Preface Connects Positionality with Activism.)

Malik, S. (2002), *Representing Black Britain: Black and Asian Images on Television.* London: Sage.

Maréchal, G. (2010), 'Autoethnography', in A. J. Mills, G. Durepos and E. Wiebe (eds), *Encyclopaedia of Case Study Research (Vol. 2).* Thousand Oaks, CA: Sage, pp. 43–55.

Mark, R. (2004), *A Century of Holiness: The Doctrine of Entire Sanctification in the Church of the Nazarene: 1905 to 2004.* Kansas: Beacon Hill.

Marlon Yearwood, M. (1999), *Black Film as a Signifying Practice, Cinema, Narration and the African American Aesthetic Tradition.* Trenton NJ: African World Press.

Martin, G., Meade, B. and Greenough, J. (2011), *A Boy, A Journey, A Dream: The Story of Basil Meade and the London Community Gospel Choir* (1st edn). Oxford, UK and Grand Rapids, MI: Monarch Books, pp. 101–17.

Marwick, M. G. (1965), *Sorcery in its Social Setting: A Study of the Northern Rhodesia Ceŵa.* Manchester: Manchester University Press.

Marx, C. (1992), *Capital: Volume 1: A Critique of Political Economy.* London: Penguin Classics.

Matsumoto, D. and Juang, L. (2008), *Culture and Psychology* (4th edn). Belmont, CA: Thompson Wadsworth.

Maxwell-Stuart, P. G. (2001), *Witchcraft in Europe and the New World, 1400–1800.* Basingstoke: Palgrave Macmillan.

Mbiti, J. (1991), *Introduction to African Religion* (2nd edn). Heinemann: England.

McCasland, S. V. (1951), *The Finger of God: Demon Possession and Exorcism in the Light of Modern Views of Mental Illness.* New York: MacMillan.

McGrath, A. E. (2001), *Christian Theology: An Introduction* (3rd edn). Chichester: John Wiley & Sons.

McMillan, M. (2007), 'Aesthetics of the west Indian front room,' in R. V. Arana (ed.) *"Black" British Aesthetics Today.* Newcastle: Cambridge Scholars.

Meier, J. (2001), 'The Beginnings of the Catholic Church in the Caribbean', in A. Lampe (ed.), *Christianity in the Caribbean: Essays on Church History.* Barbados: University of the West Indies Press, pp. 1–85.

Meier, J. P. (1994), *A Marginal Jew: Rethinking the Historical Jesus, Vol. 2: Mentor, Message, and Miracles* (1st edn). New Haven and London: Yale University Press.

Metz, J. B. (1980), *Faith in History and Society: Towards a Practical Fundamental Theology.* D. Smith (trans.). London: Burns and Oates.

—. (1986), *The Emergent Church.* New York: Crossroad.

—. (1999), *Translating the Devil: Religion and Modernity amongst the Ewe in Ghana.* London: Edinburgh University Press.

Miguez, N., Rieger, J. and Sung, J. M. (2009), *Beyond the Spirit of Empire (Reclaiming Liberation Theology): Theology and Politics in a New Key.* London: SCM.

Miles, R. (1993), *Racism after Race Relations.* London: Routledge.

Mitchem, S. Y. (2002), *Introducing Womanist Theology.* Maryknoll, NY: Orbis Books.

Moe-Lobeda, C. D. (2013), *Resisting Structural Evil: Love as Ecological-Economic Vocation*. Minneapolis: Spark House.

Moore, H. L. and Sanders, D. T. (2001), 'Magical Interpretations and Material Realities: An Introduction', in H. L. Moore and D. T. Sanders (eds), *Magical Interpretations, Material Realities: Modernity, Witchcraft and the Occult in Post-Colonial Africa*. London: Routledge, pp. 1–28.

Moore, S. D. (2006), 'Mark and Empire: "Zealot" and "Postcolonial" Readings', in R. S. Sugirtharajah, *The Postcolonial Biblical Reader*. Oxford: Blackwell, pp. 193–205.

Morrish, I. (1982), *Obeah, Christ and Rastaman, Jamaica and Its Religion*. Cambridge: James Clarke.

Muncey, T. (2010), *Creating Autoethnographies*. London: Sage.

Murrell, N. S. (2000), 'Dangerous Memories: Underdevelopment, and the Bible in Colonial Caribbean Experience', in H. Gossai and N. S. Murrell, *Religion, Culture and Tradition in the Caribbean*. Basingstoke: Palgrave Macmillan, pp. 9–37.

Myers, C. (2008), *Binding the Strong Man: A Political Reading of Mark's Story of Jesus*. New York: Orbis.

Naegeli-Osjord, H. (1988), *Possession and Exorcism: Understanding the Human Psyche in Turmoil*. Oregon: New Frontiers Centre.

Nesbitt. J. (2010), *Chris Ofili*. London: Tate.

Nichols, B. (1994), *Blurred Boundaries: Questions of Meaning in Contemporary Culture*. New York: John Wiley.

—. (2001), *Introduction to Documentary*. Bloomington and Indianapolis: Indiana University Press.

—. (2001), *Representing Reality*. Bloomington and Indianapolis: Indiana University Press.

Olmos, M. F. and Paravisini-Gebert, L. (eds) (2011), *Creole Religions of the Caribbean: An Introduction from Vodou and Santeria to Obeah and Espiritismo*. New York: New York University Press.

Onyinah, O. (2011), *Pentecostal Exorcism: Witchcraft and Demonology in Ghana*. Bryanston: Deo.

Ortner, S. (1984), 'Theory in Anthropology since the sixties'. *Comparative Studies in Society and History*, 26 (1), 126–66.

Otto, R. (1958), *The Idea of the Holy*. Oxford: Oxford University Press.

Parish, J. (2000), 'From the Body to the Wallet: Conceptualizing Akan Witchcraft at Home and Abroad', *Journal of the Royal Anthropological Institute*, 6 (3), 487–500.

Parrinder, G. (2005), 'Exorcism', in L. Jones (ed.), *Encyclopedia of Religion, vol. 3, 15 vols*. Detroit: Thompson/Gale, pp. 225–33.

Patterson, O. (1982), *Slavery and Social Death: A Comparative Study*. Cambridge, MA: Harvard University Press.

Peake, L. and Trotz, A. (1999), *Gender, Ethnicity and Place: Women and Identities in Guyana*. London: Routledge.

Peirce, C. S. (1931–58), *Collected Writings (8 Vols.)*. C. Hartshorne, P. Weiss and A. W. Burks (eds). Cambridge, MA: Harvard University Press.

Perkinson, J. W. (2004), *White Theology: Outing Supremacy in Modernity*. New York: Palgrave Macmillan.

—. (2005), *Shamanism, Racism and Hip Hop Culture*. New York: Palgrave Macmillan.

Pero, C. S. (2013), *Liberation from Empire: Demonic Possession and Exorcism in the Gospel of Mark*. New York: Peter Laing.

Peterson, D. (1995), *Possessed by God: New Testament Theology of Sanctification and Holiness*. Nottingham: IVP.

Philip Sherlock, P. and Bennett, H. (1998), *The Story of the Jamaican People*. Kingston, Jamaica: Ian Randle.

Pickering, M. (2001), *Stereotyping: The Politics of Representation*. London: Palgrave Macmillan.

Pool, R. (1994), *Dialogue and the Interpretation of Illness. Conversations in a Cameroon Village*. Oxford, UK and Providence, RI: Berg.

Prince, M. (2000), *The History of Mary Prince: A West Indian Slave*. London: Penguin.

Quicke, A. and Quicke, J. (1993), *Hidden Agendas: The Politics of Religious Broadcasting in Britain, 1987–1991*. Doncaster, UK: Dominion King Grant.

Ragin, C. C. (1992), *The Comparative Method: Moving Beyond Qualitative and Quantitative Strategies*. Berkeley and Los Angeles: University of California Press.

Reddie, A. (2012) *Black Theology*. London: SMC.

Rediker, M. (2007), *The Slave Ship: A Human History*. Harlow: Penguin Books.

Reed-Danahay, D. (1997) Auto/ethnography: Rewriting the Self and the Social. Oxford: Berg.

Renov, M. (ed.) (1993), *Theorizing Documentary*. London: Routledge.

Rich. W. C. (2013), *The Post-Racial Society is Here: Recognition, Critics and the Nation-State*. London: Routledge.

Rigaud, M. (1985), *Secrets of Voodoo*. Robert Cross (trans.). San Francisco: City Light Books.

Root, D. (1996), *Cannibal Culture: Art, Appropriation, and the Commodification of Difference*. Boulder, CO: Westview.

Roscoe, J. and Hight, C. (2001), *Faking It: Mock-documentary and the Subversion of Factuality*. Manchester: Manchester University Press.

Rose, G. (2011), *Visual Methodologies: An Introduction to Researching with Visual Materials* (3rd edn). London: Sage.

Rosen, H. (1998), *Speaking from Memory: The Study of Autobiographical Discourse*. Stoke on Trent: Trentham Books.

Rosenthal, A. and Corner, J. (eds) (2005), *New Challenges for Documentary* (2nd edn). Manchester: Manchester University Press.

Rucker, W. (2001), 'Conjure, Magic, and Power: The Influence of Afro-Atlantic Religious Practices on Slave Resistance and Rebellion', *Journal of Black Studies*, 32 (1), 84–103.

Runcie, R. (1986), *Religious Broadcasting Today. (Pamphlet Library No.13)*. Canterbury: Centre for the Study of Religion and Society.

Russell, J. (2005), *Book of the Dead: The Complete History of Zombie Movies: The Complete History of Zombie Cinema*. Godalming, England: FAB.

Sanders, A. (1995), *A Deed Without a Name: The Witch in Society and History*. Oxford: Berg.

Sanders, M. (2006), *Gayatri Chakravorty Spivak: Live Theory*. London/ NYC: Continuum.

Scandrett-Leatherman, C. ( 2011), 'Rites of Lynching and Rights of Dance: Historic, Anthropological, and Afro-Pentecostal Perspectives on Black Manhood after 1865', in A. Young and E. Y. Alexander (eds), *Afro-Pentecostalism: Black Pentecostal and Charismatic Christianity in History and Culture*. New York: New York University Press, pp. 95–117.

Segundo, J. L. (1976), *The Liberation of the Bible*. New York: Orbis Books.

Shanahan, C. (2010), *Voices from the Borderland: Re-imagining Cross-Cultural Urban Theology in the Twenty-first Century*. Cross Cultural Theologies. London: Equinox.

Shaw, R. (1997), 'The Production of Witchcraft/Witchcraft as Production: Memory, Modernity and the Slave Trade in Sierra Leone', *American Ethnologist*, 24 (4), 856–67.

Sheller, M. (2003), *Consuming the Caribbean: From Arawaks to Zombies*. London: Routlege.

Simpson, G. E. (1978), *Black Religions in the New World*. New York: Columbia University Press.

—. (1980), *Religious Cults of the Caribbean: Trinidad, Jamaica and Haiti*. Rio Piedras, San Juan, Puerto Rico: Institute of Caribbean Studies, University of Puerto Rico.

Smith, K. A. (2010), *Thinking in Tongues: Pentecostal Contributions to Christian Philosophy*. Grand Rapids, MI: Wm. B. Eerdmans.

Smith, S. A. (2009), *British Black Gospel: The Foundations of This Vibrant UK Sound*. Oxford: Monarch Books.

Smith, T. (1996), Conjuring *Culture: Biblical Foundations for Black America*. Oxford: Oxford University Press.

Sorensen, E. (2002), *Possession and Exorcism in the New Testament and Early Christianity*. Tubingen: J.C. Mohr.

Souraiu, E. (1953), *L'Universe Filmique*. Paris: Flammarion.

Spivak, G. C. (1994), 'Can the Subaltern Speak?' in P. Williams and L. Chrisman (eds), *Colonial Discourse and Post-Colonial Theory, A Reader*. New York: Columbia University Press, pp. 66–111.

Stanfield, John H. (2011), *Black Reflective Sociology: Epistemology, Theory and Methodology*. Walnut Creek, CA: Left Coast.

Stangor, C. and Crandall, C. (eds) (2013), *Stereotyping and Prejudice*. Florence, KY: Psychology.

Steel Pulse (1978), 'Soldiers' *Handsworth Revolution*, composed by Selwyn Brown, Basil Gabbidon, David Hinds, Alphonso Martin, Ronnie McQueen and Steve Nesbitt. Island Records, UK.

Stephens, M. (1998), *The Rise of the Image and Fall of the Word*. Oxford: Oxford University Press.

Stewart, D. M. (2005), *Three Eyes for the Journey: African Dimensions of the Jamaican Religious Experience*. Oxford: Oxford University Press.

Stewart, P. J. and Strathern, A. (eds) (2004), *Witchcraft, Sorcery, Rumors, and Gossip*. Cambridge: Cambridge University Press.

Sturken, M. and Cartwright, L. (eds) (2001), *Practices of Looking: An Introduction to Visual Culture*. Oxford: Oxford University Press.

Sugirtharajah, R. S. (2002), *Postcolonial Criticism and Biblical Interpretation*. Oxford: Oxford University Press.

—. (2003), *Postcolonial Reconfigurations: An Alternative Way to Read the Bible and Doing Theology*. St Louis, MO: Chalice.

—. (2006), *The Postcolonial Biblical Reader*. Oxford: Blackwell.

Sugirtharajah, R. S. (ed.) (1998), *The Postcolonial Bible*. Sheffield: Sheffield Academic.

Theissen, G. (2004), *The Gospels in Context*. London: Continuum.

Thomas, K. (1973), *Religion and the Decline of Magic: Studies in Popular Beliefs in Sixteenth and Seventeenth Century England*. London: Penguin.

Thompson, R. F. (1984), *Flash of Spirit: African and Afro-American Art and Philosophy*. New York: Random House.

Tillich, P. (1957), *Dynamics of Faith*. New York: Harper & Row.

—. (1994) *Systematic Theology*. Volume 1. Chicago: University Of Chicago Press.

Tillich, P. (ed.) (1959), *Theology of Culture*. New York: Oxford University Press.

Tinker, G. E. (1993), *Missionary Conquest: The Gospel and Native American Cultural Genocide*. Minneapolis: Fortress.

Todorov, T. (1987), *The Conquest of America: The Question of the Other*. Richard Howard (trans.). London: Harper and Row.

Turlington, S. (1999), *Do You Do Voodoo?: The Real Religion Behind Zombies and Voodoo Dolls*. Reading: South Street.

Turner, V. (1957), *Schism and Continuity in an African Society: A Study of Ndembu Village*. Manchester: Manchester University Press.

—. (1982), *From Ritual to Theatre: The Human Seriousness of Play*. New York: PAJ Publications.

Twelftree, G. H. (2007), *In the Name of Jesus: Exorcism among Early Christians*. Grand Rapids MI: Baker Academic.

Vaughan, D. (1983), *Portrait of an Invisible Man: The Working Life of Stewart McAllister, Film Editor*. London: BFI.

Walls, J. L. (ed.) (2008), *The Oxford Handbook of Eschatology*. Oxford: Oxford University Press.

Walton, J. L. (2009), *Watch This!: The Ethics and Aesthetics of Black Televangelism*. New York: New York University Press.

Walton, P. L. (2004) *Our Cannibals, Ourselves*. Chicago: University of Illinois Press.

Wannenwetsch, B. (2004), *Political Worship: Ethics for Christian Citizens*. Margaret Kohl (trans.). Oxford: Oxford University Press.

Ward, P. (2005), *Documentary: The Margins of Reality*. London and New York: Wallflower.

—. (2005), *Selling Worship: How what We Sing has changed the Church*. Milton Keynes, Buckinghamshire: Paternoster.

Warner-Lewis, M. (2003), *Central Africa in the Caribbean: Transcending Time, Transforming Culture*. New York: MacMillan.

Warrington, K. (2008), *Pentecostal Theology: A Theology of Encounter*. London: T&T Clark.

Watson, S. E. (2009), '"Good will Come of this Evil": Enslaved Teachers and the Transatlantic Politics of Early Black Literacy', *College Composition and Communication*, 61 (1), 66–89.

Webb, J., Schirato, T. and Danaher, G. (2002), *Understanding Bourdieu*. London: Sage.

West, C. (1993), *Beyond Eurocentrism and Multiculturalism vol 1: Prophetic Thought in Postmodern Times*. Monroe, ME: Common Courage Press.

White, L. (2000), *Speaking with Vampires: Rumor and History in Colonial Africa*. Berkeley: University of California Press.

Wilkinson, M. and Studebaker, S. M. (eds) (2010), *A Liberating Spirit: Pentecostals and Social Action in North America*. Eugene, OR: Pickwick.

William, K. (2011), *Pentecostalism: A Very Short Introduction*. Oxford: Oxford University Press.

Williams, T. R. (2006), 'Proclaiming the Lord's Death until He Comes: Toward a Theology of the Lord's Supper', PhD dissertation, Fuller Theological Seminary.

Wilmore, G. (1998), *Black Religion and Black Radicalism: An Interpretation of the Religious History of African Americans.* New York: Orbis.

Wilson, B. (2000), *Lies, Damn Lies and Documentaries.* London: BFI.

Wink, W. (1998), *The Powers That Be: Theology for a New Millennium.* New York: Doubleday Dell.

—. (1992), *Engaging the Powers: Discernment and Resistance in a World of Domination.* Minneapolis: Fortress.

Wise, T. (2010), *Colorblind: The Rise of Post-Racial Politics and the Retreat from Racial Equity.* San Francisco, CA: City Lights Books.

Witmer, A. (2012), *Jesus, The Galilean Exorcist: His Exorcisms in Social and Political Context.* London: T&T Clark International.

Wolfe, J. (2004), *Religion, Exploration and Slavery.* Milton Keynes, Buckinghamshire: Open University.

Young, A. and Alexander, E. Y. (2011), *Afro-Pentecostalism: Black Pentecostal and Charismatic Christianity in History and Culture.* New York: New York University Press.

# INDEX

Page numbers in **bold** refer to illustrations.